Lost Angels of a Ruined Paradise:

THEMES OF COSMIC STRIFE IN ROMANTIC TRAGEDY

✸✸✸✸✸✸✸✸✸✸✸✸✸✸✸✸✸✸✸✸

Lost Angels of a Ruined Paradise:

THEMES OF COSMIC STRIFE IN ROMANTIC TRAGEDY

Erika Gottlieb

1981

Sono Nis Press

1745 Blanshard Street,
Victoria, British Columbia, Canada V8W 2J8

ISBN 0-919462-83-9

Canadian Cataloguing in Publication Data

Gottlieb, Erika.
    Lost angels of a ruined paradise

    Bibliography: p.
    Includes index.
    ISBN 0-919462-83-9

    1. English drama—19th century—History
and criticism.   2. English drama (Tragedy)—
History and criticism.   3. Romanticism—
England.   I. Title.

PR719.T69G6   822′.051209   C81-091138-8

This book has been published with the help of a grant
from the Canadian Federation for the Humanities,
using funds provided by the Social Sciences and
Humanities Research Council of Canada.

Published by
SONO NIS PRESS
1745 Blanshard Street
Victoria, British Columbia

Designed and printed in Canada by
MORRISS PRINTING COMPANY LTD.
Victoria, British Columbia

CONTENTS

I   Introduction   7

II   "DARKNESS DEEPENING DARKNESS": Wordsworth's
      THE BORDERERS   14
      Hero, Heroine and Father   17
      Hero and Villain   27
      Images of Nature and the Cosmic Structure   36

III   "POISON IN THE WINE": Coleridge's *REMORSE*   45
      Hero, Heroine and Villain   47
      Hero and Villain   55
      The Son's Offence Against the Father   61
      Nature Imagery and the Cosmic Structure   66

IV   "SO TAKING A DISGUISE": Keats's
      OTHO THE GREAT   72
      Hero, Innocent Heroine, Villainous Enchantress   76
      Hero and Father   86

V   "THE MONSTER OF THE UPPER SKY": Byron's
      MANFRED   92
      Hero and Heroine   93
      Manfred as Villain and Hero:
        Satan in Defiance, Adam in Search of the Father   98
      Images of Nature and the Cosmic Structure   106

VI   "A HIGHER TRUTH": Shelley's *THE CENCI*   114
      The Innocent Heroine as Tragic Hero:
        Eve without Adam   116
      Father as Villain: Diabolic Creator Against his
        Own Creation   130
      Images of Nature: The Cosmic Structure   140

VII   Conclusion   153

      Footnotes   163

      Bibliography   172

      Index   182

To Paul

ACKNOWLEDGEMENTS

I am grateful to Professor Desmond Cole of McGill University for sharing with me his deep interest and knowledge in this subject, and for offering invaluable help and encouragement throughout these years.

I also wish to thank Professor Alec Lucas of McGill for incisive criticism, and Mr. Philip Cercone, Director of the Publications Programme of the Canadian Federation of the Humanities, for his sincere dedication to this project throughout its stage-by-stage development.

I

INTRODUCTION

The Romantic period was exceptionally prolific in tragic drama, and the number of plays submitted to and actually performed by the theatres in England is quite staggering. What is more, each of the major poets of the period attempted to write at least one, if not several tragedies. It is the more interesting, therefore, that in a period which is characterized by such an exceptionally strong dramatic and tragic impetus (apparent also in the representative non-dramatic work of the major writers)[1] the actual plays produced in the genre do not live up to the accepted definitions of genuine tragedy or to the literary achievement of their authors' non-dramatic works.

On the point that the period, so rich in literary talent and so full of theatrical endeavour, failed to produce great drama or genuine tragedy, critics agree.[2] Beyond this accord, explanations vary on what causes this curious phenomenon. Lack of a contemporary dramatic idiom; the consequent use of an artificial poetic diction imitative of Shakespeare and the Elizabethans; the influence of Gothic melodrama and its infectious sentimentality; the enlargement in the physical dimensions of the theatre; even the emergence of a star system is among the reasons most often cited.[3]

The importance of all these factors, individually and cumulatively, cannot be underestimated. Nevertheless, I believe that by exploring the major themes of one tragedy by each of the five major Romantic poets in the period, we may arrive at a more enlightening explanation, while also putting into proper perspective the romantic poet's particular contribution to tragedy.

This exploration, then, will pay particularly close attention to Wordsworth's *The Borderers*, Coleridge's *Remorse*, Keats's *Otho the Great*, Byron's *Manfred* and Shelley's *The Cenci*. So far there has been no extensive analysis of these five works which, as a group contain representative common characteristics of Romantic tragedy. By looking at each play on its own, in the context of the poet's other works, and in comparison with the other four plays, I wish to outline those common characteristics of theme and genre which shed light on these poets' attitude to tragedy. Exploring the major themes of

7

these five works against the philosophical, religious and aesthetic ideas of the period, some insights of this study may also naturally extend to the wider context of the relationship between tragedy and the Romantic Movement.

When examined in the light of the poets' thematic concerns, *The Borderers*, *Remorse*, *Otho the Great*, *Manfred* and *The Cenci* reveal two common characteristics. Firstly, the central part of the intrigue concerns a near-saintly heroine's loss of innocence.[4] Secondly, the major crime is an offence committed against a father or a father figure.

The first three plays, Wordsworth's *The Borderers*, Coleridge's *Remorse* and Keats's *Otho the Great* are, in contemporary parlance, costume plays. They use most of the typical conventions and stock characters of Gothic melodrama. In all of them, the intrigue centres on the wedding between the hero and the innocent heroine. The villain attempts to prevent this wedding by slandering the innocent heroine's reputation.

In the last two plays, that is, in Byron's *Manfred* and Shelley's *The Cenci*, the wedding, or rather the union between the main characters and the innocent heroine still takes centre-stage. However, in these two plays the union itself is presented as sinful. Ironically, the villain's evil is manifested not in preventing this union, but in consummating it, because it is a union of incest.

The second significant point of thematic similarity among the five plays is the hero's or villain's crime against a father or a father figure which in the most extreme case takes the form of parricide.

Ritual murder is at the very core of tragedy. It is, however, quite remarkable that in each of the Romantic tragedies under study, the target of this ritual offence (in the form of murder, attempted murder or symbolic murder) is invariably the father figure. Interestingly, this figure is father to both hero and heroine, by blood, adoption or emotional sympathy.[5] In each play the offence against the heroine's innocence is causally connected to the crime against the father.[6]

Perhaps unbeknownst to the playwright himself, each of these five tragedies is essentially the ritual enactment of a basic myth, that of man's fall from innocence, and his loss of Paradise. In this ritual, the heroine's original innocence, the crime committed against the father, as well as the crime of violating the heroine's innocence are primarily of an allegorical nature. For the Romantic poet the Fall implies Adam's loss of Eve and his alienation from their Father, that is, Man's mysterious offence against Nature and the Spirit in Nature.

8

Consequently, in each of the five plays there is a supernatural aura surrounding the heroine. Her origins are mysterious, her character is of almost superhuman perfection. These traits suggest an extraordinary, almost sacred quality. In effect, her virgin innocence is the innocence of unfallen Nature. For the romantic poet she becomes Eve, representative of the garden of Nature, which also contains the Spirit within or beyond Nature. The heroine's human, yet more than human qualities are strongly suggestive of the Romantic poet's ambivalent attitude towards the secular or sacramental significance of Nature.

The central issue that is to be resolved by the impending marriage between the hero and heroine poses a number of questions about man's potential for the attainment of Paradise. Is the world of Nature indeed unfallen, and therefore permeated with the Spirit? If so, does the natural world also contain what was formerly thought to be exclusively within the supernatural realm? Since Man's union with Nature extends to union with the Divine, is Man really able to consummate this union? Is he entitled to it? Or, is it possible that this aspiration is itself blasphemous, and, therefore, instead of the union being sacramental, will it turn out to be demonic? In other words, is Man capable and worthy of attaining Paradise?

The ritual murder of the father in each Romantic tragedy answers these questions in the negative.[7] The hero's fate shows that Man either misses the sacramental wedding with Nature and with the Spirit through Nature, or consummates a forbidden union, thereby violating both Nature and Spirit. The missed wedding between Idonea and Marmaduke in *The Borderers*, and between Erminia and Ludolph in *Otho the Great* illustrates the first; the forbidden union between Astarte and Manfred in *Manfred*, and between Auranthe and Ludolph in *Otho the Great* illustrates the second alternative.

The hero's fate also implies that due to Man's false relationship with Nature, he is driven to murdering the Father, the Spirit, in effect the image of God in man. This act is tantamount to spiritual suicide.[8]

Yet, through these five plays we also have ample opportunity to notice that the Romantic poet's obsession with the quest for and the inevitable loss of Paradise does seldom lead to genuine tragedy.

What, then, are the criteria of a tragic vision of reality, a vision that is, in turn, conducive to great tragedy? From the evidence of Sophocles's, Shakespeare's or Ibsen's works, it is apparent that great tragedy coincides with periods of transition. Tragedy conceives of evil as real and in radical conflict with the good. However, evil is also inexplicable: it is part of man's experience he has to accept and come to terms with before being able to transcend it, if indeed he can do so.

Tragedy is a statement about evil, which is organized in a special way so that while we are moved to pity and terror by the suffering of the tragic hero, we are also left with a sense of the grandeur of his struggle, and hence the grandeur of man.[9]

It is also said that in great tragedy, by facing the utmost limits of the human predicament, we also feel that there is a possibility or at least a yearning for "deliverance," or in other words, "when man faces the tragic, he liberates himself from it."[10]

Romantic tragedy does not offer a sense of this liberation or deliverance. It seldom charts the course of a downward journey, which, through the darkness, reaches the light of a new knowledge. Consequently, the five plays in question do not offer a sense of tragic catharsis, (with the possible, and partial exception of *Manfred*). The ultimate effect of the poet's ritual leads not to spritúal rebirth, but arrives at an irrecoverable loss and a feeling of waste that amounts to moral collapse, not a renewal, but a form of spiritual suicide.

To understand the thematic problems facing the Romantic poet as tragedian, we should unravel the central conflict mirrored by Romantic poetry. This profound spiritual conflict, experienced by all the major poets of the period is well articulated by M. H. Abrams:

To Europe at the end of the eighteenth century the French Revolution brought what St. Augustine said Christianity brought to the ancient world: hope... a *universal absolute*, a novel hope which sprang from the Revolutionary events sudden and complete, like Minerva. Pervasively in both the verse and prose of the period, "hope," with its associated term, "joy," and its opposites, "dejection," "despondency," and "despair," are used in a special application, as a shorthand for the *limitless faith in human and social possibility* aroused by the Revolution, and *its reflex, the nadir feeling* caused by its seeming failure—as Wordsworth had put it, "the loss of hope itself / And things to hope for..." P. XI. 6-7) (Italics mine)[11]

The French Revolution marks the "ultimate crisis of Western consciousness,"[12] a sense of spiritual crisis. As the ideal of man undergoes the critical change from belief in perfectibility to post-revolutionary disillusionment, the romantic poet seems impelled to choose between absolute affirmation and absolute despair. His attempts at tragedy can, indeed, hardly be understood without his initially "limitless faith in human and social possibility."

Abrams, however, seems to be not entirely accurate in saying that

10

this "universal absolute...sprang from the revolutionary events sudden and complete, like Minerva." The Revolution indeed made the onlooker feel that the ideal of man's natural perfectibility could now become fully realized. This ideal itself, however, was conceived as far back as Locke's concept of the "tabula rasa" and the theory of human perfectibility. The Revolution gave new impetus to the questions raised by it, and the poet-witness felt called upon to respond to this faith with new spiritual fervour. But the fundamental characteristics of the faith had been prepared by the Enlightenment with the full complexity of a philosophical or even religious system. This is the faith the Romantic poet inherited, and developed into the myth of "white romanticism."[13]

This myth is based on a fundamentally optimistic interpretation of the relationship between good and evil. One of its cornerstones is the belief that it is possible to realize the Heavenly Jerusalem in the city of the eighteenth-century philosopher. The city is founded on the "absolute hope" that the world of Nature is unfallen, perfect and accessible to human beings, offering the chance of unlimited perfectibility for natural man.

While the Book of Revelation anticipates the Second Coming as a "spiritual marriage" between God and Man, Romantic poets celebrate their millennium in the period metaphor of "sacred marriage" between Man and Nature, a union that is equivalent to the realization of the perfected city, that is, a second and lasting state of Paradise.

It is important to understand the relationship between this new faith and early Christianity. Both share the spiritual fervour and belief in an Apocalypse:

The strongest intellectual forces of the Enlightenment [says Cassirer in his summary of the period] do not lie in the rejection of belief, but rather in the new form of faith which it proclaims, and in the form of religion which it embodies... This era is permeated by a genuine creative feeling and an unquestionable faith in the reformation of the world.[14]

It is equally important, however, to establish fundamental differences between Christianity and this new faith. Here Nature is no longer seen, as in previous ages, as an imperfect sublunary world that participates in the "divine malediction" of Mutability on account of Adam's original sin. Now the heavenly regions above the moon are no longer seen as different in kind from the sublunary regions. As a matter of fact, by widening the boundaries of the natural realm, the new cosmic system has destroyed the former structure of Heaven, Nature and Hell.

11

In this infinitely enlarged region, the new world of an unfallen and perfect Nature, Man is also seen as being free of limitations. Nature's perfection and Man's perfectibility are closely related beliefs. Their connection seems to form the very basis of the new faith in the reformation of the world, a faith that gathers its greatest momentum in denying original sin.

Original sin is the common opponent against which all the different trends of the philosophy of the Enlightenment join forces. In this struggle Hume is on the side of English deism, and Rousseau and Voltaire; the unity of the goal seems for a time to outweigh the differences as to the means of attaining it.[15]

In addition to this common front against original sin, there is another important factor to consider in the background to English Romantic tragedy. The Romantic poet seems to have inherited from Shaftesbury and the Oxford Platonists the basically Platonic concept of good as light, and evil as lack of light, an idea that feeds quite naturally into the mainstream of Enlightenment social optimism, with its hopes for man's ultimate perfection through the extinction of the darkness of evil, which to them, is merely the darkness of ignorance.

The "nadir feeling" the Romantic poet experiences after the failure of the Revolution is caused not only by the collapse of a political ideal, but the loss of faith in the human ideal the Revolution was supposed to demonstrate. Faith in man's natural goodness and limitless perfectibility is part of that loss. Limitless hope is followed by absolute despair, loss of faith in man himself.

It is not Fate, God, or a cosmic catastrophe, but something within man's own heart that is responsible for the betrayal of hope; there is a flaw in human nature: "The deeper malady is better hid," cries Wordsworth's hero at his fall in *The Borderers*, "the world is poisoned at the heart" (*B*. II. 1035-1036). The "poison" of this unexpected and mysterious flaw in human nature is a significant theme throughout the five tragedies, and it threatens with collapse the entire new cosmic system created by the Enlightenment. This is the poison that leads to the demonic realm of alienation, despair and destruction, from the light-flooded realms of "white romanticism" to the demonic and dark world of "black romanticism."

In each of the five plays the hero experiences and recognizes a fall, a loss of Paradise through the "poison" of evil hidden in the human heart. This recognition would make it tempting to return to the Christian framework which offers the mystery of redemption, a road towards the re-gaining of Paradise. A return to the sacramental

12

framework, however, is impossible for the post-Enlightenment poet.

Oswald and Ordonio (respectively Wordsworth's and Coleridge's villain-offenders) as well as Ludolph, Manfred and Beatrice (the fallen heroes of Keats, Byron and Shelley) all die without recognition of the meaning of suffering, and with no hope of redemption. The romantic offender having lost innocence, dies in despair and madness.

The Romantic poet's initial reluctance to recognize the existence of evil, and the cosmic despair that follows when he finally does so, contributes to his failure of achieving the cathartic effect associated with great tragedy.

There is no doubt that Romantic tragedy offers the grand spectacle of intense conflict. Yet, somehow, this conflict often lacks the magnitude of classical tragedy which portrays Man taking a stand against the inevitable forces of evil. One often wonders whether this great conflict has not been reduced to the petulant rage of the romantic poet who has seen his exaggerated hopes of infinite possibility elude him. Isn't Romantic tragedy merely an angry lament, protesting the fact that the wax wings of Icarus can soar but not sustain the flight, and that no terrestrial Paradise is immune to the effects of mutability?

The answer to these questions may vary according to the individual poet's vision and poetic temper, but the questions do point to the central dilemma of the Romantic poet as tragedian. They are, therefore relevant to all the five plays, delineating each poet's characteristic conclusion to the Romantic quest for Paradise and the dilemma of filial rebellion.

II

"DARKNESS DEEPENING DARKNESS": WORDSWORTH'S *THE BORDERERS*

Most critics agree that Wordsworth's *The Borderers* mirrors an intense crisis in the life of the young poet, although they disagree about the nature, causes, and implications of this crisis. Campbell and Mueschke regard *The Borderers* as a document of the poet's "conquest of Godwinian pessimism."[1] They relate this to the period which followed his abandoning of Annette Vallon and their daughter, a period of profound emotional crisis in which he found the philosophy of Godwin untenable. They explore the connection between the poet's dilemma and his aesthetic creed, and state that the play is

essentially, the record of a revelation that came to him when he tried to escape the inevitable consequences of a profound natural emotional experience through a philosophy that denied the importance and validity of that very experience.... he denied the philosophy and affirmed the experience.[2]

Ernest de Selincourt, however, argues that the play is a proof of Wordsworth's unshaken belief in the Godwinian creed he finds now more attractive than ever:

now [Wordsworth] embraced the creed in all its implications, in its exaltation of reason at the expense of the passions, and of the individual against the collective will, in its insistence of the right of each man to reject all general rules of conduct and act in each situation as his independent reason prompted him.[3]

The debate is a long standing one. Légouis,[4] Campbell and Mueschke argue for Wordsworth's rejection of Godwin, Garrod[5] sees in the play proof of Wordsworth's acceptance of Godwin, and therefore calls it "immoral," while E. de Selincourt regards the play as the very embodiment of the Godwinian tenets in its "tragic optimism."

More recent commentators attempt to disengage the play from the specific focus of Godwinian philosophy, and relate it to Wordsworth's concern with more universal problems. P. Thorslev studies in it the "nascent Romantic mind,"[6] Charles Smith relates Oswald to the prototype of the romantic villain as a "mortal god,"[7] and G.

Hartman offers an existentialist interpretation of Oswald's villainy as Dostoievskian "intellectual murder."[8]

I agree with P. Thorslev that *The Borderers* is one of the first works which refers to the "darkest fears and deepest questionings of the nascent Romantic mind ... which signal the breaking up of enlightenment certainties and the coming of a more modern if also in many ways a darker consciousness."[9]

These "enlightenment certainties" should probably be understood as an entire system of metaphysical optimism, which is grounded in Shaftesbury's affirmation of a rationally comprehensible universe through which a benevolent Maker manifests Himself, a system which is also conducive to Godwin's rational positivism. When writing the tragedy, the poet experiences negation and doubt, a loss of faith in the whole "creed of idealistic youth," in the millennial hopes anticipated by the Enlightenment and made suddenly imminent in the French Revolution. Losing these hopes, the poet despairs not only of political Utopia, but also of man's perfectibility, and comes to doubt the presence of a spiritual Being guiding the Cosmos according to clearly established distinctions between good and evil. The tragedy reflects the "crisis of that strong disease," which, following the political disillusionment also called in doubt all other tenets of the Enlightenment which had given birth to the political ideal. Disillusioned by the Revolution, Wordsworth comes to doubt the very foundation of his creed, his faith in the unfallen world of Nature, in the human being who is free from original sin, and hence ultimately perfectible:

> ... now believing,
> Now disbelieving; endlessly perplexed
> With impulse, motive, right and wrong, the ground
> Of obligation, what the rule and whence
> The sanction; till, demanding formal proof,
> And seeking it in everything, I lost
> All feeling of conviction, and, in fine,
> Sick, wearied out with contrarieties,
> Yielded up moral questions in despair.
> This was the crisis of that strong disease,
> This the soul's last and lowest ebb; I drooped,
> Deeming our blessed reason of least use
> Where wanted most: 'The lordly attributes
> Of will and choice, 'I bitterly exclaimed,
> 'What hath in no concerns of his a test
> Of good and evil; knows not what to fear
> And who, if those could be discerned, would yet
> Be little profited, would see, and ask

15

Where is the obligation to enforce?
And, to acknowledged law rebellious, still,
As selfish passion urged, would act amiss;
The dupe of folly, or the slave of crime.
(The Prelude, Book XI, 297-320)

The Borderers is an exciting document, because in it Wordsworth re-examines the "enlightenment certainties" of Shaftesbury's light-flooded universe, together with Godwin's belief in the progress at the very heart of "nature's holy plan." These main tenets of the poet's youthful "creed," are now pressed for their emotional implications.

There is no doubt, then, that *The Borderers* is the record of a profound spiritual crisis. Yet, as a work of drama or tragedy it raises many a well-deserved criticism. Allardyce Nicoll, for example, describes it as a failure because of its "chaotically constructed" plot, and the unrealized dramatic characters who "remain without life."[10]

Although dramatically it is confused, indeed, the play's plot makes more sense if we recognize it as an outline to an allegorical framework, in which the poet takes a symbolic journey in search of a resolution of his cosmic dilemma. This dilemma assumes the form of dramatized spiritual debate, and this debate is at the heart not only of *The Borderers*, but probably of romantic tragedy in general: Can the human being attain Paradise, a state of perfection and wholeness that is symbolized in the "sacred wedding" between the opposites of Male and Female, Man and Nature, Adam and Eve, or hero and heroine? The villain argues for the negative, while the hero answers, or would like to answer, in the affirmative.

The first scene begins with the hero, Marmaduke, saying farewell to the band of freebooters he had disciplined and organized into a highminded group of soldiers to guard the innocent. The band warns Marmaduke against Oswald, whom they recognize as a mysterious and sinister character, but ignoring their warning, Marmaduke sets out on a journey with Oswald. Their goal is, presumably, to meet Marmaduke's bride, Idonea, whose hand was refused to Marmaduke by the girl's father, the Baron Herbert. Herbert has been a broken, blind old man since his return from the Crusades some fifteen years ago, when he was also dispossessed of his land and heritage. On their journey Oswald convinces Marmaduke that the blind old man is actually a scoundrel who is posing, not only under the Baron's title, but under the Father's title as well. Having paid a beggarwoman to furnish the necessary lies,

Oswald produces false evidence to the effect that Idonea is actually the beggarwoman's daughter whom Herbert bought in infancy so that he could sell her to the lecherous Lord Clifford when she reached maturity.

Marmaduke who has been in love with Idonea since childhood, and has also learned to admire her venerable old father as his own, finds it difficult to believe the accusation. Oswald's clever fabrication of evidence gradually convinces him, however, and he subjects Herbert to the "ordeal of the waste" by abandoning the blind old man on the moor. When Oswald admits that he wanted Marmaduke to murder an innocent in order to turn him into a criminal, it is too late to save the old man. By the time Marmaduke and Idonea meet, they learn that Herbert died of hunger and exposure, close to an abandoned chapel on a ridge of rocks.

Recognition and resolution follow. The villain is killed by the outraged band, and Marmaduke, leaving Idonea to the care of his followers, decides to live the rest of his life as a lonely wanderer "till anger is appeased / In Heaven, and Mercy gives me leave to die!" (*B*. V. 2352-2353).

The Borderers, then, presents two parallel journeys: father Herbert and daughter Idonea take a journey to regain their rightful inheritance, while Marmaduke sets out to win and wed the innocent Idonea. Both journeys are symbolic of a quest for Paradise. Due to his error in judgement, Marmaduke offends against Idonea and Herbert, and both journeys end in crime, separation and despair.

To delineate Wordsworth's conclusion to the quest for paradise, we should now inquire into the allegorical significance of the hero's offence against the innocent heroine and her father.

HERO, HEROINE AND FATHER

Many readers have recognized echoes of Shakespeare's tragedies in the language and situations of *The Borderers*.[11] Few critics, however, have pointed out the influence of Milton's *Paradise Lost* which is particularly significant to our recognition that the relationship between villain and hero resembles the relationship between Satan and Adam. And when it comes to the relationship between hero and heroine, we should recognize the influence of yet another of Wordsworth's favourite authors, Spenser, "whose genius" he considered to be of "a higher order than even that of Ariosto."[12]

Meditating upon the differences between Shakespeare, Milton

and Spenser, Wordsworth makes a distinction between Shake-speare's "human and dramatic Imagination"[13] and Milton's and Spenser's "enthusiastic or meditative Imagination":

Spenser, of a gentler nature, [than Milton] maintained his freedom by aid of his allegorical spirit, at one time inciting him to create persons out of abstractions; and, at another, . . . to give the universality and permanence of abstractions to his human beings, by means of attributes and emblems that belong to the highest moral truths and the purest sensations,—of which his character of Una is a glorious example.[14]

Wordsworth's appreciation of Spenser's "allegorical spirit" sheds light on certain general qualities in his own work, both in terms of tone, and in the approach to characters, particularly in the resemblance between the figures of Una and Idonea. In search of the "universality and permanence" of the "highest moral truths," Wordsworth in his tragedy seems to be naturally attracted to Spenser's "allegorical spirit." Marmaduke, the romantic protector of the innocent is in many ways like the Redcross Knight. Each is in search of his own version of Holiness, accompanied by a female figure who personifies Truth he is to be united with at the end of his quest.

The figure of Idonea, an obvious attempt "to create [a] person out of abstractions," approximates that of Una in her purity and innocence.

> It fortuned out of the thickest wood
> A ramping Lyon rushed suddainly,
> Hunting full greedie after salvage blood;
> Soone as the royall virgin he did spy,
> With gaping mouth at her ran greedily,
> To have attonce devoured her tender corse:
> But to the pray when as he drew more ny,
> His bloudie rage asswaged with remorse,
> And with the sight amazd, forgat his furious forse.
> (*The Faerie Queene*, I. iii. 5. 37-45)

This bears striking similarity to the image associated with Idonea's purity:

> Why, if a wolf should leap from out a thicket,
> A look of mine would send him scouring back,
> Unless I differ from the thing I am
> When you are by my side. (*B.* I. 317-320)

Una's uncorrupted relationship to Nature is a sign of her connection with the Supernatural, with the realm of the Spirit that transcends Nature. In Idonea's case, however, Nature is expected to

18

contain and manifest the Spirit. It is her love and compassion, "the eighteenth century mother of all virtues, sympathy," that assures her paradisiac harmony with the world, within and not beyond Nature. There is, nevertheless, an aura of the supernatural around her also, and her father who accompanies her on part of the journey also shares this aura.

Idonea's mission to help her father be restored to his birthright shows parallels with Una's destiny. Una appeals to the Knight (who stands for Adam, Everyman, but also for the Second Adam) to restore her royal parents to their birthright, that is to restore mankind to the Paradise he was deprived of by Satan. The "poor and innocent" Una

> ... by descent from Royall lynage came
> Of ancient Kings and Queenes, ...
> ...
>
> Till that infernall feend with foule uprore
> Forwasted all their land, and them expeld:
> Whom to avenge, she had this Knight from far compeld.
> (*The Faerie Queene*, I. i. 5. 40-45)

Idonea also sets out to restore a dispossessed parent, her old and venerable father, to a heritage from which he had been "driven a wretched outcast." In this effort, she turns to Marmaduke for protection. Marmaduke who is the protector of all the innocent, fulfills a role similar to the Redcross Knight's. Were he able to aid Idonea in her task, he would restore mankind to his birthright of innocence, and would himself also attain Paradise.

Both the Knight and Marmaduke are erring human beings who get separated from their respective companions at certain points of their journey. Una, the personification of Truth, is temporarily forsaken by her Knight and falls into the lecher's hands.

> Forsaken Truth long seekes her love,
> And makes the Lyon mylde,
> Marres blind Devotions mart, and fals
> In hand of leachour vylde. (*The Faerie Queen*,
> I. iii. lines previous to 1st stanza)

When Idonea is separated from her protector she too is suspected of having fallen into the hands of a "leachour vylde," Lord Clifford. Marmaduke decides to murder her father, first to save, and then to revenge, the loss of her innocence.

Yet, in spite of the parallels, the two journeys have a very different ending. After successfully completing his journey towards Holiness, the Redcross Knight is united with Una, as a symbol of his completion of the journey leading to Truth. Marmaduke, however, is prevented from uniting with Idonea because of his own failure to reaffirm Herbert's holiness and Idonea's purity.

Idonea, like Una in *The Faerie Queene*, also evokes a sense of awe, a sense of holiness which she shares with Herbert. Like Una, she too is the representative of Truth, Beauty, and Goodness, all of these qualities being symbolized in her sexual innocence. Her virginity is associated with an uncorrupted harmony between Self and Nature, as well as harmony within the Self. A "dutiful child" to her venerable father, she is his "Raven in the wilderness" (*B*. II. 847), and through her the blind man communicates with the "sun," the "woods resound[ing] with music," and with the whole "pleasant face of Nature" (*B*. I. 146-147). She recognizes this "pleasant face" because of her own purity which makes her open to Truth both in Man and Nature: "She hath an eye that sinks into all hearts," (*B*. III. 1316), since she is a "Spirit, spotless as the blessed."

Being in perfect sympathy with Man and Nature, her sanctity is equally apparent to wild beasts who would be sent "scouring back" at a mere "look" of hers or to "troops of armed men in the road," who would "bless" both her and her father.

Their need for each other is mutual. The heroine leads her blind old father, but she is also led by him in her judgement. She looks at him with gratitude for having saved her life at the expense of losing his eyesight: "Twice had he been to me a father, twice / Had given me breath" (*B*. III. 1607-1608). Geoffrey Hartman thinks that because of her "double birth" Idonea's archetype is a rather confusing one. Interpreting from *The Prelude*, however, it appears that Idonea's double birth anticipates a notion of Wordsworth's later poetry in which he celebrates the immanence of the Spirit in Nature by claiming that throughout the world of Nature "all things have second birth" (*P*. X. 83). Idonea's innocence consists of being in this natural and supernatural state at the same time, suggesting the miracle of the grace of Creation being repeated in the grace of redemption. For Marmaduke, she stands for the childhood Paradise that he could attain in maturity through their union.

The play deals with the lovers' tragic loss of this Paradise, a promise of which was implied in the miracle of Idonea's second birth. At the end of the play this promise seems to be withdrawn when she suffers the "double loss" of both lover and father. It should be noted, however, that Idonea is still alive, and Marmaduke bequeaths the task of her protection to his devoted band. Idonea, and with her Nature's unfallen innocence, and hence our hope for Paradise, is bequeathed to the common people, to the spirit of our "common humanity."

The ambivalence between natural and supernatural in Idonea's figure merits further examination. In *The Faerie Queene*, the Redcross Knight undertakes to redeem Man from the consequences of the Fall, harking back to Eve's original sin, by relying on Una's supernatural guidance. In *The Borderers*, however, Idonea fulfills the role not only of Una, that of the Spirit, but also that of Eve, or Nature. For the romantic poet Eve, like the world of Nature, is unfallen, innocent. The hero's tragic mistake is in doubting this innocence, in coming to believe that the "Maiden...lovely as Spring's first rose" (*B.* I. 453-454), the "fairest of all flowers" (*B.* III. 1309) could be corrupt by nature, carrying "the worm...in her" (*B.* III. 1314) from birth. Although Marmaduke is strongly drawn to believe in her even after the villain's accusations (*B.* III. 1633-1650), his intuitive awareness of her purity is not strong enough to overcome Oswald's false evidence. Therefore he turns against her, and loses her irrevocably.

Idonea represents the romantic Eve or the purity of Nature. Her role can be understood more fully in her relationship to her father. Together with Idonea, Herbert evokes a sense of awe. The very fact of his blindness suggests something verging on the supernatural, something like a prophet's spiritual vision that takes the place of physical sight. Even Oswald acknowledges that there is something in Herbert that is "venerable," something reminiscent of the sacred. It is precisely because of Herbert's archetypal attributes of the sacred that Oswald decides to appoint him as a suitable victim for the sacrifice:

> For this old venerable Grey-beard—faith
> 'Tis his own fault if he hath got a face
> Which doth play tricks with them that look on it:
> 'Twas this that put it in my thoughts—that countenance—
> His staff—his figure—Murder! (*B.* II. 922-926)
> . . .
>
> We recognize in this old Man a victim
> Prepared already for the sacrifice. (*B.* II. 1092-1093)

The beggarwoman, although she is paid by Oswald to attest to his accusations, also describes Herbert as saintly:

> Lank as a ghost and tall, his shoulders bent,
> And long beard white with age—yet evermore

As if he were the only Saint on earth,
He turns his face to Heaven.   (*B.* I. 461-464)

In his moving helplessness and innocence Herbert emerges as a
late eighteenth-century personification of Holiness, a mediator
between Man and the Spirit, an allegorical figure of the Divine
image, of the "living God" in man. In many ways he foreshadows
the solitaries in Wordsworth's later poetry, the figure of the pitiable
"beggar [who is] a kind of inverse scapegoat: instead of bearing
away the sins of the community a memory of its good services and
charities."[15] Herbert's blindness and helplessness should make him
the focus of all the rays of sympathy reflected upon him by the
community. Through this focussing of the light of love of him, he
becomes the very source of human kindness and sympathy, of a
human love that in its intensity evokes, once more, the superhuman.

Marmaduke's love for Herbert is like his love for God. It is
fundamental to his self-image as a feeling human being. Since early
childhood he has loved Herbert as his own father, without even
knowing him, and this is inextricably entwined with the awakening
of his love for Idonea:

> Though I have never seen his face, methinks,
> There cannot come a day when I shall cease
> To love him. I remember, when a Boy
> Of scarcely seven years' growth, beneath the Elm
> That casts its shade over our village school,
> 'Twas my delight to sit and hear Idonea
> Repeat her Father's terrible adventures,
> Till all the band of playmates wept together;
> And that was the beginning of my love.
> And, through all converse of our later years,
> An image of this old Man still was present,
> When I had been most happy   (*B.* I. 87-89)

The hero's love for Herbert and Idonea is associated with the
happiest memories of his childhood, repeated and reinforced in the
happiest experiences as a man. These highlights in human existence
are the moments of epiphany Wordsworth later calls "spots of time"
(*P.* XII. 208). Such moments of keen perception and intuitive awareness make their presence felt in their restorative function when
remembered in later life.

Making Marmaduke equally devoted to Idonea and her father is
typical of Wordsworth. The hero's love for the heroine had its beginning in sympathy and compassion for a poor blind old man
whom he loves as his own father. Here Wordsworth provides an
excellent illustration of the sentimental eighteenth-century transla-

22

tion of love into pity. There is, however, something peculiar in the way Wordsworth makes use of this eighteenth-century concept. In the romantic poet's definition the moments of pity and love assume a religious aura (*B.* I. 87-98), descriptive of the hero's childhood Paradise he shares with the soul's perfect mate, Idonea. Surrounded by this aura, Herbert and Idonea belong together both in Marmaduke's affections and in the allegorical structure. Adam cannot unite with Eve, his complement, as a harmonious and complete being, without gaining the Father's acquiescence. When he turns against Herbert who personifies the Father or the Spirit, he is also led to turn against Idonea, symbol of unfallen or innocent Nature. It is through his alienation from Spirit and Nature, that Man loses his chances for Paradise.

The feelings of love, pity and veneration are the very foundations of Marmaduke's faith in Man, in himself, and in the existence of the Father or the "living God."

> Father!—to God himself we cannot give
> A holier name... (*B.* I. 543-544)

When Oswald's slander shakes his faith that Herbert is Idonea's venerable father, he feels that he is losing "the firm foundation of [his] life."

> Oswald, the firm foundation of my life
> Is going from under me; these strange discoveries—
> ...involve, I feel, my ruin. (*B.* I. 547-548; 550)

Having lost his "firm foundation," he confronts the "abyss" in himself with a sense of terror which is beyond human understanding:

> ...in plumbing the abyss for judgment
> Something I strike upon which turns my mind
> Back on herself, I think, again—my breast
> Concentres all the terrors of the Universe:
> I look at him and tremble like a child.
> (*B.* II. 782-786)

In spite of Oswald's persistence in passing judgement on the alleged criminal, Marmaduke is aware that the Divine Image Herbert evokes in him moves him to love and not to judgement, and to peace instead of retribution:

> ...I cannot do it:
> Twice did I spring to grasp his withered throat,
> When such a sudden weakness fell upon me,
> I could have dropped asleep upon his breast.
> (*B.* II. 889-892)

23

Nature itself warns Marmaduke against killing Herbert. The light of the star appears to him like the light of revelation to stay his hand:

> 'Twas dark—dark as the grave; yet did I see,
> Saw him—his face turned toward me; and I tell thee
> Idonea's filial countenance was there
> To baffle me—it put me to my prayers.
> Upwards I cast my eyes, and, through a crevice,
> Beheld a star twinkling above my head,
> And, by the living God, I could not do it.
>   (*B.* II. 984-990)

When, in spite of his intuitive awareness of Herbert's innocence, Marmaduke is prepared to abandon him on the moor, he recognizes himself destroyed as a feeling human being, cut off from man and the "living God" in man: "I am cut off from man; / No more shall I be man—no more shall I / Have human feelings!" (*B.* III. 1327-1329).

The impact of Herbert's figure, even more immediately than that of Idonea, evokes Wordsworth's awe before the divinity in man, the "living God" in the human soul which Marmaduke should have recognized. As one of Wordsworth's critics states,

The essence of the Wordsworthian revolution is precisely this transfer of the 'numinous' from the remote heavenly sphere to the "very world, which is the world / Of all of us,—the place where, in the end / We find our happiness, or not at all!" (*The Prelude*, XI. 142-144)[16]

In the play Marmaduke is tested for his ability to recognize and affirm the presence of Holiness in a human character. In order to fulfill his mission as the protector of the innocent who will restore mankind to its birthright of Paradise, he should recognize that Herbert is innocent, and has a sacred bond with his daughter. He should see that father's and daughter's relationship is "mutually consecrated" (*B.* IV. 1849) like the bond between Spirit and Nature, in spite of the satanic opponent's slander. Only by succeeding in this trial could Marmaduke re-unite with Idonea and regain the Paradise of childhood which would be available to man through the gift and promise of Idonea's "double birth." Marmaduke's journey to Holiness (unlike that of the Redcross Knight) would have been successful had he recognized that Holiness is in the natural human world around him and only there. Hence, having forfeited Paradise he cannot hope for restoration in any "remote heavenly sphere."

Although Wordsworth's transfer of the numinous to the worldly sphere is fundamental to his development of the allegorical framework, this same transfer is difficult to achieve dramatically.

Herbert may stand for the archetypal image of Holiness, but he can never become a psychologically realized character in a human drama. His function, together with that of Idonea, is allegorical, and not dramatic. There is a sense about their togetherness in the play which draws attention to a static, fixed relationship. The recurring image of the blind old father being led by his daughter is more like an emblem, illustrating relationship between two ideas, (the sacred bond between those "who walk in helplessness, when innocence is with them" (*B.* II. 790-791)) than a psychological relationship.

The breaking of Herbert's and Idonea's relationship is equivalent to the liberation of evil forces. As soon as they separate from each other they become vulnerable to Oswald's manipulation, and Marmaduke becomes susceptible to deception. Indeed, Herbert has a strong premonition about the wrongness of their parting: "And are you going then? Come, come, Idonea, We must not part" (*B.* I. 296-297), and again: "Now she is gone, I fain would call her back" (*B.* I. 328). Like Herbert, Idonea also anticipates that their strength might depend on their remaining united, and she wonders when she is alone, whether "I differ from the thing I am / When you are by my side" (*B.* I. 319-320).

Together they evoke a sense of awe which tames the wild forces in Nature and in man:

> ...Troops of armed men,
> Met in the roads, would bless us; little children,
> Rushing along in the full tide of play,
> Stood silent as we passed them! I have heard
> The boisterous carman, in the miry road,
> Check his loud whip and hail us with mild voice,
> And speak with milder voice to his poor beasts.
> (*B.* III. 1330-1336)

Together they are like "two songsters bred / In the same nest" (*B.* I. 150-151), and it is only after their separation, which allows the sinister forces of nature to come to the fore, that the "dismal moor," the "bewildering moonlight" (*B.* I. 111) and the stormy rocks around the deserted chapel gain their full negative significance. Once they are separated, Herbert is led to the ordeal of the "savage waste" to be sacrificed, and Idonea is left abandoned.

The allegorical significance of Herbert's figure is slightly different on various levels of the allegory. On the political level he is the very ideal of Man the Revolution was to rehabilitate, the same ideal that

25

had been victimized and ruthlessly sacrificed by the Reign of Terror:

> Such ghastly visions had I of despair
> And tyranny, and implements of death;
> And innocent victims sinking under fear,
> And momentary hope, and worn-out prayer,
> Each in his separate cell, or penned in crowds
> For sacrifice, and struggling with forced mirth
> And levity in dungeons... (*The Prelude*, X. 402-408)

"We recognize in this old man a victim / Prepared already for the sacrifice," announces Oswald with "forced mirth" when preparing his intrigue, enacting the victimization of the innocent by the ruthless forces of the Revolution.

On the universal level, the figure of the venerable old Father stands for the Divinity in Man, man's hope for restoring the Divine Image, or the Spirit. Herbert's blindness, however, also implies a sense of loss, a loss of direction. His blindness suggests the failure of old fashioned piety: it was "from the Holy land" that he "returned sightless, and from [his] heritage... driven a wretched outcast" (*B*. II. 828-830). Throughout his journey in the play, he is in search of a convent he will never reach, and meets his death, appropriately, at a deserted chapel.

On the aesthetic or epistemological level of the allegory, Herbert's death signifies a stage in the poet's development. Wordsworth was, as it were, on the "borderline" between a materialistic sensationist philosophy, and a belief in the transcendental powers of the human mind. Herbert's death signifies a desperate moment before the revelation that Wordsworth describes later in *The Prelude*. This is the revelation in which "the light of sense / Goes out, but with a flash that has revealed / The invisible world" (*P*. V. 600-601). This experience of the paradox, however, will be resolved for Wordsworth only after the development of his mature poetry in which he will bear witness to "imagination experienced as a power distinct from Nature [which] opens the poet's eyes by putting them out."[17] In the tragedy, this paradox is not yet resolved. Herbert dies blind and abandoned, and Marmaduke acknowledges his own defeat as "darkness deepening darkness."

Unable to affirm the spiritual light that is immanent in Nature, Man offends irredeemably against himself. Being unable to wed Idonea with the blessings of her father, who, symbolically is his father also, the hero loses Paradise.

26

Dramatically, Wordsworth has the same difficulty with his villain, Oswald, that he had with Herbert and Idonea in presenting on stage everyday characters with an almost supernatural aura. Although Oswald's soliloquies are philosophically and poetically the most memorable, and he is the only character the poet wants to explain and justify in his "Preface to The Borderers," he never emerges as a human being or a well realized human character.

There is an ambivalence in Oswald's character which shows through his illogical interaction with Marmaduke. Oswald wants to betray Marmaduke into crime as an act of personal revenge. (The band elected Marmaduke and not Oswald as their captain.) At the same time, Oswald also claims that he wants Marmaduke to commit crime out of a benevolent desire, to liberate his intellect from the bondage of moral scruples.

The problem in Oswald's characterization originates from Wordsworth's problem of accounting for Satan's role in the lovers' loss of Paradise, that is, his problem of accounting for the origin of evil.

In the light of the final tragedy, the borderers seem to reveal the insight of the common people when they recognize Oswald's ties with the more than natural forces of evil: "and I have noticed / That often, when the name of God is uttered / A sudden blankness overspreads his face" (B. III. 1437-1439). They refer to him with fear and awe as the "One of crooked ways" (B. I. 8) who is guilty of "some dark deed to which in early life his passion drove him" (B. I. 15-16), identifying him with the image of Satan in the guise of the Gothic villain.

Like Spenser's infernal magician, Archimago, who can conjure up insubstantial shapes and figures, Oswald is able to conjure up false evidence from unrelated facts, and the Band fears him as the practitioner of black magic, who "hold[s] of Spirits and the Sun in heaven" (B. III. 1447) and "seek[s] for sympathy / In dim relation to imagined Beings" (B. III. 1454-1455). He himself claims to dominate nature and threatens to "raise a whirlwind" (B. II. 944) if crossed in his purpose by the beggarwoman.

His affinities with Milton's Satan contribute to his aura of supernatural evil powers. He is the Betrayer who wants to win Marmaduke's soul:

> ... now
> For a few swelling phrases, and a flash

Of Truth, enough to dazzle and to blind,
And he is mine forever... (*B*. II. 562-565)

After his loss of Heaven, Satan welcomes the regions of Hell, not with sadness, but proud defiance:

... Farewell, happy fields,
Where joy forever dwells! Hail, horrors! hail,
Infernal world! and thou, profoundest Hell,
Receive thy new possessor, one who brings
A mind not to be changed by place or time.
(*Paradise Lost*, I. 249-253)

Oswald echoes this when leading Marmaduke away from the innocence of joy and harmony into a "region of futurity," opening to him the gloomy regions of a new "intellectual empire":

... What if you had bid
Eternal farewell to unmingled joy
And the light dancing of the thoughtless heart;
It is the toy of fools... (*B*. III. 1545-1548)

Oswald claims to be a bringer of light, but he is, like Lucifer, a bringer of a sinister light, the deceptive "flash / Of truth, enough to dazzle and to blind." Like Milton's Satan, who looks to Hell saying "here at least we shall be free" (*P.L.* I. 258-259), Oswald claims that he wanted Marmaduke to commit crime in order to "set him free" from the illusions of hope and happiness. Oswald also strikes a satanic pose when surveying his new dominion, looking down from the mountaintop of Syria to the "moonlight desert and the moonlight sea," he proudly observes that Nature's "mighty objects do... elevate our intellectual being" (*B*. IV. 1809-1810). His new dominion reflects intellectual pride, solitude and despair. In this romantic interpretation, Wordsworth associates Oswald's tragic character with the sublime grandeur in Nature, a foreshadowing of Byron's treatment of his heroic villain, Manfred. When in the "Preface to The Borderers" Wordsworth admits that in spite of his evil ways, Oswald's actions indeed have "the appearance of greatness,"[18] the poet himself reveals some sympathy with his villain's satanic grandeur, particularly with his claim to unlimited freedom.

In spite of the allusions that make Oswald resemble his supernatural archetype, however, he is yet only a human being in whom "pride... borders even upon madness,"[19] not a supernatural force, but a diseased individual. He represents the discord of natural affections in an ideology in which

Isolation, disconnection, unbalance are varieties of disease. The harmony of the constant interaction among things is comparable to the health of the organism . . . [where] harmony is guaranteed, because the world is a divine life.[20]

The members of his band who fear Oswald as a magician, also look on him as a madman, and Marmaduke describes him as a "monster" and an "unhappy man." Unlike the arch enemy who made a deliberate decision to rebel against his Master and commit evil, Oswald himself was "betrayed into crime," and his sin is mainly the desire to perpetuate evil by betraying Marmaduke.

If Oswald is right in saying that crime is an act man is "betrayed into"[21] by incomplete information, evil is basically an "error," a lack of knowledge, but it is not radical or innate. If, however, the poet were to acknowledge that sin is innate and natural, then Nature itself could no longer be seen as holy and unfallen, and hence he would have to construct a new myth to account for original sin, the Fall and the dilemma of redemption. The ambivalence in Oswald's characterization is closely related to Wordsworth's uncertainty whether to present him as an erring, but potentially perfectible and responsible human being, or as an embodiment of innate, satanic depravity.

Oswald's fall is described, through flashbacks and in a roundabout way. Both the circumstances and the nature of his original error are clouded in mystery.

> . . . In my youth,
> Except for that abatement which is paid
> By envy as a tribute to desert,
> I was the pleasure of all hearts, the darling
> Of every tongue—as you are now. You've heard
> That I embarked for Syria. On our voyage
> Was hatched among the crew a foul Conspiracy
> Against my honour, in the which our Captain
> Was, I believed, prime Agent . . .   (*B.* IV. 1684-1692)

The nature of this "foul conspiracy" is left vague and undefined. Oswald reproaches the captain for his undefined treachery, and the captain reacts by striking him for his insolence. Outraged, Oswald leaves the captain marooned on a desert island, and he is encouraged in this action by the cheering crew.

The fact that Oswald is "betrayed into crime" by the crew is central to the allegorical structure in which the crew is the collective source of evil. Being jealous of Oswald, an exceptional individual, the crew conspires against him and leads him to abandon the captain of their ship. Although they know that their master is innocent, their laughter drowns out his anguished cry as the ship leaves him behind. Their cruelty, ruthlessness, and malice is the original and rationally inexplicable source of evil. Through the crew of the ship Wordsworth presents the revolutionary reversal of the traditional social structure as a riot, a mutiny which leads to destruction, and ultimately to chaos. Revolution is presented here as the victimizer of innocence through the elimination of lawful authority.

What is the degree of Oswald's complicity in and responsibility for this crime against lawful authority and human sympathy? He does not examine the evidence of the captain's guilt, but accepts it because it feeds the violent and hostile passion he had already developed against him, the germ of his rebellious negation and defiance. Yet, if his gullibility, or willingness to believe the crew is the full measure of his responsibility, this would still leave a number of unanswered questions about the crew's initial motive for its crime, about the nature and the origin of evil. It is significant that these unanswered questions are presented against the background of a mysterious and distant past, and through flashbacks.

In the dramatic action, however, Wordsworth does not give much attention to or details about the crew's crime. Neither the motives nor the circumstances of this distant act are clearly defined or explained, as if the poet were much less interested in the mystery of original sin, than in man's reaction to finding himself guilty.

Having found himself "betrayed into crime," Oswald responds to the loss of his innocence with a philosophy of despair, pride and defiance. He interprets his suffering as a process that alienates the exceptional human being, but also sets him above the rest:

> Great actions move our admiration, chiefly
> Because they carry in themselves an earnest
> That we can suffer greatly.   (B. III. 1536-1538)

Oswald also argues that man should not be held morally responsible for his actions because our impulses follow the laws of physical necessity.

> Action is transitory—a step, a blow,
> The motion of a muscle—this way or that—
> 'Tis done, and in the after-vacancy
> We wonder at ourselves like men betrayed:
> Suffering is permanent, obscure and dark,
> And shares the nature of infinity.   (B. III. 1539-1544)

30

Oswald is convinced that the physical laws of Nature operate quite independently of will, or moral responsibility, since the universe is itself without a spiritual being, and has no ethical dimensions. Having taken this stance, he rejects remorse as something irrelevant to the unethical principle beyond the universe: "Remorse— / It cannot live with thought: think on, think on / And it will die" (*B.* III. 1560-1562). Remorse would be meaningful only if man had belief in the divine design that rules the world according to the principles of law, justice, and mercy. Oswald, however, conceives of the Infinite as inscrutably obscure and dark, like the permanent darkness of suffering. Therefore he presumes that it is only "in darkness and in tempest that we seek / The majesty of Him who rules the world" (*B.* II. 615-617). This statement of despair and the denial of the benevolent spirit also justifies Oswald's satanic experimenting with evil. Yet his satanic role stems only from his "false conclusion" to or interpretation of his original loss of innocence.

Although Oswald enjoys the posture of a satanic villain, his offence is significantly different from the sin of Milton's Satan. Oswald is not fully responsible for his first crime; he becomes a criminal only when alienating himself from his fellow man in despair. His pride in his fall is "unnatural" because it cuts him off from the sympathy of the rest of humanity. He claims that he has no need of human sympathy, because of his exceptional, non-human or more than human stature, and claims that he had manipulated Marmaduke's beliefs only in order to share with him this stature. His argument, however, is self-contradictory.

> Compassion!—pity!—pride can do without them;
> And what if you should never know them more!—
> He is a puny soul who, feeling pain,
> Finds ease because another feels it too.
> If e'er I open out this heart of mine
> It shall be for a nobler end—to teach
> And not to purchase puling sympathy.
> (*B.* III. 1553-1559)

He considers himself to be above the need of sharing human sympathy, but what is his "nobler" purpose that he wants to reach? And why should he want to teach it if he had no desire to communicate with or influence a disciple? He describes his isolation as the freedom of absolute independence, yet he feels a strong need to draw Marmaduke into his confidence, admitting "fellowship we must have, willing or no." This "fellowship" immediately introduces the loss of absolute independence or liberty: "Ay, we are coupled by a

31

chain of adamant / Let us be fellow-labourers, then, to enlarge / Man's intellectual empire" (*B.* IV. 1854-1856).

Oswald's conception of freedom is paradoxical. Even when he insists on being free, he is the slave of his own past, of his crime, and craves the fellowship of another criminal with whom he can enter the bond of a "chain of adamant."

Yet Oswald's flawed philosophical argument, like that of Milton's Satan, is far from unattractive. Although he is ruthless in arguing for the spirit of liberty, he also asserts the need of genius to examine law and tradition anew. Encouraging Marmaduke to make his own law, he acts true to the spirit of the Romantic outlaw as tragic hero. His argument is given dignity and power when rendered through the images of the sublime in Nature, the "moonlight sea and the moonlight desert," "the lonely mountaintop," "the torrent of the cataract," and the "solitude" of the "eagle." Oswald represents the attractiveness of the "tempestuous loveliness" of despair, of the sublime defiance of Satan.

In *The Borderers* Wordsworth raises the question: what would it entail to succumb to the sublime argument of the satanic Oswald?

By listening to his 'betrayer,' Marmaduke severs himself from Idonea and from his band, and both these separations have tragic consequences. In separating from Idonea, he cuts himself off from the innocence of a childhood Paradise and from the promise of finding a second Paradise in sexual love. Only in such a state of alienation can Marmaduke be tempted to take on the role of judge, and thereby murder the spirit of kindness and love, the image of God in man.

Himself "blinded" by Oswald's negation, Marmaduke's murder of the blind Herbert is at least as much an act of suicide, as it is an act of "intellectual murder."[22] By killing Herbert whom he loved as a Father, he destroys something vital in his own soul: the "living God" of love, innocence and hope for renewal. What is left for him is merely the desire to meet the mercy of death.

Oswald, Herbert and Marmaduke may be seen as personifications of various aspects of Wordsworth's intellectual and spiritual crisis following the disillusionment with the French Revolution. As described in *The Prelude*:

> In such strange passion...
> ... I warred against myself—
> A bigot to a new idolatry—
> Like a cowled monk who had foresworn the world,
> Zealously laboured to cut off my heart

From all the sources of her former strength;
And as, by simple waving of a wand,
The wizard instantaneously dissolves
Palace or grove, even so could I unsoul
As readily by syllogistic words
Those mysteries of being which have made,
And shall continue evermore to make
Of the whole human race one brotherhood.

(P. XII. 75-87)

It is as Marmaduke that he fell into error, being "betrayed by reasonings ... false." It is as Oswald that he fell into the role of the self-destructive "wizard" who is like Satan's apprentice Archimago, or Satan himself, in being powerful enough to "wave the wand" and "dissolve palace or grove." This image of the destructive and self-destructive wizard appears again in the "Preface to The Borderers" where Oswald is said to be demolishing the very "groves that should shelter him."[23] The magic of Oswald's "syllogistic words" reduced Marmaduke's whole world to "shadows" by eliminating its element of human sympathy, by "unsouling" the vital "myteries of being which have made ... of the whole human race one brotherhood."

Although in *The Prelude* the poet describes how these different aspects assumed an inner war, how he "warred against" himself, in the play the two sides of the warfare are not developed with equal philosophical vigour. Neither does Wordsworth's internal warfare lend itself to the staging of an effective dramatic conflict.

On the political level of the allegory Oswald represents the ruthless activist who ridicules moral scruples. He is an allegorical presentation of an energy that found its distorted embodiment in the Reign of Terror that "plucked up mercy by the root" (*P.* X. 332), and made "the crimes of the few spread into the madness of the many" (*P.* X. 336). Oswald's merciless sacrifice of the helpless victim Herbert, parallels the energy of political revolutions that Wordsworth came to distrust through his disillusionment with the French Revolution.

Marmaduke will conclude through his experience with Oswald that political action is useless or of dubious significance, because "The deeper malady is better hid; / The world is poisoned at the heart" (*B.* II. 1035-1036). Yet there is no real dramatic conflict between hero and villain. Marmaduke turns against the venerable father and paternal authority, just as Oswald did when he had turned against his captain, the master of his ship. The poet makes clear that the revolutionary reversal of paternal authority leads to guilt, suffering and alienation.

Oswald assumes Man to be evil, and Nature indifferent to man. All his ruthless acts follow from his alienation, which is, ultimately, due to a "false conclusion" (*P.* XI. 187). This false conclusion is, in effect, the argument of Shaftesbury's atheist who perceived the universe as a "wide waste" of chaos, and not a well ordered harmonious whole designed by a benevolent Divinity.[24]

To refute the satanic villain's accusation, Marmaduke should affirm Nature's perfection and immediate accessibility; he should affirm the invincible innocence of Idonea. It is because he failed to affirm that the bond between Nature and Spirit (that is, between Idonea and her father) is "mutually consecrated," that he destroys himself, and "a wanderer...[he] must leave" his lost Paradise. There is no doubt that the Paradise was an earthly one and having lost it there is no compensation in afterlife. The vagueness of the language, "Providence," "Heaven's mercy," "Heaven's eye," or a "soul in bliss" should not obscure this dilemma. In Wordsworth's world Man should find Holiness in his earthly journey. Since the spiritual realm is not distinct from the natural one, Marmaduke's loss, therefore, is irrevocable, and so is his final experience of Nature as a hellish "waste" where his story will leave a monument: "raise on that dreary Waste a monument / That may record my story" (*B.* V. 2326-2327).

Leaving the Paradise of his first innocence, Marmaduke has no hope for restoration because he feels himself cursed by Nature through the curse of Idonea: "I am accurst: All nature curses me, and in my heart / *Thy* curse is fixed" (*B.* V. 2204-2206).

Marmaduke cannot argue convincingly against Oswald. He does not personify affirmation, only a desire for affirmation, and neither his intellectual argument nor his character is developed with sufficient vigour to serve as Oswald's effective dramatic opponent. While Oswald's character conveys cosmic despair about a materialistically conceived universe, Marmaduke's pathetic figure personifies the weakness of the counter argument: he is a weak, ineffective spokesman for sympathy and intuition, the potentially transcendent faculty of the mind that should, but is unable to "master" Oswald's argument.

Oswald is right, then, in saying that Marmaduke "blended to [his] wish" like a "Fool and a Coward" (*B.* V. 2318), without much resistance. The fact that Marmaduke personifies the weakness and perplexity of the poet's affirmative philosophy also renders him weak dramatically.

Nevertheless, Marmaduke's weakness and defeat is not complete at the end of the play. His greatest shock is in discovering that the word "I" became "filled with horror" (*B.* V. 2167-2168). When Idonea asks him, "hast thou pursued the monster?" Marmaduke answers, weighed down by remorse, "I have found him" (*B.* V. 2192). Having set out to conquer evil in the outside world, he found the monster within himself, and responds to the discovery with the shock of moral crisis, and even temporary madness (*B.* V. 2022-2039). Then, by facing up to his responsiblity, he responds to Idonea. "I am the man" (*B.* V. 2207) and confronts his fate in the spirit of acceptance.

He acknowledges Oswald's victory, but feels he is not totally defeated:

> ... there was a plot,
> A hideous plot, against the soul of man:
> It took effect—and yet I baffled it,
> In some degree.   (*B.* V. 2142-2145)

Although the satanic villain conspired against the soul of man, his plot did not totally accomplish what it intended. Marmaduke is not won over by Oswald's ruthless materialism. The very intensity of remorse and grief makes Marmaduke recognize the power of passion and sympathy. Through this suffering he can start his lonely pilgrimage to find a new image of God: "a wanderer must I go / The Spectre of that innocent Man, my guide" (*B.* V. 2344-2345). We are left, by the end of the play, on the "borderland" between faith outworn and lost, and the coming of a new faith in Man and Nature.

The murder of Herbert is like the ritual murder of the spirit of pious affirmation. The poet has to confront the intellectual doubts and questions of an Oswald before he can attain a higher level of affirmation, an affirmation that will absorb and transcend negation and despair. The play opens the way to a change from Herbert's outdated orthodox piety to the "natural piety" of the "sensitive soul."

The dialectical movement in the poet's own spiritual journey allows for the formulation of a paradox. Marmaduke, the Romantic Redcross Knight failed to recognize Holiness. Nevertheless the poet goes further on his own journey leading to his new "creed" of affirmation, a creed which celebrates the light of the spirit revealed both in Man and in Nature.

35

It has been said of Wordsworth that "he loved Nature as a reality, man as an idea"[26] and this statement also draws attention to some of the strengths and many of the weaknesses in this early work, his only attempt at drama, or tragedy.

While the tangled plot and the unmotivated characters make the dramatic action difficult to follow, the images relating to Nature are complete and lucid, and they sustain the character portrayal and the dramatic action symbolically. The characters are indeed hard to comprehend without the corresponding images from Nature. For example, Oswald compares Herbert to a "withered tree" to be "hewn down" and Marmaduke explains to Herbert the old man's own condition when describing to him a ragged tree on the moor:

> Here is a tree, ragged, and bent, and bare,
> That turns its goat's-beard flakes of pea-green moss
> From the stern breathing of the rough sea-wind;
> This have we, but no other company: (*B.* III. 1294-1297)

Archetypally the tree is a mediator between human and super-human realms, and this fits in with Herbert's function as a mediator, the representative of the Divine Image. In other instances he is referred to as the "venerable Grey beard," and since Marmaduke suspects Herbert of having become an instrument of lechery, it is this image which is transformed into the lecherous "goat's-beard." The tree turns away from the "rough sea wind," from the tempestuous energy of intellectual inquiry and revolutionary denial, an energy formulated in terms of wind and storm images throughout the play.

The person most often related to these storm and wind images is Oswald, the villain. He describes his fall, as being "betrayed into crime" by the crew of his ship. The reason for the original crime, however, that is, the crew's "foul conspiracy against [his] honour" is left vague and undefined. What we see in graphic detail, instead, is his depression which follows the committing of the crime. His anguish is described through images of the surrounding world of nature. His mental conflict is acted out exclusively in the natural landscape, most specifically through the images of falling and rising winds:

> ... The wind fell:
> ...
>
> On a dead sea under a burning sky,

> I brooded o'er my injuries, deserted
> By man and nature;—if a breeze had blown,
> It might have found its way into my heart,
> And I had been—no matter—do you mark me?
> (*B.* IV. 1692-1702)

The clumsiness of the dialogue reflects the speaker's excitement. Oswald interrupts himself and leaves the sentence unfinished, drawing attention to the significance of the "breeze" that could have changed the entire course of events. What Oswald is bewailing here is the lack of a creative and loving spirit in the human soul, as if anticipating the famous image of the "corresponding breeze" in *The Prelude*, the breeze that inspires the energies of Nature and the human mind. It is the creative spirit that links Man with Nature.

After Oswald deserts the captain, the whole ship suffers from the lack of wind or breeze, from the "dead calm" upon the sea: "I know not how he perished; but the calm, / The same dead calm continued many days" (*B.* IV. 1743-1744). This seascape of Oswald's journey is strongly reminiscent of the Ancient Mariner's enchanted journey, which also externalizes a spiritual experience. In Coleridge's poem, the Mariner's spiritual agony follows from his unaccountable and mysterious offence against Nature in the killing of the Albatross. For Oswald, spiritual agony seems to be a direct punishment for his revolution. By turning against the Captain of his ship, he turned against his master or Father, and the "dead calm" of the sea, and the laughter of the riotous mob are twin aspects of his own guilt which follows the revolutionary reversal.

Rebellion is followed by a period of acute shame and inactivity which ended in his decision to "burst forth" in any "possible shape of action" for redeeming his "lost peace." As soon as he made this decision, he regained the energy that in the period of shame has been turned against the self. Immediately he feels that his "Ferocity subsided in a moment, like a wind / That drops down dead out a sky it vexed" (*B.* IV. 1784-1786). He regains a "salient spring of energy" to be channelled "from action up to action." In these images Oswald describes how the storm of destructive revolution is followed by dead calm, and then by the "ferocity" of guilt feeling that he relieves by newer, and by now, quite deliberate acts of evil.

The pattern of the wind imagery, the storm followed by the dead calm, has sinister connotations. When he wants to scare the superstitious beggarwoman, Oswald describes himself as a magician, the devilish manipulator of the wind, and threatening to "raise a whirlwind" (*B.* II. 944), he identifies with this destructive element.

The wind as destructive force is also associated with other characters. Herbert finds his death in a storm while trying to reach a deserted chapel whose bell is rung by the wind: "that Chapel-bell ... its fitful stroke / Can scarcely be the work of human hands," it is "the wind" (*B.* IV. 1651-1653) that acts "like some evil spirit" (*B.* IV. 1664).

Marmaduke also describes his feeling of loss and the turbulence of his spirit by complaining, "how the wind howls" (*B.* IV. 1765). When Herbert turns to nature for re-assurance, he turns to the "earth-loving wind" (*B.* III. 1263) among the flowers, but the wind is, ironically the very force that leads him to his death. In this play the wind is a sinister force of a revolutionary energy being led astray, and the destructive movement of this energy is followed only by "dead calm," and the "impotence of death."

The energy here is far from the creative and shaping energy of the "corresponding breeze," it is the energy of discord, of the revolutionary "storm of great events" (*P.* XI. 374) historically, and of the stormy "perturbations of a youthful mind" (*P.* XI. 373) on the personal level; of Man being alienated from Nature and from the Spirit on the most universal level. Creative energy is contemplated as possibly a malicious or destructive force, both in the cosmos and in the human mind. The poet questions whether the mind can find its bond with Nature and the Infinite in any form other than in storm and tempest: "It is in darkness and in tempest that we seek the majesty of Him who rules the world." The pattern of the wind and storm images, therefore, seems to be in accord with the play's dramatic resolutions: Herbert's death, Oswald's death without hope for redemption, and Marmaduke's lonely wandering "by pain and thought compelled to live, / Yet loathing life" (*B.* V. 2351-2352).

There is, however, another image related to the wind, which suggests the possibility of restoration. When Idonea refers to her birth and rebirth as "twice had he [Herbert] been a father, twice gave me breath," the "breath" of the creative spirit contains symbolic foreshadowing of the "corresponding breeze." The image is associated with hope, a new birth out of Idonea's "double loss," but this image of hope is not translated into the dramatic action.

The images of light and darkness support the overwhelmingly negative connotations of the wind imagery in the dramatic action.

Darkness predominates, and the images of blindness emphatically underline this impression. Herbert is "blind as the grave," the beggarwoman is afraid of being "struck blind," the band complains of having acted "blind as moles," Marmaduke of having been de-

38

ceived and "blinded," and Oswald is described in the "Preface to The Borderers" as a person who is "blind to truth."

In his death scene Herbert cries out against the darkness and the tempest: "My child,—my child—dark—dark—I faint—this wind / These stifling blasts—God help me!" (*B*. IV. 1657-1658). Marmaduke describes the dungeon "dark—dark as the grave," and his final assessment of Oswald's test is that it was "darkness deepening darkness."

Although there is a surface opposition between the powers of light and darkness, the images of light are usually connected with the false light of illusion, or even betrayal. Idonea complains of the "bewildering moonlight" that led her to the "dismal moor," and Herbert dies on this moor alone, without even the "pitying moon." Neither is the beggarwoman, who sees the cheerful light of a glow-worm in the stormy night, sustained by this source of light. In her distress she sees it as a symbol of God's mockery of, or indifference to human misery:

> The darkness overtook me—wind and rain
> Beat hard upon my head—and yet I saw
> A glow-worm, through the covert of the furze,
> Shine calmly as if nothing ailed the sky:
> At which I half accused the God in Heaven—
> You must forgive me.   (*B*. I. 423-428)

She doubts the spiritual light shining through the natural which is blasphemy in Wordsworth's mature formulation of his belief in Nature.

Marmaduke repeats this blasphemy when he denies that the light of the star that appears in the dungeon carries the light of revelation. At first when Marmaduke enters the dungeon to kill the sleeping old man, he is stopped by seeing Idonea's reflection on the old man's face. Innocence and love produce light enough to illumine the dark cave. This light is reinforced by the light of the star through the crevice.

> 'Twas dark—dark as the grave; yet did I see,
> Saw him—his face turned toward me: and I tell thee
> Idonea's filial countenance was there
> To baffle me—it put me to my prayers.
> Upwards I cast my eyes, and, through a crevice,
> Beheld a star twinkling above my head,
> And, by the living God, I could not do it.
> (*B*. II. 984-990)

This is one of the few instances in which God is mentioned (apart from the euphemisms of Heaven, Providence, and so on) and it is, emphatically the "living God" that Marmaduke summons here. The incident represents the divine revelation coming to the mind ready to perceive and receive it through a sympathetic awareness of the oneness of Man and Nature.

Marmaduke, however, later denies this "living God" and his message revealed through Nature. When he believes Oswald's slander, he succumbs to a mood of cosmic despair: the light of the star was merely a "twinkling atom" that could not dissolve the "creed built into the heart of things," the creed of an unethical and absurd universe.

> Now I could laugh till my ribs ached. Oh, Fool!
> To let a creed, built in the heart of things,
> Dissolve before a twinkling atom!...
> (*B.* III. 1218-1220)

He is "betrayed into" denying spiritual light; the feeble light of the star could not overcome the darkness of the universe abandoned by God.

It is only after a period of spiritual restoration that Wordsworth will affirm that the stars and the glowworms are equally manifestations of the Spirit, of light

> To penetrate the lofty and the low;
> Even as one essence of pervading light
> Shines, in the brightest of ten thousand stars,
> And the meek worm that feeds the lonely lamp
> Couched in the dewy grass. (*P.* XIX, 272-275)

But in this play of darkness, light is seen only in the "blinding flashes" of Oswald's despair that illuminate a scene of evil and suffering.

The poet seems to be in despair about the mind's ability to find the light of Truth. Although the natural landscape is handled as a means of revelation, the revelation assumes sinister, negative connotations. For example, when Oswald describes his transformation from a passive victim of his own guilt into a free and amoral being thirsting for action, he relates this transformation to his sudden recognition of a cosmic principle revealed through the natural landscape:

> ...from the top of Lebanon surveyed
> The moonlight desert, and the moonlight sea:
> In these my lonely wonderings I perceived
> What mighty objects do impress their forms

To elevate our intellectual being;
And felt, if ought on earth deserves a curse,
'Tis that worst principle of ill which dooms
A thing so great to perish self-consumed.
—So much for my remorse! (*B*. IV. 1806-1814)

Oswald, the lonely figure on the mountaintop, confronts the Sublime in the Infinite through the beauty of the "moonlight desert" and the "moonlight sea," and asserts that the human mind is a mirror of the majestic forms of Nature through its own lonely grandeur and solitude. He also dismisses the traditional system which would associate such moral concerns as remorse or redemption with the heights, or Heaven. To Oswald this cosmic region is expressive of nothing but solitude and vacancy.

The close relationship between the natural and the mental landscape seems to be in accord with Shaftesbury's theory of the sympathy between the natural and the moral universe, and this concept will later re-appear with firmer conviction in Wordsworth's *The Prelude*. There he celebrates "Nature's secondary grace" that "her works present ... Apt illustrations of the moral world" (*P*. XIX. 272-275). Nature is a mirror of man's consciousness, and as Wordsworth's favourite images indicate, it is a mirror of calm and undisturbed water.

In this early work of tragic questioning, however, the mirror-like relationship between the moral and the natural cosmos introduces a disturbing dilemma. When Oswald describes his own state of mind, he evokes a wild and turbulent landscape, as he "followed on, through woods of gloomy cedar, / Into deep chasms troubled by roaring streams" (*B*. IV. 1804-1805). In addition to describing a state of mind, the stage-setting of "troubled" waters, and stormy gusts also makes the whole world of *The Borderers* emerge as a dark and sinister cosmos, as if Nature were the source of the darkness and cruelty which reigns in the moral cosmos of the mind.

Through all their manifestations in this tragedy, the images of Nature contribute to the emergence of the central unifying symbol of a desert or a waste. Neither Oswald nor Marmaduke shed human blood; they yield up the condemned victim to the cruelty of Nature, confident that it will execute their intentions. The background is the "dismal moor," and together with the flashbacks to scenes from the past, it emphasizes barrenness, waste, cold, and hunger. Oswald's victim, the captain perishes because of cold and hunger upon the barren rocks of a deserted island, just as Herbert dies of cold and starvation at the foot of the rocky deserted precipice.

41

The image of Nature as a wasteland fulfills a complex function. If Nature is nothing but a wasteland, man might be "betrayed into crime," since he is by necessity also abandoned in the cosmos, without any natural guideline to distinguish between good and evil, or to find the reflection of a moral principle in the world around him. In this sense, man is "betrayed into crime" through his very existence, and he perpetuates this act of betrayal in the spiritual waste of his own heart, as experienced by the poet when "a sense / Death-like, of treacherous desertion, felt / In the last place of refuge—my own soul" (*P*. X. 414-415).

The images of the physical and spiritual wasteland describe the whole world as a waste without a central benevolent design. Betrayed and betraying, Marmaduke abandons Herbert to this wasteland, yielding him up to the cruelty of Nature which is devoid of the Spirit. In his anguish he cries out for the "living God" to appear to him, as the living force that Herbert had experienced and represented before: "If once, why not again, / And in this desert?" (*B*. III. 1395-1396), the anguished cry of man in search of a new "creed" from the desert of emptiness.

In the reflection of the poet's "inner storm," Nature in *The Borderers* emerges as a menacing "waste" of storms, torrents, and useless, unjustified destruction. In this waste Man is made to lose his innocence either as a "victim" or a "dupe" of betrayal.

Wordsworth's early view about the cosmos raises some interesting questions about the "new mythological construction" introduced by the Romantic poets. In his survey of English Romanticism Northrop Frye draws a contrast between the new romantic cosmology and that of the traditional Christian mythology which has influenced if not completely determined our view of the world and man for almost two thousand years.

Frye describes the traditional cosmos to be "best understood as a structure on four spatial levels,"[27] consisting of Heaven, Paradise, Nature and Hell, with a "moral principle incorporated into it: God is good, hell bad and the human level of nature, [that is, Paradise] better than the physical one."[28] The spatial expression of this "moral principle" is an ascending movement, where man is looking for the good in the height associated with Heaven and the Father. In contrast, the downward movement is associated with evil, pointing at the depth of Hell.

In Frye's explanation, the "new mythological construction"[29] of romanticism introduces a "revolutionary reversal" in the spatial expression of the moral principle. The regions of Heaven, formerly associated with the spiritual or the supernatural, come to assume the significance of evil as "alienation" while the moral good becomes associated with a search for "identity," and this assumes an inward or downward movement directed at a "deep cosmic center."

The concept of the "revolutionary reversal" of the cosmic structure raises interesting questions in *The Borderers* and in the other four tragedies as well.

Their study suggests that on a stage set for Gothic melodrama, Wordsworth inadvertently dramatizes the myth of the loss of innocence, or Man's loss of Paradise. The four stock characters re-enact this drama in a way which also reflects the poet's vision of the cosmos, and the "moral principle incorporated into it." The following diagram delineates the correspondence between the stock characters and the cosmic regions.

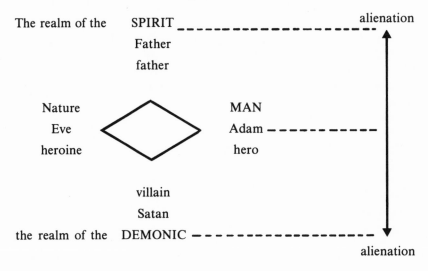

The wedding between hero and heroine with their father's blessings would celebrate the union of Adam and Eve in Paradise in harmony with their Father, or the harmony between Man, Nature and the Spirit in Nature. Having succumbed to the villain, the hero loses Eve, and suffers from the alienation between Man, Nature and Spirit: he descends into the demonic realm of alienation and even temporary madness. In Keats's, Byron's, and Shelley's tragedies this also proves to be the realm of death. At the end the hero is radically separated from the "pleasant countenance of nature," that is, from his mate and their common father; he suffers the irredeemable separation between Man, Nature and Spirit.

The nature images of Wordsworth's play delineate only a certain phase of the movement Frye described as the "new mythological construction" of romanticism. The play seems to end with the hero's shock upon recognizing the criminality of the sudden "revolutionary reversal." Having turned against the saintly old Herbert, the stock character of the father who evokes all the traditional associations with the Father or the Spirit, Marmaduke experiences a sense of spiritual vertigo, the loss of the "firm foundation" of his life. He comes to see the "abyss" of emptiness opening up as a result.

The images of height are indeed associated with alienation, as Northrop Frye suggested. The "barren rock" on which the ship's captain is exposed to death is a place of lonely agony and so is the ridge of rocks where Herbert dies.

Wordsworth's hero is indeed struck with the emptiness of regions previously associated with Heaven or the Father. Yet he fails to recognize the emergence of a new cosmic centre. His real tragedy consists of the loss which follows here the reversal, or partial reversal, of the traditional structure. He experiences the collapse of all moral structures, the loss of any "firm foundation," and faces the "abyss" of emptiness and terror.

Marmaduke feels that Man committed an irredeemable offence against Nature and Spirit. Hence he descends to the villain's satanic realm, to alienation, a descent Wordsworth himself cannot find tenable for long either psychologically or philosophically.

III

"POISON IN THE WINE":
COLERIDGE'S *REMORSE*

Both Wordsworth's *The Borderers* and Coleridge's *Remorse* deal
with the desire for marriage betwen a hero and heroine, which is
frustrated by the machinations of the satanic villain. In *The Borderers*
the villain is strong enough to prevent the wedding, whereas in
Remorse the lovers win out.

Remorse is set in sixteenth-century Spain. The villain, Lord
Valdez's younger son, Ordonio had tricked his older brother Alvar
into leaving his native Spain. Then Ordonio hired assassins to have
him murdered with the purpose of winning the hand of Alvar's
betrothed, Teresa. Alvar, however, overcame the assassins, and had
the last one, Isidore, confess that the attempt of murder had been
instigated by Ordonio.

The play begins with the hero's return after six years of absence.
He puts on a disguise to test Ordonio and Teresa and make them
feel remorse. Ordonio, however, is deceived by his brother's disguise,
and hires this stranger in Moresco clothes to perform a magic trick
with which he wants to win Teresa who is still faithful to the hero.
Lord Valdez, who is also Teresa's guardian, agrees to this trick,
having found it impossible by other means to force her into marriage
with Ordonio.

Ordonio wants the magician to present, under mysterious circumstances, the girl's miniature portrait which she once entrusted
to her lover as a keepsake and which fell in the hands of Ordonio. He
trusts that seeing this portrait, Teresa will regard it as proof of her
lover's death.—Alvar who is a gifted painter, agrees to the performance, but he prepares a surprise. Instead of Teresa's portrait, he
presents a painting depicting the attempt at his own assassination.
At the end of this performance Monviedro, the cruel Inquisitor,
appears to throw the 'magician' into prison. Ordonio, who is a
strong supporter of the Inquisition, willingly agrees to this imprisonment, the more so, since he is frightened by the magician's
unexpected knowledge of the truth.

Being afraid of betrayal, Ordonio now proceeds to trap and kill
his own agent, the Moresco chief, Isidore. Then he descends into
the dungeon to poison the magician, but Alvar declares his true

identity, and offers forgiveness to Ordonio. Ordonio, however, feels
so guilty about Isidore's recent murder that he cannot accept forgiveness. When Isidore's widow, Alhadra arrives to take revenge,
Ordonio submits his life to her willingly, preferring death to a life
that is haunted by guilt but lacks faith in redemption.

After killing Ordonio, Alhadra leaves the stage with a prophecy
about the downfall of all oppression such as Ordonio stood for.

> I thank thee, Heaven! thou hast ordained it wisely,
> That still extremes bring their own cure...
> . . .
>
> The strong holds of the cruel men should fall,
> Their temples and their mountainous towers should fall;
> Till desolation seemed a beautiful thing,
> And all that were and had the spirit of life,
> Sang a new song to her who had gone forth,
> Conquering and still to conquer!   (V. 1. 265-269; 274-279)

Like the young Coleridge in his "Religious Musings," Alhadra
looks forward to the Apocalypse of Revolution. She welcomes the
fall of the "temples" of clerical oppression, embodied in the play by
the Inquisitor, and the "towers" of political tyranny, represented by
Ordonio and to some extent his father, Lord Valdez. She anticipates
a millennium as universal liberation.

Consequently, Alvar's liberation and the reunion of the lovers is
accompanied by the general rejoicings of armed Spanish peasants
who rush to the scene with no other purpose than to celebrate
this event. In spite of his former tyrannical insistence that Teresa
marry Ordonio, Lord Valdez now needs no persuasion to take part
in the general rejoicings. Significantly, he ignores his dead son,
Ordonio, as if implicitly condoning Alvar's assessment of the situation: "Delights so full, if unalloyed with grief, / Were ominous"
(V. 1. 285-286).

The play ends with Alvar delivering a short homily on triumphant
Conscience that is always in agreement with Intuition and Imagination, the uncorrupted inner voice that is ultimately the just instrument of fate guided by Providence.

> ...In these strange dread events
> Just Heaven instructs us with an awful voice,
> That Conscience rules us e'en against our choice.
> Our inward Monitress to guide or warn
> If listened to; but if repelled with scorn,
> At length as dire REMORSE she reappears,
> Works in our guilty hopes and selfish fears!

Still bids, Remember! and still cries, Too late!
And while she scares us, goads us to our fate.   (V. 1. 286-294)

The play ends with a neatly worked out scheme of poetic justice, instead of a cathartic effect. Conscience is God's spirit in the human heart, the "inward Monitress" of the "inner light" and "inner sound." Teresa and Alvar listened to this inner guidance, while Ordonio was trying to "repell it with scorn." Therefore, in Ordonio's case, Conscience reappears in the form of self-destructive remorse, in the "guilty hopes and selfish fears" that entangle him deeper in the consequences of his originally evil deed. Alvar's sermon makes it seem just that Ordonio should die for his initial disobedience to the "inward Monitress"; it celebrates the triumph of a poetic justice which assumes the role of "Just Heaven," or Providence.

HERO, HEROINE AND VILLAIN

At first glance *Remorse* appears to be an allegory about restored and triumphant faith. In spite of evidence that should convince a non-believer, Alvar refuses to believe the rumour about Teresa's "pollution," and decides to confront her and seek proof. Similarly, in spite of the rumours and apparent evidence of Alvar's death, Teresa follows a "surer light" than that of the senses, and refuses to give up her faith in her lover's return. Alvar's final speech asserts that the intuitive faculty, whether it is called Faith or Imagination, ultimately triumphs over the brutish materialism of factual evidence. Having expelled Ordonio, the materialist Satan, from their garden, the lovers are reunited in their regained Paradise.

In terms of character, both Teresa and Alvar are unrealized abstractions. Their dramatic interaction consists of stereotyped set pieces in the form of monologues or asides, and of rather erratically arranged and anti-climatic duets about the "trances" of love, faith and intuition. Allegorically, however, they re-enact the "spiral movement"[1] of the romantic quest which in this work goes through three stages. It begins with Paradise and a sense of being one with Nature; a fall from this state by separation and the consequent falling into self-division; and finally a re-integration at a higher level, the re-gaining of a mature and somehow everlasting Paradise.

When Coleridge wrote *Osorio*, the first version of *Remorse*, he agreed with Shaftesbury about evil being subordinated to the good. In his "Religious Musings" he maintains that even if evil makes a temporary appearance in the form of apparently "fiendish deeds,"

47

God teaches "Good through Evil, by brief wrong / Making Truth lovely" (195-196). In the play this "brief wrong" is Alvar's absence. Ordonio's "fiendish deeds" make the lovers face a final trial before the consummation of their union which realizes Truth, Beauty and Goodness through its ultimate perfection.

Like Idonea in *The Borderers* Teresa also fulfills an allegorical function as the hero's complement. She describes herself and Alvar as "twins" and is described by Alvar as "not mine but me." The lovers' meeting place is the "rock" surrounded by the "grove of firs" (I. 2. 295), symbolic of the combination of the male and female in a state of perfection. Their union, is like the "love of Adam and Eve in Paradise," which Coleridge defines as "a union of opposites, a giving and receiving of the permanent in either, a completion of each in the other."[2]

We hear from Teresa that before the temporary "fall" of their separation (an unexplained and rather obscure event in the play) the lovers' world "imitated Heaven."

> Those blessed days that imitated heaven,
> When we two wont to walk at eventide;
> When we saw nought but beauty; when we heard
> The voice of that Almighty One who loved us
> In every gale that breathed, and wave that murmur'd!
> (IV. 2. 99-103)

Like the heroines of Wordsworth, Keats and Byron, Teresa is a childhood companion to the hero, and their pre-adolescent love is like the Paradise of childhood. From Teresa's above description, the young lovers appear like Adam and Eve wandering in their garden. Theirs is a terrestrial Paradise, because both Nature and Man are unfallen, and in the presence of the Spirit. Hence the lovers hear "the voice of [the] Almighty One" through every voice in Nature.

It is worth noticing that Coleridge uses "Heaven" and "Paradise" interchangeably. When Teresa phantasizes about an after-the-grave reunion with Alvar, she describes the scene as

> To be in Paradise, and with choice flowers
> Build up a bower where he and I might dwell,
> And there to wait his coming! (I. 2. 43-45)

This scene seems to be identical to "those blessed days that imitated Heaven," but the meeting of the earthly lovers can be called "blessed," only in a Romantic framework in which the union between Adam and Eve itself creates Paradise.

48

Teresa is described as "angelic and saintly"; yet Coleridge insists that all her extraordinary goodness and intuition flows merely from an uncorrupted relationship with Nature. Thus, her virginal innocence, like that of Wordsworth's Idonea, is symbolic of unfallen Nature, and this "sacred sympathy" gives her insight into the mysteries of human nature as well. While she could not have any clue or evidence, Teresa rightly suspects Ordonio of crime and hypocrisy, "There is mystery," she observes, "And guilt does lurk behind it." (IV. 2. 44-45)

Through intuition Teresa defeats Ordonio's attempt to deceive her, and her strength of faith in Alvar's existence has a force that equals any "conjurer's power."

Her faith in Alvar's return has the "magic" of creative imagination which forms its own world by simply imagining it. She insists that her inner voice and inner light are reflections of Truth revealed in Nature.

> These rays that slant in through those gorgeous windows,
> From yon bright orb—though coloured as they pass,
> Are they not light?—Even so that voice, Lord Valdez!
> Which whispers to my soul, though haply varied
> By many a fancy, many a wishful hope,
> Speaks yet the truth: and Alvar lives for me!   (III. 2. 26-31)

Father Valdez is himself shortsighted, and scolds Teresa for giving "religious faith" (III. 2. 34) to her wishes and fancies. She proves, however, that by dreaming her "trances" she was really listening to the "inward voice" and following the "surer light" of her intuition that is ultimately equivalent to the "inward Monitress" of Conscience, that is, to the instrument of Providence. For Coleridge, intuitive awareness of Truth, revealed through Nature, has a power very similar to the creative power of Imagination. He makes both of these powers appear really undistinguishable from the "religious faith" in question, as well as from one another.

Another example of Teresa's intuitive wisdom (although not of Coleridge's ability to create a sense of dramatic probability) is her being attracted to Alvar in spite of his disguise as a magician. She is capable of ignoring his base appearance:

> ...A Moor! A sorcerer!
> No, I have faith, that Nature ne'er permitted
> Baseness to wear a form so noble   (IV. 2. 8-10)

Since Teresa believes that beauty in Nature reflects the presence of the "Almighty," she takes the magician's noble beauty as proof of a noble nature. She perceives in him a "kindred lustre" to Alvar's, and again through mere sympathetic insight, she is able to foretell with great precision what will happen to him when exposed to Ordonio, the personification of "Coward Treachery":

> What if in yon dark dungeon coward treachery
> Be groping for him with envenomed poignard—
> Hence, womanish fears, traitors to love and duty—
> I'll free him.   (IV. 2. 112-115)

Her remarkable insight is coupled with similarly remarkable courage to descend into the darkness of the dungeon, an act in which innocence confronts experience: "that fell dungeon which thou ne'er hadst sight of" (IV. 2. 19).

Unlike Wordsworth's Idonea who is a passive sufferer, Teresa expresses her steadfast innocence by resisting Ordonio; Lord Valdez calls her the "wild Teresa" who, in spite of his warnings, obtains the key and descends to the dungeon to save the Moor. Her innocence is not that of blissful ignorance; it is an ability to resist evil (although in this play it never really becomes very tempting to succumb). She takes the risk of confronting the darkness, and faces extremity: "Oh! / If I faint? If this inhuman den should be / At once my death-bed and my burial vault?" (V. 1. 46-48). In spite of her fears she resolves to free the hero because "womanish fears" are "traitors to love and duty." When with her taper she conquers the darkness, the truth is revealed: "Ah! who art thou? Nay, I will call thee Alvar!" (V. 1. 87-88).

Although Alvar's reunion with Teresa stands for their regaining of Paradise, Alvar is more than Adam. Once receiving his Eve, and with her a perfected state of being, he becomes the Second Adam, a romantic definition of the Messiah. To become this seems to be within the capacity of Everyman who reaches a sense of oneness with the whole, a sense of "sacred sympathy" between Man and Nature:

> When he [man] by sacred sympathy might make
> The whole one Self! Self, that no alien knows!
> Self, far diffused as Fancy's wing can travel!
> Self, spreading still! Oblivious of its own,
> Yet all of all possessing! This is Faith!
> This the Messiah's destined victory!
> ("Religious Musings," 153-158)

Alvar's fate in the play is the allegorical enactment of this "destined victory," the triumph of true faith over evil in all its forms, not the least of which is clerical oppression. When the hero is thrown into the dungeon by the Inquisitor, the act illustrates the Church's pretense of "honour[ing] God" while "rejecting Christ,"[3] a situation that reinforces the contrast between Alvar's true faith and that of Father Monviedro, the Inquisitor. On the more universal level, Alvar acts out the "destined victory" of the Messiah as the bringer of the light of Truth through Love. The emphasis on the redemptive power of Love is typical of Coleridge, who prays to it as to a Deity:

> ... Infinite Love,
> Whose latence is the plenitude of All,
> Thou with retracted beams, and self-eclipse
> Veiling, revealest thine eternal Sun.
> ("The Destiny of Nations," 23-26)

The light images associated with Alvar identify him as Infinite Love, the light of the "eternal Sun" of Truth, Goodness, and Beauty. When Teresa recognizes in the Moor that "kindred lustre," that is the "reflected light" of "Alvar's "almost spiritual light," in effect, she recognizes the "retracted beams" of this "eternal Sun." After the short "self-eclipse" of this light in the dungeon, Alvar emerges and reveals his identity, and this revelation is synonymous with the happy union between the lovers.

Although the hero's victory is like the "Messiah's destined victory," Alvar is also Everyman or any man who is able to carry "his Maker's Image undefaced." Thus he describes how he "redeemed" the would-be assassins from murder:

> But by my looks, and most impassioned words,
> I roused the virtues that are dead in no man,
> Even in the assassins' hearts! they made their terms,
> And thanked me for redeeming them from murder.
> (I. 2. 287-290)

If he is the redeemer, it is so because he believes that through his "looks and words" he can make his fellow-man feel the same "sacred sympathy" that he himself is radiating.

There is an ambivalence about natural and supernatural elements in both Alvar's and Teresa's characterization. To some extent this ambivalence may be related to the language of the religion of sentimental love. This convention[4] was fashionable in both the melodrama and sentimental novel of Coleridge's day, and had an influence on *Remorse*, clearly demonstrated by the play's overwhelming concern with the heroine's innocence.

Alvar is told by the would-be assassin that Teresa may be partner to the villain's crime. The first step, therefore, in Alvar's quest for Truth is the testing of the heroine. It is noteworthy that at their very first meeting (I. 2.), Alvar discovers that Teresa is innocent of crime. Still, he resolves to leave her, assuming her to be married to Ordonio, and hence not innocent sexually. At this point Ordonio's guilt is as clear to Alvar as it is to the audience. Yet, in an outburst of pious resignation, Alvar announces his giving up Teresa, and his intention to respect the sacred bond of marriage which he assumes may have a cleansing effect even on criminals:

> Her husband—aye her husband! May this angel
> New mould his canker'd heart!... (I. 2. 362-363)

The inconsistency in Alvar's behaviour at this stage indicates the code of the religion of sentimental love. The villain in this convention plays the role of the satanic seducer, and the heroine's loss of sexual innocence outside of marriage is tantamount to the Fall. Marriage, however, is regarded as a kind of redemption that might endow the heroine with powers of an "angel" to "new mould" the villain's "canker'd heart."

At the same time, Alvar's words attribute a symbolic significance to the heroine's purity that goes beyond the conventions of the sentimental code. Even after Alvar is convinced of Teresa's innocence of the crime and regards her merely as a victim, he is still ready to leave her when he thinks that she was sexually "stained" or "dishonoured." Believing her "dishonoured [in] soul and body" is tantamount to losing faith in the holiness and purity of unfallen Nature. At this point, in his despair, Alvar is ready to go into exile, and abandon his father's estate and his betrothed, although both of these he ought to have regarded as his birthright.

A turning point in Alvar's faith occurs when he hears that Teresa and Ordonio are still not married (II. 2.). He responds to this shock according to the theatrical convention of Gothic melodrama that portrays deep emotion like a fit of madness.

> A: Are you not wedded, then? Merciful Heaven!
> Not wedded to Teresa?

To this Ordonio answers by observing the questioner's strange reaction:

> O: Why, what ails thee?
> What, art thou mad? Why lookst thou upward so?
> Dost pray to Lucifer, Prince of the Air?
> (II. 2. 120-123)

The revelation of Teresa's sexual innocence awakens in the hero an emotional intensity normally associated with the regaining of religious faith. He declares himself "guilty of folly," of having committed blasphemy by having doubted Teresa: "And I did curse thee, At midnight on my knees, thee a traitress, thee dishonoured." When she proves worthy of adoration because of her intact innocence, her portrait becomes a "holy image" which Alvar would not "profane." "I will not profane thee, holy image, to a dark trick." He blames himself for having succumbed to doubt and for having discarded her picture. There is, as a matter of fact, quite a powerful suggestion that it is only through re-claiming the heroine's "holy image," that Alvar himself will be able to reveal the true image of perfection, his "Maker's image undefac'd."

To arrive at the allegorical significance of Teresa and of her union with the hero, one should also examine her relationship to the villain, the only threat to the lovers' wedding.

Ordonio's and Teresa's relationship creates some curious contradictions in psychological motivation. Coleridge himself acknowledged that Ordonio's jealousy is probably not developed well enough to be a sufficient motive for the murder of his elder brother. It is, he admits a "curiously modified love for a beautiful female (which is nowhere developed in the play)."[5] Ordonio shows indeed very few signs of being in love with Teresa. He talks about her with scorn when planning for the magician's trick that is to deceive her:

> Her lover schooled her in some newer nonsense!
> Yet still a tale of spirits works upon her.
> She is a lone enthusiast, sensitive,
> Shivers, and can not keep the tears in her eye:
> And such do love the marvellous too well
> Not to believe it. We will wind up her fancy.　(II. 1. 36-41)

Not only is his language cynical and loveless when he describes Teresa, but he shows scarcely any signs of being acquainted with her, let alone appreciating or understanding her true nature. He assumes her to be easily impressed by the "marvellous," when in fact she holds sorcery so distasteful that she leaves the magic performance that he staged for her before it reached its climax.

Although Ordonio's dramatic role is that of the satanic seducer of Gothic melodrama, and he is, in effect, Satan responsible for the loss of the lovers' first Paradise, Coleridge characterizes Satan as weak, vague, and cowardly. Ordonio wants to possess Teresa, but not out of his passionate love or physical desire for her. He seems to be contemptuous rather than jealous of the intimacy between her and the hero. Alvar in describing the lovers' last meeting speaks of the purity of their exchange of "chaste endearment" (II. 2. 164), but

Ordonio who had witnessed it contemptuously describes love as a bewitchment of the sense:

> Fondly caressing him, her favour'd lover,
> (By some base spell he had bewitched her senses)
> She whispered such dark fears of me forsooth,
> As made this heart pour gall into my veins. (II. 1. 48-51)

The scene is an important one. The "poison" of evil seems to have entered like "gall into [the villain's] veins" at this very moment. He is like Satan, the evil spirit who spies upon the lovers in their garden:

> But I had traced her, stolen unnotic'd on them,
> And unsuspected saw and heard the whole. (II. 1. 56-57)

In general, Ordonio's feeling is far removed from sexual jealousy. It is more like a striving for mastery over Alvar through the possession of Teresa. It is an abstract goal, and consequently he sounds more indignant than desperate about her resistance:

> This, then, is my reward! and I must love her?
> Scorn'd! shudder'd at! yet love her still? yes! yes!
> By the deep feelings of revenge and hate
> I will still love her—woo her—win her too! (IV. 2. 168-171)

He would like to win and possess Teresa without love, and therefore he would only "pollute" or corrupt her. In contrast to Alvar, Ordonio lacks the potential to truly "wed" the innocent heroine; he cannot affirm Man's "sacramental marriage" with an unfallen Nature, which also implies loving and joyous affirmation of the Spirit in Nature.

Such an affirmation seems to be impossible for Ordonio even before he had committed his crime. Teresa cannot accept him from the outset because of his dark and joyless nature (I. 2. 79-84), and it is ultimately his inability to rejoice which is responsible for his defeat.

It is worth noting that while the dramatic conflict is based on Ordonio's attempt to win Teresa, there is very little direct communication between the two. Ordonio keeps sending messengers to communicate with her, uses his father to induce her into marrying him, and makes no attempt to know, understand or win her.

The absence of dialogue reinforces Ordonio's allegorical function as the personification of evil. To Coleridge, inclined to Shaftesbury's Platonism, evil is more of an absence of the good than an active force in the world. Within the individual, too, it is less of a force than the lack of it, a spiritual impotence. If Ordonio undertakes the role of a treacherous Satan, it is because, being spiritually impotent, he is unable to enter the lovers' Paradise.

Although Ordonio may play the role of Satan, his weak character suggests that Coleridge sees nothing superhuman about evil. Ordonio does represent the force of division responsible for the separation of the lovers, but his evil acts seem to emanate from the very human disease, the division within the self. This is the disease that renders him unworthy and incapable of wedding Teresa, and thus achieving, through "sacred sympathy," Man's union with the Spirit through Nature.

Neither Ordonio's desire to possess Teresa, nor his hatred of his older brother have much psychological or dramatic credibility. These two emotions are nevertheless at the very core of the allegorical framework. The exploration of their "meaning" is crucial to the understanding of the tragic dilemma in the play.

HERO AND VILLAIN

Just as Alvar is defined by his relationship to the heroine as both Adam and the Second Adam, so is the villain identified by his archetypes. As the destroyer of the lovers' first paradise, he fulfills the role of Satan, but as the betrayer of Alvar as Redeemer, he relates to the archetype of Judas.[6] In addition to these two, the nature of the crime evokes still another parallel. Ordonio's original crime is an attempt at fratricide, and the two brothers' conflict in the play has links with Cain and Abel: the crime of the jealous brother against the saintly one.

The parallel is consistent. Cain's jealousy is aroused by the fact that Abel is in a state of grace, his sacrifice to God accepted, while Cain is, unaccountably in a state of disfavour. Ordonio's jealousy is aroused by the fact that Teresa accepts Alvar as her "favoured" lover because of his joyful disposition (equivalent to being in a state of grace), while rejecting Ordonio because of the "dark brows" of his joyless temper.

Although these parallels are significant, of even more significance is the particular way in which Coleridge uses the myth. First, he reverses the original relationship between the Biblical brothers by making the saintly 'Abel' become the exemplary older brother, Alvar. Then his 'Cain,' Ordonio fails in his desire to kill the good brother and destroys himself in the attempt. To add a third and essential difference, Coleridge has the good brother return and offer redemption to the fratricidal brother.

Coleridge's approach to the Cain-Abel conflict seems to be consistent. In another treatment of the story, "The Wanderings of Cain,"[7] he again makes Abel return as Cain's potential redeemer. Once more, he concentrates on the connection between sin and redemption, and pays little attention to the original crime.

Several critics have discovered similarities between Ordonio's character and that of his author. They also speculate on Ordonio's conflict with his older brother as a transferral of the poet's relationship to this father. Beverly Fields approaches the Cain-Abel conflict in the play by analyzing Coleridge's relationship to Frank,[8] an older brother who died shortly after the poet's father. A. Fox sees the Cain-Abel parallel to be that between the poet and his older brother George,[9] whom Coleridge considered a fatherly figure, loved and possibly resented at the same time.

It is indeed significant that Coleridge turns Cain into a rebellious younger brother offending against a rather fatherly, older Abel, and I will return to this reversal in the next section. Just as important, however, is to notice that the two brothers in this play are not psychologically individualized characters. In their conflict they externalize their author's spiritual dilemma.

What Ordonio and Alvar re-enact in the play is the abstract conflict between good and evil within the same psyche, the struggle between the "Cain and Abel of the mind." Alvar may be an older brother in the play, but the essential features of his character do not represent either Frank or George: they are Samuel Taylor Coleridge himself. Alvar is the creative artist as magician and successful lover, the image Coleridge aspires to. At the same time, the villain personifies the object of the poet's frequent complaint, the spiritually impotent personality which loses sight of creative joy. Ordonio represents the erratic despair of Coleridge in his moods of dejection.

The conflict between these two projections is therefore an inner conflict. It is a genuine conflict deeply and intensely felt in its psychological and spiritual manifestations, but it is one that does not survive the transfiguration into drama.

The relationship between these two images of the one personality comprises important aspects of the play. While Ordonio fits the mould of the satanic villain of Gothic melodrama, he is probably the least powerful of all romantic villains. When he wants to kill he hires an assassin; when he wants to use magic, he hires a magician.

This tendency to deputize is part of Ordonio's passive, somnambulant state, and Alvar would like to stir him so "That he may wake as from a dream of murder" (V. 1. 95). Ordonio describes his ordering of his brother's murder as a "phantom thought" that was given reality by an "over-ready agent." As if living a nightmare, he finds his actions unaccountable even to himself, and out of proportion to their consequences.

Unlike Wordsworth's defiant villain, Ordonio is not insensitive to the sufferings of others. He cannot forgive himself for the pain caused to Isidore's orphans. He dies humiliated, ashamed and guilt-ridden, crying to his brother, "curse me with forgiveness." He is neither a sadist like Shelley's Count Cenci who enjoys the power of inflicting suffering, nor is he secretly proud of his flaw like Byron's Manfred. Ordonio destroys others as a consquence of his own blindness to joy and coldness to love. This is a constitutional incompleteness which results not only in an absence of light and harmony, but also in a lack of dramatic intensity.

Like Wordsworth's Oswald and Byron's Manfred, Ordonio is a solitary, who "in this world / ... found no fit companion." (IV. 1. 108-109). Unlike the other villains, however, he has no heroic dimension at all. It looks as though Coleridge had an extremely bad case of conscience over his 'loner' villain and was unwilling to grant him that so potent Gothic mixture of heroism and criminality that would give him stature. The heroism which usually goes together with the romantic son's rebellion against his father and extenuates his lonely pride, is absent in Ordonio.

Manfred's creative daring to confront the unknown or Oswald's courage to extend man's intellectual empire even at the cost of damnation, that is, the Promethean streak in the Romantic Satan is alien to Ordonio. In sharp contrast, the heroic or Messianic qualities of Prometheus are consistently attributed to Alvar, this superhuman bringer of light. He combines the qualities of the artist as magician and successful lover, and is the liberator of the oppressed as well.

Coleridge often expressed dislike for the way the ancient Greek poets presented Prometheus, because, in his figure, they "jumbled together" the roles of "Redeemer and Devil."[10] Coleridge takes pains to avoid attributing any negative qualities to his hero, while denying all positive qualities to his villain. Alvar is the sole representative of both the warmth and the "spiritual and almost heavenly light" of the Sun. Ordonio is constantly complaining about darkness and cold. Light is brought forth from the very joy with which Alvar regards the world around him; he exudes the light of affirmation while Ordonio is fatefully blind to that joy. His evil actions stem from his joyless, dark condition, his lack of spiritual power to "rejoice."

In the last act Ordonio descends into Alvar's dungeon, and, pretending gaiety, offers him a cup of wine. Alvar recognizes, however, that there is a "drunken anguish" that belies Ordonio's "revelry." His joy is not sincere, there is "poison in the wine." In refusing the wine, Alvar also explains the real cause of Ordonio's miserable condition. The inability to rejoice sincerely, makes Ordonio less that human. Life, even in the lowest form of being, means sharing in the divine joy inherent in Nature, and thus available to all:

> Yon insect on the wall,
> Which moves this way and that its hundred limbs,
> . . .
>
> . . . has life Ordonio! life, enjoyment!
> And by the power of its miraculous will
> Wields all the complex movements of its frame
> Unerringly to pleasurable ends!   (V. 1. 127-134)

Alvar argues eloquently for Coleridge's "Optimist." The "poison" of evil means being out of harmony with the "miraculous will" that wields the movements of every creature "unerringly to pleasureable ends." In this universe, gloom or dejection is an unnatural state. At the same time, Alvar fails to point out that the individual creature's will to share in the Divine Will is indeed "miraculous," a state of grace, a gift. As such, offenders like Ordonio can do very little on their own to attain this desirable condition, one that is naturally enjoyed by all who are not cursed with disease. Being refused by Teresa for his joyless nature points to the cause and to the further development of Ordonio's misery, the cause of his evil, his fallen condition.

According to Coleridge's notes, and the "confessional" strain in most of his later poems, he is preoccupied with a "Fall of some sort or other,"[11] because he experiences this as psychological reality. This preoccupation leads him further and further away from his youthful optimism, especially since impetus for social optimism also disappeared in his disillusionment with the French Revolution. He arrives at a "deep conviction" that "man is a fallen creature," because he is "diseased in his will."[12]

Certain contradicitions in Ordonio's fate already in the first version foreshadow Coleridge's wrestling with the dilemma, the "deep conviction" in the Fall, and the optimistic, revolutionary hope to explain it away. Yet, even in the period of growing pessimism, there is evidence in Coleridge's work of a desire for transplanting such orthodox terms as "fall, guilt and redemption" into a post-Enlightenment, secular framework. An early, but typical example of this desire is "Dejection: An Ode."

Here the poet divorces evil as "the disease of the will" from the theological context and transposes it into a psychological framework. He celebrates "Joy" as the natural state of mind, and the germinal force of all vital energies "Which wedding Nature to us gives in dower / A new Earth and new Heaven, / Undreamt of by the sensual and the proud—" ("Dejection: An Ode," 68-70). In the play this is the "wedding" that consummates Alvar's naturally joyful and happy state, the condition of love and creativity. Such a "wedding," however, is impossible for Ordonio. He is one of the "proud" who isolate the self from the whole. He also stands for the "sensual" philosophy of empiricism that regards Nature merely as matter devoid of Spirit, and therefore renders it accessible only through the evidence of the senses. This joyless condition of the "sensual and the proud" however, seems to be both cause and consequence of a disease, as if the "jarring dissonant thing" were punished for his condition of misery with even greater misery.

Alvar, the personification of creative joy and affirmation would like to redeem Ordonio, the personification of dejection and ensuing evil. As noted above in another context, the conflict between the two characters is really that between two states of mind. Yet a psychological interpretation of good and evil may not yet resolve the dilemma of finding redemption for the evil brother. Even if Ordonio's state of deprivation means only the departure of Joy, this state seems to be as hard to deal with as the departure of grace. Ordonio in the play seems to personify the "dull pain" experienced by those whose "disease of the will" polluted or paralyzed the fountains of their spirit. Even if only a human disease, the pain seems incurable, because the sufferer-sinner "may not hope from outward forms to win / The passion and the life whose fountains are within."

The setting for Ordonio's final crime defines the nature of his disease and foreshadows his punishment. The cave is a hellish pit that contains, within its darkness, an even deeper and darker abyss. This is the abyss into which Ordonio hurls his own agent, Isidore, and it is through this act that he will meet his own death. The abyss may suggest the infinity of evil. It is also symbolic of infinite and unredeemed suffering, presenting the "pollution," "poisoning" or draught of those spiritual powers whose "fountains are within."

> ...its horrid sides
>
> ...
>
> ...still groaning well,
> Which never thirsty pilgrim blest, which never
> A living thing came near—unless, perchance,
> Some blind-worm battens on the ropy mould
> Close at its edge.   (IV. 1. 55-61)

It is in this dried-out well that Isidore meets his death, and Ordonio seals his own doom. When, in the last act, Alhadra arrives to take revenge, the desperate Ordonio willingly submits his life to her, as in an act of suicide. By having hurled his own agent into that "still groaning well" of the "hellish pit" in the cave, Ordonio blocks the fountain of his own spirit, and consummates the act which began with his attempt on the life of his older brother, his "Maker's image undefaced." In the final analysis, murder is an act of spiritual suicide.

Ordonio's fate in the play illustrates a complex problem. On the one hand, it seems to illustrate Coleridge's earlier assertion that in the perfectly designed and just processes of Nature, "Cain's... victorious murder" is actually no more than his own "Blind suicide" ("Religious Musings"). On the other hand, Alvar's entire dramatic role hinges on his success to redeem his evil brother by making him feel remorse. Yet, not only does he fail in redeeming him, but by showing him the picture of the past, inadvertently he tosses Ordonio even further into the pit of evil, and propels him towards his only irredeemable act, the murder of Isidore.

Alvar's mission, then, of reaching out to Ordonio is a failure. Somehow, it seems, there can be no real communication between the two brothers in the play. Abel is incapable of redeeming Cain, because Cain cannot redeem himself. Even though the poet made an attempt to translate the concept of grace into "Joy," he can offer no means through which the sufferer could replenish the dried out spiritual fountains once Joy had departed, since "Ah! from the soul itself must issue forth / A light, a glory, a fair luminous cloud / Enveloping the Earth ("Dejection: An Ode," 53-55).

Wordsworth's drama suffers from the lack of radical conflict, since the characters of villain and hero suggest a sense of continuum. (In turning against Herbert, the hero merely repeats the villain's original offence against the Captain of his ship, against the Father.) In contrast, Coleridge makes an unmistakably sharp distinction between hero and villain, an energetic "Redeemer" and an extremely weak and unconvincing "Devil." Yet the result is not any more effective as drama: the sharp dichotomy causes the two brothers to emerge as representatives of two distinct and remote modes of being, with no possibility for interaction.

To shed more light on Coleridge's difficulty in resolving the two brothers' interaction, we should examine it in the context of the second major romantic theme, the rebellious son's relationship to the father.

THE SON'S OFFENCE AGAINST THE FATHER

In *Remorse* Coleridge transfers the romantic son's offence against the father into the offence of a rebellious younger brother against a near-saintly older brother. Yet, by attempting to murder Alvar, who is his "Maker's image undefac'd," Ordonio assumes the guilt of the romantic son's spiritual rebellion against the Father or the Maker. Coleridge also makes Ordonio justify this rebellion with his philosophical creed, Atheism, which, in turn, seems to follow from his joyless temper.

Using the somewhat pious moralist, Alvar, as his spokesman, Coleridge argues that Ordonio's alienation from the "life, enjoyment" (V. 1. 131) manifest in the universe amounts to blasphemy, the sin of the Atheist who denies the existence of a Benevolent Creator. Ordonio identifies himself as such a sinner when he accuses Nature of being a joyless and cold mechanism, devoid of the Spirit, and responsible for having "forced [him] into" his own strange shape "by accident or malice" (IV. 1. 108).

Alvar blames Ordonio for his gloomy disposition, and implies that it is a result of immature posturing: "at his mother's looking glass he would force his features to a frowning sternness." Dismissing Ordonio's pessimistic vision, Alvar seems to follow Shaftesbury's interpretation:

Nothing beside ill humour [says Shaftesbury] either natural or *forced* can bring a man to think seriously that the world is governed by any devilish or malicious Power. I very much question whether anything, beside ill humour, can be the cause of atheism.[13]

In Alvar's description, Ordonio's negation is the result of such "forced" ill humour, because "Nothing beside ill humour can give us dreadful or ill thought of the Supreme Manager."[14]

Yet, although Ordonio explains and justifies his offence against his older brother, by denying the presence of the spirit in Nature, that is, by denying the spiritual authority of the Maker, Ordonio's

61

character does not convey the defiant energy associated with the other villains. This is probably due to the fact that in Coleridge's play it is Alvar who identifies with the political aspect of revolution and liberation. In contrast to Ordonio, Alvar is an optimist, who believes in the Spirit within and beyond Nature, and appropriately, he also possesses the 'magic' power of art. Politically, he is in alliance with the oppressed and sympathetic to the powers of their liberation. These two alliances also make him an appropriate personification of Imagination, a liberating spiritual force.

It is Alvar who acts out the romantic son's political, emotional and imaginative revolution, while Coleridge makes Ordonio pay for the religious-spiritual implications of the same revolution. Hence Ordonio's character remains a rather weak and unconvincing foil to Alvar's larger-than-life and almost entirely flawless hero.

Coleridge's attitude to the son's rebellion is becoming even more interesting if we examine the stock character of the father in the play. To do so, we should also compare *Remorse*, written in 1817, to the first version of the tragedy, *Osorio*, written in 1797.[15]

In *Osorio* the characters are marshalled so clearly into the camp of good and evil, that there is an unmistakable separation between the father's oppressive and the son's liberating forces. The father, Marquis Velez, is a figure of tyrannical paternal authority, closely associated with the Holy "Father," the Inquisitor who personifies the cruelty of clerical oppression. Together they threaten the heroine with disinheritance or the convent if she refuses to give up the hero and accept the villain as her husband (*O*. IV. 268-304). The close alliance between father Velez and Father Francesco stands for the alliance between the "patient folly of Superstition" and "mitred Atheism" on the philosophical level of the allegory, and for the alliance between "Worldly Power" and "Organized Religion" on the political level. That the Inquisitor accompanies Lord Velez in most of his scenes illustrates Coleridge's conviction "that the Babylon of the Apocalypse does not apply to Rome exclusively; but to the union of Religion with Power and Wealth, wherever it is found."[16]

As for Lord Velez himself, he is not only a tyrant, but also a fool. He approves of the villain's trick to win the heroine, and cannot see through his web of intrigue. His blind trust in the villain and the Inquisitor illustrates the dependence of the "patient folly of superstition" on "mitred Atheism."

In this early version of the tragedy the hero stands for the "new faith" of revolution directed against the evil of any form of oppression. After he is thrown into prison by the Inquisitor, the heroine obtains the key to his dungeon from their common foster mother. The old woman recites a long tale about how the key had been used before to release an innocent peasant boy thrown into prison for worshipping God in Nature and not in the Church. Both the offence and the liberation of the offender foreshadow the hero's fate and identify his alliances. "The Foster Mother's Tale" reinforces the father's association with the Organized Church and oppression ("the union of Religion with Power and Wealth") while the hero is associated with Nature worship and revolution.

The sharp separation between the father's oppressive and the good son's liberating forces works for a straightforward dénouement in *Osorio*, where, in the fourth act the Inquisitor is attacked, then defeated and carried away by the Moors and Alhadra. At the end of the play, the villain is led away to his execution by these same powers. Since the hero was thrown into prison by the various machinations of the oppressors (the Inquisitor, in alliance with the villain and his father), it stands to reason that the political power that defeats the oppressor should also be responsible for the hero's liberation. Once the hero is liberated, hero and heroine unite, and *Osorio* ends with Alhadra's manifesto of the revolutionary destruction of "temples" and "high towers." Since it was only political oppression that stood in the way, the lovers' reunion may indeed be celebrated as universal liberation, or the coming of the millennium.

Osorio, in spite of its chaotic plot and tendentious use of allegory had a certain charm, and the energy of conviction. The world of *Remorse* lacks both.

In *Remorse*, written twenty years after *Osorio*, Coleridge seems to feel far less certain about revolution, millennium, or the powers at its disposal. The alliance between the father and the Inquisitor, Father Monviedro, is less sharply focussed, as if Coleridge no longer wanted to emphasize the alliance between paternal authority with tyranny and oppression. Old Valdez, in this play, is less of a tyrant than a shortsighted old man. He does not threaten Teresa, only warns her not to let herself be overheard by the Inquisitor: "What if Monviedro or his creatures hear us! / I dare not listen to you." (IV. 2. 34-35)

Both Lord Valdez and the Inquisitor have more limited and less clearly defined roles in *Remorse* than in the first version. Thus, for example, the Inquisitor is still instrumental in throwing Alvar to prison at the end of the third Act, and we should expect that Alvar's liberation should signal the Inquisitor's defeat. Yet he simply disappears from the play after Act III. Since we hear nothing about his deposition, we should assume that his power is still unbroken at the end of the play.

There is a similar ambiguity about the character of Lord Valdez. This old man, called "Father" both by the hero and the heroine, makes a stern appeal to make Teresa marry Ordonio, and goes as far as assisting Ordonio in tricking her. Yet, at the end of the play he suddenly becomes the benevolent figure of sacred paternal authority, offering blessings to Alvar and Teresa, both of whom accept it with respect and affection.

In the 1795 version of his "Allegoric Vision" Coleridge satirizes the Organized Church which presents the alliance between Superstition and the "mitred Atheism" of hypocrisy; the Organized Church is the enemy of true Religion. In the 1811 version of the same work, however, Coleridge changes his position. By now the Organized Church became identified with true Religion, fighting against the alliance between Catholicism and Superstition. Consequently to these changes in ideology, in *Remorse* the wicked Inquisitor represents only the abuses of Catholicism, and not the structure of Organized Religion in general. Most likely this shift also explains why the "The Foster Mother's Tale" with its openly pantheistic and revolutionary, anti-clerical connotations is left out from this play.

There are some striking inconsistencies in *Remorse* due to certain ideological, and possibly theological changes that took place in Coleridge's mind between the writing of first and second versions. The play still ends with rejoicings over the lovers' union, as if it signified a universal triumph over evil. Yet, in spite of Ordonio's death, the world of *Remorse* is not really free from evil.

Even if the hero's father, Lord Valdez assumes now the rather unexpected role of benevolent paternal authority, the Inquisitor's oppressive powers have not been explicitly checked.

Also, in the first version violent revolutionary energy seems to be vindicated in Alhadra's final manifesto, as a ruthless but ultimately justified force in action, "conquering and still to conquer."—In the second version, however, the addition of Alvar's pious final words render Alhadra's manifesto less effective, and bring into doubt its validity. The conflict between Christian ethic and romantic millennium via revolution has become much sharper here than in the first version. Consequently, while Alhadra is still directly responsible for the villain's defeat and the hero's liberation, Coleridge also finds it necessary to make Alvar sermonize about the superior forces of Conscience and Providence. In other words,

Remorse ends with a strangely contradictory message, as if asserting that Alhadra's "deed of blood" was both directed and disapproved of by Alvar's "Just Heaven."

Although both versions end happily, the happy ending is somewhat forced in both cases. Coleridge's choice of titles, *Osorio* (the name of the villain in that version) and *Remorse*, would indicate that the writer's major concern lies in his villain's character, the nature of his guilt and the chances of his redemption. In order to end on a note of celebration, the poet has to abandon this concern in both versions. The villain's defeat in *Osorio* implies that evil is unnatural, and therefore ultimately self-destructive. The same defeat in *Remorse* asserts the powers of Providence which ultimately rewards the just by eliminating the evil. In neither case, however, does the writer offer a means for the sinner to redeem himself.

There are, then, many curious contradictions, evasions and inconsistencies in the plot, tone and characters of *Remorse*. Yet, one really cannot attribute this to Coleridge's lack of dramatic skills or consistency. Unlike Wordsworth, Coleridge was an eminent critic of drama, an expert in theatre, and poet of great dramatic ambition.[17] Rather, it seems to me, one should recognize that the particular shortcomings of this tragedy follow quite directly from Coleridge's having an extremely bad conscience about the two major themes of the romantic tragedian: the hero's claim for Paradise and his rebellion against the father who may stand in the way of consummation.

At any rate, Coleridge is the only one among the five tragedians to be examined in this study for whom the son's rebellion against the father appears so problematic that it has to be approached indirectly. Not only does he transfer this dilemma to that between a rebellious younger and a rather fatherly older brother. He also separates the political from the spiritual-religious aspects of the rebellion, and allows the hero to express sympathy for the former, while making the villain pay by eternal damnation for the latter. (Coleridge's own interpretation of the Promethean myth suggests that the "Redeemer" will redeem and liberate mankind without acting out the problematic ritual of filial rebellion against the tyrannical skygod. The spiritual aspect of filial rebellion still has to remain in the domain of the "Devil," or so Coleridge insists.)

In a letter written a few years after the completion of *Remorse*, Coleridge criticizes Wordsworth's treatment of Nature in his poetry as

The vague, misty, rather than mystic, confusion of God with the world, and the accompanying nature-worship, ... the trait in Wordsworth's poetic works that I most dislike as unhealthful, and denounce as contagious;[18]

Ironically, the effusions of hero and heroine in *Remorse* sound very much like echoes of the same pantheistic nature-worship, as if Coleridge himself found Wordsworth's vision "contagious."

As a matter of fact, the terms of the eighteenth-century nature worship, the very language of the "enthusiast," appear quite strange coming from the mouths of characters ostensibly living in sixteenth-century Spain. Thus Alhadra describes her husband as a gentle soul who "worships nature in the hill and valley / Not knowing what he loves, but loves it all (I. 2. 244-245), while the villain describes Teresa as an "enthusiast" whose "lover schooled her in some newer nonsense," that is, in worshipping God in Nature and not in the orthodox church.

Is it possible, then, that Coleridge himself might be responsible for the pantheist's "confusion of God with the world?" To answer this question, one should pay closer attention to the way the natural world appears in Coleridge's tragedy.

Wordsworth's *The Borderers* presents a unified picture of Nature, although it is not at all characteristic of the serenity of the poet's mature vision. There is a feeling here of Nature being "red in tooth and claw," and the cruelty of natural forces is an important factor in the deaths by exposure of Oswald's victim, the captain, and Marmaduke's victim, Herbert.

In Coleridge's *Remorse* there is no unified feeling about Nature, although, through the profusion of natural descriptions, the poet makes Nature a vital presence in the play. The images of Nature, however, show a dichotomy similar to that in Coleridge's characterization of villain and hero. For the lovers, Nature exists as the idealized, artificial, almost perfumed world of rococo pastoral, as opposed to the wild and dark world of the "sensual and the proud." The fallen figures see Nature in these dark images because they cannot "wed" her in a mood of creative joy, the prerequisite of insight. (Ordonio cannot wed Teresa, while Alhadra is also widowed at the end.)

It seems that Coleridge believes that ultimately everybody is responsible for his vision of the world, and he uses images of the natural landscape not only as a backdrop to character, but as inter-changeable with the mental landscape of the character whose consciousness it reflects. Thus the images associated with Teresa emphasize that the lovers perceive Nature as serene, benevolent, gentle, and beautiful:

"To watch those skiey tints, and this green ocean;" (I. 2. 21)
"To be in Paradise, and with choice flowers / Build up a bower..."
(I. 2. 43-44)

Both Teresa's and Alvar's effusions about Nature suggest something beyond merely perceiving the pleasant aspects of Nature. They suggest a more organic relationship between object and seer, as if by dreaming, and daydreaming about the world, the dreamer had a power to "fashion forth" the kind of world he wanted. To "shape sweet visions" about "past hours of delight" is shown to be, through the lovers fate in the play, an effective way for the re-gaining of the past hours.

In contrast, the landscape associated with Alhadra and Ordonio emphasizes the horror and darkness of nature as perceived by the "sordid solitary things," the alienated beings who see the world of Nature reflect their solitude. Once more, it appears that the characters are responsible for the natural landscape that serves as their background. Ordonio *chooses* to confront his slave in the dark cavern, while only a "few steps away" "bright moonshine" illuminates the world. There is a suggestion that the darkness of Nature follows from an almost voluntary blindness on the part of the perceiver who is not able, or refuses, to read in the mighty alphabet of the Book of Nature:

For all that meets the bodily sense I deem
Symbolical, one mighty alphabet
For infant minds; ("Destiny of Nations," 18-20)

Lacking insight into God's presence in Nature, man is a "jarring, dissonant creature," or, in other words, a "sordid, solitary thing." These epithets describe both Ordonio and Alhadra in the play. Their failure is the failure to feel sacred sympathy, when "by sacred sympathy [man] might make / The whole one self! Self, that no alien knows!... This the Messiah's destined victory!" ("Religious Musings," 153-158). Since she became a "sordid solitary thing," Alhadra's natural background is the tumult of "precipices and mountains": we meet her in a "wild mountainous country" or alone

67

among "the mountains by moonlight." The lovers, however, are associated with the infinite tranquillity of sea and sky, and with the creative breath of the "pleasant sea-breeze." Their union achieves serene perfection through uniting the opposites of Male and Female, the Sun and the Moon, the masculine "rock" and the feminine "fir grove." The emblem of this perfection is the recurring image of their meeting place a "rock" encircled by a "fir-grove" (III. 2. 120; I. 2. 294-295).

Like Alhadra, Ordonio sees Nature in terms of wild and malicious forces. Existence appears to him a hunt in which he is the "hunted tiger" whose eyes "glare under its hunter's torch." Alhadra wants to leap at the Inquisitor with a wild "tiger's plunge, and hurl... him down the rugged precipice" (I. 2. 194-195). Before his conversion by re-gaining faith in Teresa's "holy image," even Alvar tends to emphasize the wild aspects of nature. He asks that "Remorse might fasten on [the offenders'] hearts, / And dig with poisonous tooth... / As the gored lion's bite!" (I. 2. 310-312).

Ordonio sees Nature with the eyes of the cynic; he mocks Alvar for collecting plants under the light of the moon and mocks the enthusiast for believing in superstition when expecting to find the Spirit as "a serviceable imp under every leaf." For Ordonio Nature exists like a mechanism of cause and effect, without magic, without beauty and without a guiding Spirit. Coleridge describes Ordonio's blindness as the materialist's inability to see the first cause beyond cause and effect. To see Nature as an "infinite series of causes and effects" evokes in Coleridge a vision of "a string of blind men, whose infinite blindness supplies the want of sight," with no one "at the head to guide them."[19]

Ordonio's vision of Nature teems with images of beetles, vermin, weeds, cold dampness, and darkness. He discourses on human interaction, which he decribes to be as erratic and meaningless as the course of "air bladders" in a "puddle," and asserts the supreme indifference of Nature to human values:

> Say, I had laid a body in the sun!
> Well! in a month there swarm forth from the corse
> A thousand, nay, ten thousand sentient beings
> In place of that one man—Say, I had *killed* him!
> (III. 2. 107-110)

In this instance Coleridge should have admitted to borrowing from Voltaire's poem on the Lisbon catastrophe.[20] What is signficant, however, is that Coleridge borrows these bitter words to put into the mouth of his villain. Ordonio uses these dark images to rationalize his desperate and ruthless actions committed in the past. In other words, Coleridge does not concede the validity of Ordonio's vision of Nature; he makes the reader perceive this negative vision as a sign of the villain's insincerity or shortsightedness. In doing so, the poet insists that the ugliness of the world is not a reality; it exists only because of the villain's imperfect vision.

If there is no unified feeling about the poet's vision of Nature in the tragedy, it is mostly due to a didactic separation according to which the pleasant images are exclusively associated with the good, and the unpleasant images with the bad characters.

The landscape that is most closely associated with Ordonio is the cavern, the central tragic image with sinister connotations. It is dark, damp, and horrible, the natural habitat of criminality. Ordonio damns himself in this "hellish pit" by hurling his victim into the abyss under the cavern—a spiral structure of images that suggests the depth of infinite darkness. It is worth noting, however, that the cavern scene is not the only one located underground: half of the fourth, and the entire fifth act take place in subterranean settings. Ordonio and Isidore confront each other in the cavern, and in the last act the two lovers and the brothers meet in the dungeon.

As Northrop Frye has pointed out, the Romantic cosmos takes the poet "to confront his destiny in a creative center, usually not in the heavenward movement of earlier poetry, but in the deep interior."[21] He also points out that "the world of the deep interior in Romantic poetry is morally ambivalent, retaining some of the demonic qualities that the corresponding pre-Romantic lowest level had."[22] Frye's explanation also seems to accord with Carl Jung's treatment of the cave imagery in dreams, where it is often the source of both the demonic and the positive energies of the unconscious.

It is typical of Coleridge's attitude to tragedy that his play includes two distinctly different subterranean scenes: the natural scene, the cavern in which Ordonio kills Isidore; and the man-made cave, the dungeon into which Alvar is hurled by the Inquisitor, and out of which he emerges triumphant. To Coleridge, the separation between the creative and demonic energies of the unconscious is complete. Instead of one, he makes his characters confront two "cosmic centers": the cavern is a "hellish pit" from where there is no escape—yet it is a natural entity; the dungeon, although an "inhuman den" of social injustice, is man-made, and therefore a place where evil gets destroyed and the good emerge ultimately as victors.

When Ordonio descends into the cavern, he throws his slave, an

69

extension of himself, into an even deeper and darker chasm, the "still groaning well" under the cavern. This image is suggestive of the infinity of evil that leads to deeper and deeper darkness, and makes return to life impossible. Since Ordonio through this deed is himself killed, Coleridge seems to insist that the demonic impulse is criminal and self-destructive, while Alvar the creative and liberating impulse, is self-rewarding or self-redemptive.

At the same time, and indicative of an underlying dilemma in the play, the cavern which is the only inescapable centre, and the equivalent of hell and endless self-damnation, is a natural construct. The dungeon, however, the centre that leads to light through the darkness, is man-made, a social construct.

Having mercilessly separated "Devil" from "Redeemer" within his own "Prometheus," Coleridge makes his "Redeemer" confront evil only in its social manifestation, through the dungeon, and ends the play by insisting that Alvar's confrontation with evil must inevitably end with victory. At the same time, he makes his "Devil" confront evil in its natural abode, and the outcome of this confrontation is deeply problematic.

The central natural image of evil is "poison," and in the play this image is charged with ambiguity. Ordonio's evil is like "poison," because it is an alien matter that infects the otherwise healthy natural organism, an external ingredient that can, and should be removed from the natural world. At the same time, it is also described as a "poison tree," a natural organism that has its own roots and laws of growth in the human heart. This image implies that evil is innate in man, and therefore not accidental, but also part of Nature.

If Nature, then, is not innocent of evil, can the world still contain the Spirit—and with the Spirit, the hope of redemption—in the Natural realm? Or is this to come, if at all, only through the "transnatural" realm?

Images of light and darkness seem to answer the question in a way more convincing than Alvar's didactic soliloquies about man's natural goodness and the victory of the good through the providential processes of Nature. Images of light and darkness indicate two lines of development. Alvar, the disguised light of Truth, is thrown into prison to emerge, with the help of Teresa's "taper," triumphantly, as the victory of this light. In this process, the victory of light illustrates that evil as a social phenomenon is eliminated. The real centre of darkness, however, is the "hellish pit" of the cavern, and there is no light emerging from this centre for either of the three characters who confront its darkness. (Ordonio lures Isidore into the cavern, and Alhadra who follows Isidore, is convinced of his murder there.)

All three characters who had to confront the centre of darkness within the natural construct of the cavern, have confronted the darkness within themselves. Facing this darkness is inevitable, inescapable and unredeemable, because it is a darkness pertaining to Nature as well as to human nature; it is a darkness that offers no salvation within the natural realm.

IV

"SO TAKING A DISGUISE":
KEATS'S *OTHO THE GREAT*

The wedding of the hero is still in the centre of *Otho the Great*, as it is in *The Borderers* and *Remorse*. As in the first play, the villain's intrigue prevents this union. Yet even more unfortunate than this missed union is the fact that the hero celebrates another, fatal wedding under the spell of a beautiful but villainous enchantress.

In "Lamia," "La Belle Dame Sans Merci," and to some extent in the "Fall of Hyperion," Keats attaches a similar significance to the hero's union with a superhuman female, an act equivalent to his descent into the demonic realm of madness or death. Ludolph, the hero of *Otho the Great* dies in the morning following his wedding night, driven insane by the recognition of his irrevocable error.

It is probably characteristic of the increased pessimism and melancholy of the "second generation" of Romantic poets that the heroes of Keats, Shelley and Byron all die at the end of the play with no hope for redemption. After an initial error, Coleridge's hero, Alvar, triumphs and marries the heroine; Wordsworth's hero, Marmaduke, feels hopelessly defeated, but begins a journey for mercy or redemption. Ludolph is the first of the three tragic heroes encountered in this study for whom the tragic fall is equivalent to death.

Furthermore, in Coleridge's and Wordsworth's plays the evil villain expresses doubt or denial, while the good hero is the spokesman for Man's paradisiac union with Nature. Keats, Byron and Shelley, however, each explore the mystery of a forbidden, demonic or incestuous union, as if debating whether Man's claim for the paradisiac union is itself forbidden and self-destructive.

Like the unsuccessful dramas of Wordsworth and Coleridge discussed in the two previous chapters, Keats's *Otho the Great* can be approached best as the dramatization of a spiritual autobiography. Keats also uses his hero's story for the externalization of an internal crisis. He presents the hero-lover at the crossroads between two brides who stand for two images of Nature. The hero has to choose at the peril of his life, the poet at the peril of working out his salvation between the two.

Keats is highly conscious of the ties between himself and his hero.

With admirable self-mockery, he makes much of the close connection between the jealous lover in the play and the brooding tragedian. He writes to Fanny Brawne:

I leave this minute a scene in our Tragedy and see you (think it not blasphemy) through the mist of Plots, speeches, counterplots and counter speeches—The Lover is madder than I am—I am nothing to him—he has a figure like the Statue of Maleager and double distilled fire at his heart.[1]

The poet's letters reveal a close connection between personal, philosophical, and aesthetic concerns. In Keats's love poems to Fanny, his violent jealousy is obviously that of the "hot-blooded Ludolph," whom he describes to her as a "lover [even] madder than I am." Although Keats's jocular tone in the letter seems to imply that his hero is a somewhat exaggerated self-portrait, certain characteristics of the model are nevertheless recognizable, particularly in his dilemma concerning the two faces of Fanny. In one letter he calls her his "brilliant reality" in contrast to the deceptive temptations of poetry and of the Imagination. Yet, at other times he sees her as a temptress beckoning him to ascend to paradise, only to bitterly disillusion him the moment he would complete his journey and achieve his goal. He writes to her:

I have been reading lately an oriental tale of a very beautiful colour—It is of a city of melancholy men, all made so by this circumstance. Through a series of adventures each one of them by turns reach some gardens of Paradise where they meet with a most enchanting Lady; and just as they are going to embrace her, she bids them shut their eyes—they shut them— and on opening their eyes again find themselves descending to earth in a magic basket. The remembrance of this Lady and their delights lost beyond all recovery render them melancholy ever after. How I applied this to you my dear...[2]

The gentle reproach to Fanny for "enchanting him so deeply" is emphasized and reiterated in the love poem of "torturing jealousy" in which he cries out to her to let no hand "break the sacramental cake," begging her not to betray him to the "wintry air" of destruction and mortality.[3]

Whether or not Keats was fair in his assessment of Fanny's role in their personal relationship, he associates her with two opposing images of Paradise, and hence even the personal and sexual dilemma becomes part of a much broader, universal dilemma, debated by all the five romantic poet-playwrights in their tragedies: Is man entitled to his claim to Paradise? Should he be able to attain the perfection and even immortality implied in the sacramental wedding, this sacred union between Nature and Man in an unfallen world and hence in the presence of the Spirit?

This question receives favourable answer in Coleridge's *Remorse* because the play ends in the harmony between hero, heroine, and their father, re-enacting the harmonious resolution of the Romantic drama between Adam, Eve and their Father—the union between Man, Nature and Spirit.

In Keats's play, however, the hero's search for Paradise becomes a sinister, self-destroying and frustrating journey, in which the beautiful enchantress leads the hero not to Paradise, but to the demonic realm of chaos, equivalent to alienation, madness and death.

The motives for Ludolph's actions, and most specifically the circumstances of his death, are mainly responsible for the weakness of the work as a psychologically credible or dramatically coherent work of art. Yet it is precisely this weakness in dramatic technique which draws attention to the poet's underlying concern: we can make sense of Ludolph's apparently illogical movements and bombast once these are viewed in the context of an allegorical presentation.

The villain is Duke Conrad, who incites the young prince Ludolph to rebel against his father, Emperor Otho. When, however, his Hungarian subjects also turn against Otho, Conrad decides to join the Emperor, who now considers himself indebted to Conrad for his victory over the Hungarians. Set against this background, the villain's intrigue moves in two directions, and it has two intended victims. Prince Ludolph and the innocent Erminia are both victims of the villain's deception, and of their own innocence.

By inciting Ludolph to rebellion and later making him go over to the Emperor, Conrad manages to become Otho's favourite. Through this phase of the intrigue, Conrad also wins the Emperor's favour for his sister, Auranthe, and manages to get his long-sought royal permission for a wedding between her and Ludolph. Auranthe, however, is the secret mistress of Knight Albert, a fact which had been almost betrayed by a ladder once left against her window. The second part of the intrigue has Conrad and Auranthe trying to fix Auranthe's shame on the innocent Erminia. They not only want to clear Auranthe of suspicion, but also turn the Emperor against the innocent Erminia, his orphaned niece brought up like his own daughter, and the intended wife of his son Ludolph.

The entanglement of the dramatic plot is often arbitrary. For example, in order to make Erminia get acquainted with Gersa, the young Hungarian King and presumably her future husband, the playwright has her retire into a convent and then has all the sisters from that convent fall into the hands of Gersa as his prisoners. Erminia's finding of Auranthe's letter to Conrad in which she gives away her secret guilt is also far-fetched. Erminia, the young Hungarian's prisoner is made to go through her captor's spoils of war, and find the letter which had fallen out of Conrad's pocket at a previous skirmish with the Hungarians. These various twists and loops of the entanglement are almost impossible to follow at first reading. Yet the plot is not the single most important contributor to the failure of the play as drama. The most obvious weakness seems to concern not so much the plot, but the central character, his fate, motivation and his strangely grotesque and often inexplicable behaviour.

Although the background to Ludolph's tragedy is ostensibly the medieval Hapsburg Empire under the reign of Emperor Otho, Ludolph's fate makes sense only if related to the enchanted world of fairy tale of romance. Having fallen under the spell of Auranthe, the false enchantress, Ludolph abandons Erminia, the innocent heroine, victim of the villain's slander. At the end, discovering Auranthe's corruption, Ludolph decides to take revenge, but when he finds that all the participants in the intriuge against him have already met their death, he goes insane and then also dies in a state of madness.

The whole intrigue or entanglement, that is the rational element of the plot which is essentially Brown's contribution,[4] is not entirely incongruous or incredible in terms of human motivation. It is mainly Ludolph's reaction to the disentanglement of the intrigue, revealed in Act V, which renders the play so extremely grotesque and absurd a composition.

This act, probably the only one that is exclusively Keats's work,[5] begins in the forest. Revengeful and incensed, Ludolph meets Auranthe just after Auranthe's former lover Albert, and her brother Conrad fought a fatal duel. Before dying, Albert admits his guilt, begs for Ludolph's forgiveness and advises him not to pursue his revenge. Ludolph, however, is incensed more than ever, and he drags Auranthe back to the palace. In the next and last scene we hear the frightened and confused courtiers' reaction to Ludolph's insane behaviour, and then hear Ludolph announce his intention to kill Auranthe. Finally, when he discovers that she is dead, Ludolph also dies, the reader is never too sure whether as a result of a final fit of madness or of a broken heart.

In some respects he resembles Wordsworth's innocent hero, Marmaduke, whose "crime" stands for an error in judgement, a fundamentally epistemological dilemma the romantic poet cannot successfully translate into a psychologically or ethically valid human situation. Ludolph's sudden passion for Auranthe, and his violent anger followed by madness and death upon the consummation of their wedding, makes us aware that for him, the lovers' union stands for much more than just marriage with another being. His strangely exaggerated "soaring" while desiring the union, and his violent and finally fatal despair upon the discovery of Auranthe's duplicity indicates that for Keats, the lovers' union has an allegorical significance that is beyond, or perhaps apart from, the world of human drama.

HERO, INNOCENT HEROINE, VILLAINOUS ENCHANTRESS

Except for Ludolph, all the other characters have some credible motives for their behaviour. Conrad's greed, Albert's passion, and Auranthe's ambition are credible motivations for characters conceived in terms of the natural, everyday level of human behaviour. It is only Ludolph's character which removes the story from the realm of historical reality into that of demonic romance, and from drama into allegory.

Although, like Ludolph, Albert had also been passionately attracted to the beautiful Auranthe, he is not blind to her ambition and ruthlessness. Neither is he blind to the moral evil she and her brother instigate against Erminia. Having received his knighthood from the Emperor, Albert feels doubly guilty for inadvertently having contributed to his son's deception: in Auranthe Ludolph worships Albert's long-time mistress as the goddess of purity and innocence. In resolving his conflict, but resolving it too late, Albert comes close to the credible portrayal of a tragic predicament (not unlike Isidore, the basically honest but weak and compromised agent in Coleridge's play).

Neither are we particularly hard-pressed to find believable motives for the two villains' actions. Conrad's character evokes nothing more superhuman or satanic than the typical Machiavellian villain who acts ruthlessly out of self-interest or greedy ambition. Conrad's flight of ambition leads him naturally in the direction of Auranthe's golden crown, the goal he can obtain only through ruthless intrigue.

Auranthe herself is not a representative of superhuman or diabolical evil. If at the end she appears to Ludolph a "witch," a "cocka-trice," or "demon," it is mainly on account of Ludolph's own "soaring," that is, his exaggerated worship of her beauty, his own enchantment. The demonic connotations of her corruption follow essentially from Ludolph's exaggerated claims on her purity and goodness; it is because he expected her to be a goddess, that the recognition of her human corruption makes her appear as super-naturally evil. Once she is revealed to be a fallen creature, her beauty becomes for Ludolph the symbol of demonic deception; yet she remains a demonic creature only in Ludolph's eyes.

To the other characters, indeed, to the reader, Auranthe appears to be an ordinary young woman trying, at least in the beginning, to cover up for her first passion. Although later she becomes a ruth-lessly ambitious creature, prepared to give up her first lover and deceive her intended husband in order to get the throne, there is nothing particularly "demonic" about her actions. She would use Ludolph for securing her ambition, but she is no "demon" bent on his destruction. Neither is she demonic in the way she reacts to her misfortunes in the last act when she mourns Albert's death, and suffers from a sense of remorse strong enough to drive her to suicide.

For Ludolph, however, she becomes the symbol of the beauty of Nature, a beauty that proves sinister and deceptive. His disillusion-ment culminates when he confronts Auranthe in the midnight forest after she had fled her nuptial chamber in the palace. In an ironic reversal of Ludolph's paradisiac expectations, the forest becomes a place of demonic chaos, the dark cosmic centre of the whole world as Hell. Ludolph describes this as "an oven of dark thickets," which is set in a "oppressive shade." It is the very centre of darkness, of the absence of light. In this image, Hell is not the centre of active evil, but the centre of inevitable nothingness, where Ludolph fears being "sucked to death." In line with his dread of emptiness, he is afraid that Auranthe will "melt...into air," and the guilty conspirators will be "free as the dark air."

Ludolph clearly resembles Wordsworth's Marmaduke and Coler-idge's Alvar in the magnitude of his disappointment in love. This disappointment attains cosmic significance as it comes to stand for loss of faith in the purity of Nature and in the perfectibility of Man. Yet, Ludolph is also different from Marmaduke and Alvar; for him, the disillusionment assumes a finality that can be met only by madness, and consequently by death or suicide. By discrediting Erminia's innocence Ludolph denies the innocence of Nature and enters the demonic realm from which he cannot return.

Some of the dramaturgical weaknesses of the play are due to its affinity with romance, the world of the enchanted forest, and the demonic realm that is also part of this world. Thus, one of Ludolph's most absurd speaches deals with his violent anger against Auranthe, upon capturing her in the forest:

> Auranthe! What can he mean?
> What horrors? Is it not a joyous time?
> Am I not married to a paragon
> 'Of personal beauty and untainted soul?'
> A blushing fair-eyed Purity! A Sylph,
> Whose snowy timid hands have never sin'd
> Beyond a flower pluck'd, white as itself?
> . . .
>
> . . . safe from my revenge;
> I cannot catch you—You should laugh at me,
> Poor cheated Ludolph,—make the forest hiss
> With jeers at me—You tremble; faint at once,
> You will come to again. O Cockatrice,
> I have you. Whither wander those fair eyes
> To entice the Devil to your help, that he
> May change you to a Spider, so to crawl
> Into some cranny to excape my wrath?   (V. 2. 19-25; 32-40)

This bombastic outburst of venom, cruelty and savage despair, also refers to some unexplained code of honour. The speech becomes easier to fathom if we recognize that it echoes another "demonic romance." Wieland's *Oberon* had great influence on Keats in the period of writing his drama, and W. Beyer has pointed out that Ludolph's speech in the forest echoes that of Oberon, whom Wieland describes as the King of Love and of the spirits of Nature:

Wieland's Oberon is king of daemons, as in Platonic myth. Like Diotima's Love in the "Symposium," 'He is a great spirit [diamon], and like all spirits he is intermediate between the divine and the mortal.' Thus Oberon is the 'guardian god,' a 'kind of genius whose protecting grace' is felt like that of a tutelary angel. The awful ruler of all nature, he is 'a spirit,' a 'wood god' whose minions (no mere diminutive fairies they!) are 'angelic.'[6]

Ludolph's outburst at Auranthe sounds grotesque and exaggerated in the context of a human situation. His wrath and cruelty become understandable, however, if we realize that to him Auranthe's offence signifies the fall of the whole world of Nature. Ludolph's despair upon her fall thus assumes cosmic proportions. The fact that his desperately angry words recall those of Oberon, the god of Love and Nature, also adds special significance to the hero's own death at the end of the play. His fall, in effect, personifies the failure of he divine principle of love in the cosmos.

In discussing the effect of Wieland's work upon Keats, Beyer draws attention to some fundamental similarities between *Otho the Great* and "Lamia," particularly when it comes to the punishment of the two enchantresses. At the end of his "demonic romance," Keats effects Lamia's transformation into her initial shape of a serpent, whil the vengeful Ludolph also calls Auranthe a snake and "cockatrice," as if ready to inflict upon her the pain of such a transformation.

The play shows that Keats was preoccupied with Oberon's powers of inflicting "grievous torment" and transformation as penance for impurity and sensuality, and with his curse upon the sensual "joys that seduce" and their high-priestess, the deceitful woman who is the "bosom snake."[7]

Beyer elaborates on the similarity between Lamia and Auranthe by comparing their fate to that of Oberon's erring queen, Titania, in Wieland's tale:

Now the sin that evoked the curse upon the queen and Auranthe is clearly sexual and ethical. But the complexity of Lamia's nature—of her who is part sensual and mortal African queen and part pure and heavenly Titania, part "real woman" and part symbol of a psychic power—this complexity makes the cause of Lamia's penance more difficult to understand.[8]

While aware of their parallels, Beyer makes a distinction between the varied complexities of Lamia and Auranthe. He feels that Keats has a "sexual and literal conception"[9] of Auranthe's sins, as opposed to the "spiritual and symbolic"[10] sins of Lamia. A close examination of *Otho the Great*, however, makes clear that Auranthe's "sexual and literal" sin is merely a vehicle for a "spiritual and symbolic" one.

Beyer's distinction notwithstanding, Keats uses the love story and its sexual connotations in similar ways both in "Lamia" and in *Otho the Great*. Both works reveal significant characteristics of "demonic romance" and indicate an allegorical creation.

Both Lamia and Auranthe are deceivers or enchantesses, and Beyer's explanations of Lamia's allegorical significance is equally illuminating on the subject of Ludolph's Auranthe:

That her "sweet sin" is against love is clear. But this "love" is no longer sexual alone: it was conceived, I think, as in the "pleasure thermometer" in *Endymion*, as the highest form of the Love divine, as a spiritual ideal . . .[11]

Both Ludolph's violent anger against the enchantress and his death following hers, originate from the intensity of his total commitment to Auranthe, and through Auranthe to a spiritual ideal. To Ludolph, Auranthe's beauty is a token of Nature's perfection and of the presence of the Spirit. From their wedding, he expects the perfection and immortality associated with Paradise, the realization of spirituality through sensual beauty, the presence of the "Love Divine" in Nature.

When in love with Auranthe, Ludolph sees their union as a token of immortality. He would not exchange his lot either for the music of the heavenly spheres, or for the winged chariots of Apollo, images associated with immortality in the Christian and the Greek myths respectively.

> Though heaven's choir
> Should in a vast circumference descend
> And sing for my delight, I'd stop my ears!
> Though bright Apollo's car stood burning here,
> And he put an arm to bid me mount,
> His touch an immortality, not I!
> This earth, this palace, this room, Auranthe!
>
> (III. 2. 39-44)

Ludolph's commitment to Auranthe appears strangely exaggerated to the outsiders, and they wonder, "How deep she bewitch'd him!" (III. 2. 14); "He Soars!" (III. 2. 37); "Past all reason" (IV. 2. 37); and Otho is puzzled and concerned that this "soaring" might be the consequence of a magic spell.

> This is a little painful; just too much.
> Conrad, if he flames longer in this wise,
> I shall believe in wizard-woven loves
> And old romances; but I'll break the spell.   (III. 2. 45-48)

He asks his son: "come, come, a little sober sense, Ludolph!" and regrets that Ludolph lives "still in extremes!" (III. 2. 235).

In that state of madness that follows disillusionment, Ludolph admits that through his love for Auranthe he laid claim to immortality and infinite delight. Had Auranthe's beauty been the beauty of innocence, through their wedding they would have entered the realm of the immortals.

> ...Methought I heard,
> As I came in, some whispers,—what of that?
> 'Tis natural men should whisper; at the kiss
> Of Psyche given by Love, there was a buzz
> Among the gods!—and silence is as natural.   (V. 5. 26-30)

The glitter of the royal palace is nothing like the immortal splendour he had envisioned for his wedding of Auranthe whom he assumed to be innocent.

> These draperies are fine, and, being a mortal,
> I should desire no better; yet, in truth,
> There must be some superior costliness,
> Some wider-domed high magnificence!
> I would have, as a mortal I may not,
> Hanging of heaven's clouds, purple and gold,
> Slung from the spheres; gauzes of silver mist,
> Loop'd up with cords of twisted wreathed light,
> And tassell'd round with weeping meteors!
> These pendent lamps and chandeliers are bright
> As earthly fires from dull dross can be cleansed;
> Yet could my eyes drink up intenser beams
> Undazzled,—this is darkness,—when I close
> These lids, I see far fiercer brilliances,—
> Skies full of splendid moons, and shooting stars,
> And spouting exhalations, diamond fires,
> And panting fountains quivering with deep glows!
> (V. 5. 31-47)

Having discovered Auranthe's corruption, he lost his claim to Paradise. Auranthe, the "soft moon" whom he wanted to protect with the "tenderest clouds," has betrayed him, taking away from him "skies full of splendid moons."

After his vision of paradisiac splendours, he now sees the world deprived of light, and even the palace is "yes—this is dark—is it not dark?" The morning that follows the wedding, brings with it a darkness, in direct contrast to Ludolph's foolish expectations of more than mortal splendours. The magnificent dream of Paradise is inevitably followed by disillusionment and bitterness. "My Lord, 'Tis late; the lights of festival are ever / Quench'd in the morn ... 'Tis early dawn." (V. 5. 48-51).

The morning 'darkness' which brings the grey daylight of disillusionment upon the dazzling dream of enchantment is reiterated several times in the play, as the "morn peers with disrelish, grey, barren and cold," just as the old priest's "grey browed" visage carries with it the threat of disillusionment to Ludolph's passion for Auranthe.

Ludolph saw the perfection of Auranthe's beauty as the "fair completion of all delicate nature's wit," that is the "magic chance" of attaining Paradise in Nature. Her "deep blue eyes" and "twin-arch'd ebon brows," together with her "white temples ... Cheeks fashion'd tenderly on either side [are] / So perfect, so divine that our poor eyes / Are dazzled with the sweet proportioning, / And wonder that 'tis so,—the magic chance!" (V. 5. 61-67).

Her beauty enhanced by innocence, would have assured the lovers' union with the "magic chance" of Paradisiac perfection, and hence immortality. The very first shadow of a doubt concerning her purity makes Ludolph experience the threat of the "ashes" of mortality: "I cannot doubt—I will not—no—to doubt / Is to be ashes!—wither'd up to death!" (III. 2. 193-194).

Yet, under the veneer of immortal beauty, Auranthe is a fallen mortal, and so, discovery of her fallen state spells death to Ludolph's "soaring" flight to immortality. Her beauty is revealed as mere mask over the skeleton of death: "Her lips—I swear no human bones e'er wore / So taking a disguise" (V. 5. 69-70).

Because her beauty implies the promise of Nature's perfection, her moral flaw comes as a shock he can hardly accept: "aye, you shall see her, / And wonder at her, friends, she is so fair— / She is the world's chief Jewel" (V. 5. 71-74).

Even after he had discovered the truth beneath the disguise, Ludolph still recalls the illusion of her unblemished beauty with a nostalgia associated with a lost world of immortality and innocence. Keats envisioned that world in the gold and green splendour of Arcadia or Paradise: "Sweeping into this presence, glisten'd o'er / With emptied caskets, and her train upheld / By ladies, habited in robes of lawn, / Sprinkled with golden crescents" (V. 5. 84-87).

After acknowledging the loss of his dazzling vision, Ludolph comes to sum up the essence of his tragic loss in a way that is highly characteristic of the Romantic tragic hero: "Sad, that the fairest creature of the earth— / I pray you mind me not—'tis sad, I say, / That the extremest beauty of the world / Should so entrench herself away from me, / Behind a barrier of engender'd guilt!" (V. 5. 91-94). To this exclamation one of the ladies present responds with an "Ah! what a moan!" (V. 5. 95).

The broken pattern of Ludolph's speech indicates that his words herald the approach of his "tragedy madness" which will gradually lead to his "tragedy death." Both of these states Keats has learned to regard as rewarding clichés in obtaining the right audience reaction. At the same time, there is some unmistakably true pathos here which stems most probably from Keats's identification with his hero. Ludolph admits here that he had not reckoned with the "engender'd guilt" which lurks beyond the illusion of Auranthe's perfect beauty. In effect, the appearance of beauty might only be a

82

transitory mask upon the face of the human being, a sinister guise to cover up for the "human bones," the skeleton of mortality.

Ludolph's faith in Auranthe and in their Paradise meant being blind to the mortality lurking beyond the beauties of Nature, death being the due of Man's fallen state: "A barrier of guilt! I was the fool. / She was the cheater!" (V. 5. 103-104).

To understand the allegorical significance of Ludolph's tragic loss, we now turn to the examination of the various concepts of Paradise as articulated by the characters. Both Ludolph and Auranthe have different images of Paradise, as indeed each character conceives of his own version.

Since Keats's direct identification with Ludolph is complete, his artistic control over him is understandably lax. He makes an attempt, however, to enter into the other characters with a certain degree of objectivity. Still, a dramatic relationship between Ludolph and the others is virtually nonexistent. We see very little of the interaction between Ludolph and Auranthe, except seeing him admire her beauty. The lack of dialogue between the lovers is, once more, an indication that the poet's "dramatic business" is only a vehicle for the exploration of an allegorical relationship. Auranthe scarcely exists as a human being in Ludolph's eyes. She stands for a number of abstractions but has no distinctive traits or character.

As for Auranthe's awareness of Ludolph, there is very little in the play that would indicate that she regards him as anything other than a tool of her ambition. She dreams of Paradise as a dream of power, and the image that haunts her is that of the gracious queen handing out provinces to her favourites. Her awe of the golden crown describes her image of Paradise: "For a golden crown / With a queen's awful lips I doubly thank you! / This is to wake in Paradise!" (I. 1. 86-88). In her universe, the golden crown becomes associated with the tempting fruit of Paradise. This image is slightly transformed, due to Keats's recurring notion of Paradise as Arcadia, and the fruit of Paradise is used interchangeably with the immortal fruit of the Hesperian tree from Greek mythology:

> ... O, thou golden Crown,
> Orbing along the serene firmament
> Of a wide empire, like a glowing moon;
> And thou, bright sceptre! lustrous in my eyes,—
> There—as the fabled Hesperian tree,
> Bearing a fruit more precious! graceful thing,
> Delicate, godlike, magic! must I leave

Thee to melt in the visionary air,
Ere, by one grasp, this common hand is made
Imperial?   (IV. 1. 78-87)

In Auranthe's dream Albert, her former lover, is the snake who threatens to deprive her of this Paradise of the golden throne and the golden crown of power. Consequently she calls him "A snake, / A scorpion, sprawling on the first gold step, / Conducting to the throne, high canopied" (IV. 1. 14-16)

The unreality of the characters' vision of Paradise is accentuated by the images of soaring desire and winged flight towards a state not fit for humanity. Naturally, the dreamers are met by disillusionment and destruction. Thus Auranthe and Conrad nurture their desire for Paradise in the "eagle's nest" of their ambition for power and gold.

The images of gold, archetypally symbolic of the regions of perfection and eternity are used ironically throughout the play. Ludolph's dazzlement by the "golden beauty" of Auranthe; Albert's dubious honesty which should be impeccable as "gold current"; the mature wisdom of the Emperor that should be like the golden "sheafs of the ripening sun"; Conrad's dream of "gold bullions" and Auranthe's vision of the "golden crown"; these are all comments on man's false concept of Paradise, and on his presumptuousness of flying too high up into the regions of immortality.

The unreality of the Paradisiac dreams is also reinforced by the indication that man's hopes and aspirations are more of the substance of dreams, and that man's whole existence is as insubstantial as the dreamworld.

At first, when confronted with the accusation against Auranthe, Ludolph hopes it to be as unreal as a "nightmare, which a man forgets in the new dawn." Ironically, however, the new dawn proves that the nightmare has been reality, and Ludolph who is still unable to act, dies a nightmare death, paralyzed and unable to put up a fight.

Ludolph's behaviour makes his predicament appear so unreal that the courtiers view it as a "sleeping fancy," and they feel "Grievously ... tantaliz'd, one and all— / Sway'd her and there, commanded to and fro / As though we were the shadows of a dream / And link'd to a sleeping fancy" (V. 5. 1-4). At the end of the play this sense of unreality appears as the punishment for the hero's dazzling dream of Paradise, and he dies in a grey dawn which he perceives as dark as the night. He bids farewell to his survivors in the dawn, "She is gone—I am content—Nobles good night!" (V. 5. 190).

Having learnt about Auranthe's corruption, he still cannot return to the innocent Erminia, although he asks her angelic forgiveness for his error: "Ah! gentlest creature, whose sweet innocence / Was almost murder'd; I am penitent, Wilt thou forgive me?" In spite of her forgiveness, however, he cannot think of union with her because he is still too deeply committed to Auranthe. Having learnt that Auranthe is dead, Ludolph himself "staggers and falls into (the courtiers' arms and) dies."

He is punished with insanity and death for the wrong choice, caused by his fascination with the false "Jewel" of Auranthe's "visionary" or insubstantial beauty, and by his inability to recognize and affirm the purity of Erminia, the "simplest flower of the world's herbal."

In her simplicity, Erminia is the very essence of angelic purity, that of the "fair lilly blanch'd / Still with the dews of piety" (III. 2. 123-124). It is, ironically, this unassuming simple flower, however, who would have had the potential to "soar" with Ludolph to Paradise, since she is "like an angel newly—shent, / Who veils its snowy wings" (III. 2. 125-126).

Young Gersa wins Erminia because he had recognized her innocence, and discovered her true being in spite of slander: "The swan, soft leaning on her fledgy breast, / When to the stream she launches, looks not back / With such a tender grace; nor are her wings / So white as your soul is, if that but be / Twin-picture to your face" (II. 2. 101-103). Innocence has a significance which surpasses that of the specific human situation, and Gersa draws our attention to this when he announces that vindication of Erminia's innocence means to him more than his throne: "Today, for the first day, I am a king, / Yet would I give my unworn crown away / To know you spotless" (II. 2. 106-108).

Because of his intuitive belief in the innocence of unfallen Nature, Gersa may achieve a state of Paradise; because of his error, Ludolph is led to self-destruction aggravated by the fact that he is the last of his line.

When she is deprived of her uncle's fatherly protection, Erminia seeks the protection of her spiritual father, the old Ethelbert who stands by her throughout her misfortunes. Having known her from infancy, Ethelbert describes her as the embodiment of Nature's purity, and of its vital process:

> Watch'd her, as anxious husbandmen the grain,
> From the first shoot till the unripe mid-May,

> Then to the tender ear of her June days,
> Which, lifting sweet abroad its timid green,
> Is blighted by the touch of calumny;
> You cannot credit such a monstrous tale. (II. 2. 133-137)

Gersa's good fortune lies in not crediting the "monstrous tale" against the innocence of unfallen Nature. Ludolph who accepted another image of Nature suffers a strange transformation as a result. Having discovered Auranthe's pollution, he comes to see the very principle of growth and fertility as a destructive force rather than a life-giving one. To him the natural process appears as a process of ecstatic but also treacherously destructive delights. In his bitterness at this point, Ludolph turns against the sun which ripens the grapes, because he feels that the very principle of fertility impels the wine god, Bacchus, to commit suicide at the highest point of his ecstasy.

> Certes, a father's smile should, like sun light,
> Slant on my sheafed harvest of ripe bliss—
> Besides, I thirst to pledge my lovely Bride
> In a deep goblet: let me see—what wine?
> The strong Iberian juice, or mellow Greek?
> Or pale Calabrian? Or the Tuscan grape?
> Or of old Aetna's pulpy wine presses,
> Black stained with the fat vintage, as it were
> The purple slaughter-house, where Bacchus' self
> Prick'd his own swollen veins? (V. 5. 116-125)

The image of Bacchus, the god of fertility, ecstasy, and intoxication, committing suicide, is a telling foreshadowing of Ludolph's own death.

In his yearning for the ecstasy of Paradise, the hero came to deny the innocence of the "simplest flower" of Nature, and as a result he is faced with madness and destruction by the demonic realm.

HERO AND FATHER

As in *Remorse* and *The Borderers*, in *Otho the Great* the hero's offence against the heroine parallels an offence against the father.

Keats develops the father-son relationship on two parallel lines. Otho pardons the rebellious young Hungarian prince, Gersa, and then he most generously welcomes and pardons his own rebellious son, Ludolph. Both "sons" begin in a state of rebellion against their King and Father, and refer to their return to Otho as the prodigal son's return to the father. ("As to my father's board I will return," promises Gersa to Otho, while Ludolph says thanks for his

86

father's generosity by exclaiming, "Stead one fatted Calf / Ten hecatombs shall bellow out their last" at the feast of their conciliation.)

The parallels between Gersa and Ludolph as two sons, are numerous. The grateful Gersa emphasizes that he regards Otho as his own father ("Thy father—almost mine," he explains to Ludolph). That the story of this quasi-prodigal son has a happy ending is due to his using his favour with the father well. In spite of the villains' intrigue, Gersa recognizes the heroine's innocence. Thus in their future wedding he may fulfill Otho's original expectations and affirm the continuity inherent in the natural order.

Like Gersa, Ludolph is a noble rebel. He remembers his father's kindness to him in childhood, and, in the disguise of a mysterious Arab, protects Otho on the battlefield. When he is questioned about his "anxious love" that made him protect the same father "whose bitter days he vext with bad revolt," Ludolph acknowledges that

> 'Twas done in memory of my boyish days,
> Poor cancel for his kindness to my youth,
> For all his calming of my childish griefs,
> And all his smiles upon my merriment.   (I. 3. 40-43)

Although he acknowledges that his father had shown him generosity, he wants to rival him even in this regard.

> Yes, yes, I know he hath a noble nature
> That cannot trample on the fallen. But his
> Is not the only proud heart in his realm.
> He hath wrong'd me, and I have done him wrong;
> He hath lov'd me, and I have shown him kindness;
> We should be almost equal.   (I. 3. 55-60)

He wants to overthrow his "father's tyranny" because of his feeling of having been deprived of his affection in later years:

> There will I be, a most unwelcome guest,
> And parley with him, as a son should do,
> Who doubly loathes a father's tyranny;
> Tell him how feeble is that tyranny;
> How the relationship of father and son
> Is no more valid than a silken leash
> Where lions tug adverse, if love grow not
> From interchanged love through many years.   (I. 3. 94-101)

He is also resentful that by insisting on marriage to Erminia, "my father's iron lips have sworn divorcement 'twixt me and my right," that is, the right to choose another bride, Auranthe. Seeing Otho's concern as a sign of tyranny, Ludolph accuses him of a lack of love, although even in this moment of anger, he does not deny Otho's "love of justice":

> And ... with all his love of justice,
> When will he take that grandchild in his arms,
> That, by my love I swear, shall soon be his?
> This reconcilement is impossible. (I. 3. 118-121)

When, in the scene of reconciliation, Ludolph understands the full measure of Otho's generosity, he acknowledges himself his debtor. By this he also acknowledges that his rebellion has been a mistake, due to his blindness to Otho's true love. The son repents having been a "mad conspirator" against the father's "sacred head."

> O thou good Man, against whose sacred head
> I was a mad conspirator, chiefly too
> For the sake of my fair newly wedded wife,
> Now to be punish'd, do not look so sad! (V. 5. 138-141)

In spite of the hero's repentance, his fall follows from his initial rebellion and from his insistence on marrying Auranthe. As a result of his mistake, he is unable to produce the offspring he would have placed into his father's arms and does not fulfill Otho's desire for the continuation of the family line. Otho expresses desire for such offspring, when he points at his ring on Auranthe's hand "Keep it, my brightest daughter; it may prove / The little prologue to a line of kings" (I. 2. 19-20), and when he looks on his son's wedding he sees the dawn of a new age not only for the family, but also for the world:

> What are the cities 'yond the Alps to me,
> The provinces about the Danube's mouth,
> . . .
>
> To these fair children, stars of a new age?
> Unless, perchance I might rejoice to win
> This little ball of earth, and chuck it them
> To play with! (III. 2. 18-25)

Through his wrong bridal choice, Ludolph fails to produce heirs for Otho. Thereby he breaks the continuity of the Nature cycle, and also fails to put a seal on the son's conciliation with the Father.

To understand Keats's treatment of the conflict between young and old, presented as the conflict between son and father, one must also consider the other father figure in the play.

Old Ethelbert is the Holy Father and protector of Erminia. In order to defend Erminia, he has to reveal Auranthe's secret. Yet Ludolph registers almost insane hatred against Ethelbert at the very moment of his appearance, even before the old man could utter his accusations. "What portent,—what strange prodigy is this?" Ludolph cries on seeing Ethelbert enter the palace. Later when Auranthe faints on hearing the still-veiled accusations, Ludolph calls Ethelbert "Satan," wants to "stab him" and threatens him with torture and execution.

> ... Hast no sense of fear?
> No ounce of man in thy mortality?
> Tremble! for, at my nod, the sharpen'd axe
> Will make thy bold tongue quiver to the roots,
> Those grey lids wink, and thou not know it more!
> (III. 2. 84-88)

Ludolph's intense hatred of the old man is another instance of a strangely illogical relationship which makes sense only in an allegorical, as opposed to a psychological or dramatic framework. This becomes clear as Ludolph's insane outburst of hatred continues:

> Thine arms from forth a pulpit of hot fire
> Shall sprawl distracted!   (III. 2. 91-92)

The conflict between young and old is more explicit here than in either Wordsworth's or Coleridge's tragedy. Keats's hero gives vent to the Romantic son's rebellion against the old. Yet in this case the rebellion is not against authority, but against aging. He dreads the old as a reminder of his own mortality, and the futility of his aspirations. His disdain of the "grey brows," "rheumed eyes," and "grey lids" of old Ethelbert is probably an expression of fear in the face of the "grey and lightless morn" which follows the night of his dazzling dream of beauty and Paradise. (The same kind of sobering glance of reality destroys Lycius's dream of Infinite beauty in "Lamia." Hence Lycius's dread of his old tutor Apollodorus whose disillusioned glance forces Lamia, the beautiful bride, to disappear.)

Ludolph turns to young Gersa seeing him as a natural ally against the league of the old. By jeopardizing youth's hope of Paradise, the old become part of the "league of Devils."

> ... Gersa, you are young
> As I am; let me observe you face to face;
> Not grey-brow'd like the poisonous Ethelbert,
> No rheumed eyes, no furrowing of age,
> No wrinkles where all vices nestle in
> Like crannied vermin—no, but fresh and young
> And hopeful featur'd. Ha! by heaven you weep
> Tears, human tears—Do you repent you then
> Of a curs'd torturer's office! Why shouldst join—
> Tell me, the league of Devils? Confess—confess
> The Lie.—   (IV. 2. 80-89)

Yet, just as he does against Otho, Ludolph proves to be wrong in his violent antagonism against Ethelbert. Otho's initial disapproval of Auranthe, the enchantress, and Ethelbert's unwavering support of the innocent Erminia represent what should have been the hero's correct choice. Offending against these old men, the rebellious young hero is led to irredeemable error.

It is probably equally significant that although both Otho and Ethelbert are on the right side, they are unable to prevent the fatal error. Otho himself was made to consent to Ludolph's and Auranthe's union, while Ethelbert, although he insists upon Erminia's innocence, arrives too late to prevent the fatal wedding.

Although Ludolph's offence against both the innocent heroine and the father are simultaneous, they are not causally connected. It is not the initial rebellion against the father, in this case the prodigal's error, which has the tragic consequences. He errs irredeemably, by wedding the enchantress instead of the innocent heroine, after returning to his father. In this play, then, conciliation between son and father does not save the son from his fall.

Keats's presentation of Ludolph's error as something irrevocable and irredeemable raises some significant questions about the poet's treatment of Fall and redemption. Seemingly Ludolph merely suffers the consequences of wrong judgement, of being deceived by illusion, and not recognizing the true essence of reality. His error being a mental event, one normally does not consider it as fatal, irrevocable or of tragic significance. Yet, when Keats translates the fall into an internal event, he also makes his hero face a dilemma with no possible help from the outside. That he is all alone with his dilemma is of great significance in understanding his tragedy.

Keats's metaphysical speculations about man's salvation in the "vale of Soul-making"[12] and his search for a "system of Salvation which does not affront our reason and humanity"[13] may clarify why he presents Ludolph's mental error as irredeemable. In search of a "grander system of salvation than the christ[e]ain religion,"[14] Keats sets up his own system of "Spirit-creation," in which the immortal element of the divine spark, the "Intelligence," undergoes a transformation in the "human heart," within the "Elemental space" of the "World." Keats describes these immortal elements as the "Intelligences" or "atoms of perception—they know and they see and they are pure, in short they are God."[15]

Keats's concept of salvation, as suggested in his speculation, obviously does not rely on a personally imagined, anthropomorphic Divinity. Both salvation and the Fall are transformed into a purely epistemological dilemma, pertaining to the question of knowing or failing to know.

Although Ludolph is grateful for the Creation, for the childhood watched over by his father's loving eyes, when making his fatal decision he faces the individual's solitude. Presented with the tragic dilemma about the two possible aspects of Nature, Man can no longer expect help from a personally perceived and effectively benevolent Father.

Although the first part of the play may resemble the prodigal son's return, it is significant that after reconciliation, the son still finds himself alone and unaided in the only real dilemma which is at the heart of his tragedy. Being entirely on his own, he is also cut off from any course of spiritual redemption after his fall into intellectual error.

V

"THE MONSTER OF THE UPPER SKY": BYRON'S *MANFRED*

Manfred's theme is fundamentally the same as that of the other four romantic tragedies: Man's fall from innocence and his claim to Paradise. Thematic links with the other plays are self-evident. In the centre of *Manfred* is the hero's union with an innocent heroine, although this union assumes the form of forbidden incest. This offence against the heroine also offends against the common father whose blood Manfred contaminates and spills symbolically through the incestuous union and the consequent destruction of the family line.

The overall structure shows a sense of circular completion. The play starts at midnight with Manfred trying to reach out to the dead Astarte, evoking the supernatural realm. It also ends at midnight when the demonic force appears uninvited. The play culminates in the magician-hero's duel with the Devil, and with his declaration of independence both from the infernal spirits of the underworld, and from the redemptive powers of Heaven represented by the saintly Abbot.

The structure in which a magician evokes the spirits in the first scene and faces his final confrontation with the spirits in the last one makes comparison with Marlowe's *Doctor Faustus* inevitable.[1] Faustus is to pay with eternal life for committing blasphemy and signing the pact with the Devil with his own blood. In his last hour he is unable to "leap up" to Christ and participate in the mystery of redemption, although even "half a drop" of the redeemer's blood could pay for the sins of a believer. At the end he is dragged to hell straight from the study in which he damned himself by his blood crime.

Manfred's most obvious offence is not blasphemy. He suffers for having been a lover, and as a lover his 'Hell' is the loss of Astarte after the 'blood crime' of their incestuous union. Yet, like that of Faustus, this crime also grows out of an insatiable "thirst of knowledge" and experience.

For Faustus the initial offence, the breaking of the taboo, is connected with his insatiable thirst to enter the secrets of the universe, the sin of the scholar originating in his study. Dissatisfied with human limitations, he wants to reach beyond these, and win a "dominion" that "stretches as far as doth the mind of man." In his yearning for the Infinite he claims the prerogative of deity, and announces, "A sound magician is a demigod / Hence, tire my brains, to get a deity."

The Faustian aspiration beyond Manfred's crime becomes apparent when he describes his youthful explorations, up to his love affair with Astarte at which point he breaks off:

> ...and with my knowledge grew
> The thirst of knowledge, and the power and joy
> Of this most bright intelligence, until—   (II. 2. 94-96)

Manfred's love for Astarte was both the culmination and the end of the mounting "power and joy" accompanying his explorations for Infinite knowledge and experience.

Yet, there is an interesting difference between the fates of Manfred and Marlow's Doctor Faustus. Faustus takes his punishment after he signed his pact with the devil and enjoyed the resulting delights before the spectators' eyes; for Manfred offence, delight and punishment are darkly but inextricably linked together as elements of a single mysterious event in the past, of an "all nameless hour." Paradoxically, this event signified both the reaching of, and the fall from Paradise. In addition to the ambiguity created by this paradox, the way Manfred's old servant describes this long past event, he may equally refer to an incestuous union between brother and sister or to a Faustian hero's trafficking with the demonic realm (III. 3. 34-47).

Guiltridden, Manfred acknowledges that his outcast state is the ultimate consequence of Faustian man's insatiable search for spiritual powers, of the magician's proud claim for the "fathers' lore." Yet, unlike Faustus, he still seeks forgiveness through magic, that is through the forbidden fruit of the "Tree of Knowledge."

Also, as a lover, Manfred admits to having committed an offence against his "fathers' blood," and his entire cosmic journey is in search of expiation for the "all nameless hour" of the incestuous embrace. Yet, he also yearns to re-live that embrace in the re-union with the lost Astarte. He acknowledges the forbidden nature of Paradise, yet regards it as enticing as ever.

HERO AND HEROINE

Although *Manfred* is a play of great passion, ostensibly about the "half-maddening crime" of incest, the play is marked by the absence of a heroine. When she makes an appearance at all, Astarte is an almost entirely silent apparition, a phantom who scarcely does more than echo the last words of Manfred's questions. Her dramatic character is the culmination of all the other innocent heroines encountered so far. She is an abstract, non-corporeal presence, obviously an allegorical personification of a particular aspect of the hero's self. Indeed, she is less than a presence. Astarte is an inverted being, the absence of something that had been vital to the hero, the loss of something essential, a cause for complaint.

Like the other heroines, Astarte had been the hero's childhood companion, the only human being in this case with whom the hero enjoyed the "chain of human ties." She is the childhood Paradise, a shelter from loneliness and isolation. Without her the world of Nature changes into the hell of emptiness. Nature is barren of the vital warmth, and Manfred can no longer love the Mother Earth in her absence:

> For I have called on thee in the still night,
> Startled the slumbering birds from the hushed boughs,
> And woke the mountain wolves, and made the caves
> Acquainted with thy vainly echoed name,
> Which answered me—many things answered me—
> Spirits and men—but thou wert silent all.   (II. 4. 135-140)

Astarte's absence from Nature makes Heaven itself look empty: "gazed over heaven in vain search of thee ... your likeness ... speak to me." It is this emptiness which makes the world turn into the hellscape of spiritual barrenness, a limbo in which Manfred stagnates at the beginning of the play.

When, in the opening scene he bemoans the fact that the "Tree of Knowledge is not that of Life," he describes his anguish as the suffering of Adam following the eating of the forbidden fruit, and the expulsion from Paradise.

In the Romantic poet's rendering of the myth of Eden, expulsion from Paradise is equivalent to Adam's separation from Eve, or Man's alienation from Nature. Manfred complains about a "vigil" which does not allow him to sleep and forget his guilt and loss. "Vigil" refers to his mourning of Astarte as well as to physical and spiritual insomnia. Having lost Astarte, he is cast out of the natural cycle alternating between energy and peace, day and night, consciousness and lack of consciousness.

Having reached out for the "Tree of Knowledge," he lost his grip on the Tree of Life. Having offended against the Father, he caused the destruction of Astarte.

The circumstances of Astarte's destruction have bewildered many a reader, and invited a great deal of speculation. Although a sensitive and enthusiastic reader of Byron, Goethe evades solving this mystery and imposes his own interpretation.[2] According to this, Manfred's profound sense of guilt is caused by his tribulations over an illicit love affair with a beautiful Florentine lady whose husband found out about their affair and killed her ("her blood was shed,") and therefore Manfred had to kill him in revenge ("I have shed / Blood, but not hers—and yet her blood was shed;")

The mystery surrounding Astarte's figure creates a sense of tension, and it may invite ingenious critical interpretations of Byron's psychological or sexual dilemmas. Thus, when Manfred describes the circumstances of her death, he admits that it was the flaw in his own heart that caused her death: "My heart . . . broke her heart; / It gazed on mine, and withered" (II. 2. 118-119). This original flaw, something previous to the actual sin of incest, may refer to Manfred's sin of pride, or, as Wilson Knight would have it, to homosexuality.[3] For the purposes of this analysis it only needs be said that Manfred's union with Astarte had been sufficient to heal his alienated self. Their union, therefore, appears to have been, if only temporarily, a shelter of Paradise. On its most universal level, then, the relationship between hero and heroine is an exploration of the tragic conflict between guilt and limitless desire, while the poet's strategies are directed to overcome guilt and re-affirm desire.

When preparing for the confrontation with Arimanes, Manfred reflects on the historical examples of people who had tried to extort an answer from Fate. He recalls the Spartan monarch who "slew / That which he loved, unknowing what he slew, / And died, unpardoned," (II. 2. 185-186). The parallel between this and his own case is clear "had I never loved / That which I love would still be beautiful, / Happy and giving happiness" (II. 2. 193-195). Oscar Wilde's "all men kill the thing they love"[4] sounds like a reiteration of Manfred's anguished cry in this scene. The thought is also the keystone of the romantic poet's articulation of tragedy. Although it is associated with what appears to be man's crime, to lose innocence is actually beyond man's knowledge or responsibility. Nevertheless, the hero has to suffer the consequences and die unpardoned and unredeemed. Man kills because he loves; he loses Paradise because he claims Paradise.

Time and again, Byron emphasizes the extremely strong connection between Manfred's individual sin and the cosmic mystery of the Fall and Creation. The connection is introduced by the Seventh

Spirit, the personification of Manfred's ruling star and a reminder of his great promise and fall:

> The Star which rules thy destiny
> Was ruled, ere earth began, by me:
> It was a World as fresh and fair
> As e'er revolved round Sun in air;
> Its course was free and regular,
> Space bosomed not a lovelier star.
> The Hour arrived—and it became
> A wandering mass of shapeless flame,
> A pathless Comet and a curse,
> The menace of the universe;
> Still rolling on with innate force,
> Without a sphere, without a course,
> A bright deformity on high,
> The monster of the upper sky!   (I. 1. 110-123)

At first sight Byron's cosmology seems remarkably close to a Christian, even to an orthodox medieval, world picture. It draws a distinction between the eternal perfection of the "upper sky," in contrast to the "sublunar" world which has been reduced to imperfection and mutability on account of Adam's sin. Originally intended to be a "fresh and fair world," the star of Manfred's destiny became a "pathless comet and a curse." Now it is a "monster"; yet it still carries the memory of the perfection once possessed in its paradoxically "bright deformity." Earlier Manfred delineated this same condition by describing himself as a "wandering hell in the eternal Space," a planet which due to a cosmic catastrophe has been reduced to the "burning wreck of a demolished world."

The cosmic catastrophe which hurled the star of eternal perfection into the abyss of chaos is the direct consequence of the mysterious "Hour," presumably the same "all nameless hour" in which Manfred tasted the forbidden fruit of the "Tree of Knowledge." Since the star had existed in its immutable perfection "ere earth began," it signifies that the ominous "Hour" which "arrived" in its fateful necessity is identical to the Hour of Creation. Manfred's personal fall in the "all nameless hour," therefore, is inextricably linked with the earth's fall through the Hour of Creation, and with the loss of that permanent perfection that belonged to the celestial bodies of the "upper sky."

Although the Seventh Spirit embodies Manfred's personal fate, he also identifies the hero as Everyman, whose guilt is man's universal condition, and Manfred's self-image is hardly understandable without this double exposure of personal and cosmic catastrophies.

His sense of guilt for Astarte's destruction stems from feeling ethical responsibility for the individual's fall. At the same time, he also claims to be a sacrificial victim of the "curse" connected with man's universal condition. He is the victim of the Fall into imperfection, confined to the Earth, his spirit separated from its rightful celestial abode.

The cosmic analogy also draws attention to the duality between villain and hero in Manfred's own character. The "pathless comet'[s]" regrettable fall from paradisiac innocence identifies Manfred with Everyman or Adam. Since this event also implies, however, a fall from Heaven to Hell, the Seventh Spirit's description also reinforces the analogy between Manfred and the fallen "Spirit of the Air," Satan. This dual role as Adam and Satan also determines the ambivalence of his relationship to the heroine.

As her name implies, Astarte is the "clear bright star" of perfection, the mirror image of the higher self (II. 2. 105-118) that shows to Manfred, the "fallen comet," the perfect beauty he had lost. Yet, she is also an elusive, mocking and even demonic apparition. When Manfred's ruling star, the Seventh Spirit, assumes the shape of Astarte, it serves as a scornful reminder of the hero's loss of his celestial position. When he reaches out to re-possess this taunting vision, he fears it to be but a "madness and a mockery." These fears are indeed well grounded; unable to clasp her, Manfred "falls senseless" in frustration and despair.

Like Adam, Manfred is drawn to Astarte, his chosen Eve, in whose embrace he would again be "most happy." In his role as Satan, however, he cannot help identifying himself with the "poor erring Spirits," who were "never allowed to return" to the heavenly abode because of their descent to the beautiful daughters of earth. Therefore, the consummation of Manfred's and Astarte's love is also like the embrace between earthly and celestial regions. It is the moment of Paradise, yet it destroys the daughter of the Earth, and bars the "erring Spirit'[s]" return to Heaven.

Their union is simultaneously the consummation of the paradisiac moment, and that of their Fall, one inextricably contained within the other. Therefore, if the hero as Adam wants to claim Man's title to Paradise, he also finds it necessary to affirm his own fall. Hence the proud defiance of Manfred as villain, cosmic rebel, or Satan.

The fact that the moments of Fall and Paradise are simultaneous, sheds further light on the hero's problematic relationship to the Father, and on the "curse" pronounced on him by the Father. In *The*

Borderers, *Remorse* and *Otho the Great* the hero's fall from innocence is the result of his being fatally deceived by the villain. In these
plays the Romantic Adam falls merely because in his ignorance he is
deceived by Satan. Manfred is the first hero who is not deceived.
Here the locus of the tragic fall is not an error in judgement; it is a
"curse" the hero is knowingly obliged to fulfill. It is this "curse" and
not his ignorance that makes him love, and through loving, destroy
Astarte, just as it is his "curse" to have fallen from the state of eternal
star into that of a destructive and self-destroying comet. Since the
fatal "Hour" which on multiple levels sweeps together in its sexual
embrace both the Fall and Creation, the course of Manfred's actions
is just as inevitable as that of the comet. His fall is a pre-ordained and
inevitable cosmic catastrophe.

Manfred's spiritual anguish, then, is not connected with his
acceptance of the incestuous union as evil. On the contrary, he
affirms this experience as the moment of attaining Paradise, and
defies the Power which imposes on him the "curse" of consequences.
His satanic stance stems from his "deep despair without the fear of
Hell," and ultimately from his refusal to "justify the ways of God
to man."

MANFRED AS VILLAIN AND HERO: SATAN IN DEFIANCE,
ADAM IN SEARCH OF THE FATHER

In *Manfred* Man's tragic alienation from Nature and the Spirit is
acted out through the hero's search for an absent heroine and an
absent father.

> ... I have not named to thee
> Father or mother, mistress, friend, or being,
> With whom I wore the chain of human ties;
> If I had such, they seemed not such to me—
> (II. 2. 100-103)

Manfred claims to have no relatives on the human scale, either by
blood or choice. The way the old servant Manuel describes his one-
time Master, Manfred's father was a carefree soul of revels with
whom the stern Manfred could find very little in common. It is
possible, however, to read the old servant's account in a way that
suggests that Manfred was brought up as an orphan. When Manuel
says, "Ere Count Manfred's birth, / I served his father" (III. 3.
14-15), this could imply that his service with the father terminated
at or before the son's birth.

There are many indirect indications that Manfred was an orphan. The only reference to a mother in the play, is the reference to "Mother Earth," and the only human relative he acknowledges is his gentle and protective sister.

Yet, whether he knew his father and disliked him, or did not know him at all, Manfred feels guilty for having offended against him by loving Astarte "as we should not have loved." The fact that the mother is not even mentioned in the play, and it is the gentle Astarte who fulfills the role of the mother to Manfred, also increases the son's guilt vis-à-vis the father.

His offence implies the polluting and destruction of the family line, the "pure warm stream" which ran in the "veins of my fathers." Although the story implies that it is Astarte who is destroyed as the result of the "fatal embrace," Manfred also insists that the blood shed was his own as well:

> I say 'tis blood—my blood! the pure warm stream
> Which ran in the veins of my fathers, and in ours
> When we were in our youth, and had one heart,
> And loved each other as we should not love,
> And this was shed: (II. 1. 24-28)

He admits guilt for Astarte's destruction, but his ultimate sin is self-destruction: "I have shed / Blood, but not hers" (II. 2. 119-120) and "was my own destroyer, and will be / My own hereafter" (III. 4. 139-140). The sin of murder, therefore, is ultimately the sin of self-destruction, or suicide, the breaking of the continuity of the family line and of the nature cycle. Like the fallen mountain in the Alpine scenery, the fall of the tragic hero also leaves a "gap in the clouds," and it is "filling up / The ripe green valleys with Destruction's splinters; / Damming the rivers" (I. 2. 94-96). Manfred's fall, his forbidden love for Astarte, resulted in the damming of the "pure warm stream" of the father's blood, and in the destruction of the potentially "ripe green valleys," of the promise of progeny. It is, therefore the offended father's blood which rises up to colour the clouds, and shut him out from Heaven:

> I say 'tis blood—my blood! ...
> ...
>
> ... but still it rises up,
> Colouring the clouds, that shut me out from Heaven,
> Where thou art not—and I shall never be.   (II. 1. 24-30)

The angry cloud of the father's blood that shuts Manfred out of Heaven is an important image in establishing the hero's relationship to the Father. The image works in combination with a number of related images. The hero's fall makes the river turn into mist ("Damming the rivers with a sudden dash," the gigantic mountain in his fall "crushed the waters into mist, and made / Their fountains find another channel" (I. 2. 96-98). The mist turns into clouds ("The mists boil up . . . clouds rise curling fast beneath me" (I. 2. 85-86). Finally, the angry "red cloud" re-appears on the pinnacle (III. 3. 36-37) as if warning Manfred of the infernal spirit who is "robed as with angry clouds" (III. 4. 65) when he arrives to remind Manfred of the Father's wrath.

When musing on the Alpine scenery, both the Hunter and Manfred comment upon the clouds. The Hunter sees the rising mists a sign of danger he wants to warn Manfred about:

> The mists begin to rise from up the valley;
> I'll warn him to descend, or he may chance
> To lose at once his way and life together.   (I. 2. 82-84)

Although the hunter describes the mist in physical terms, the obvious hint is to the spiritual danger in the mist where Manfred might indeed "lose his way and life."

As for Manfred, he looks at the same white clouds as yet another reminder of the depth of Hell, and of the angry clouds shutting him out of Heaven:

> The mists boil up around the glaciers; clouds
> Rise curling fast beneath me, white and sulphury,
> Like foam from a roused ocean of deep Hell,
> Whose every wave breaks on a living shore,
> Heaped with the damned like pebbles,—I am giddy.
> (I. 2. 85-89)

Condemned to his Hell, Manfred feels neither love nor humility towards the biological or spiritual father whom the chamois hunter worships. When the hunter calls out to him "For the love of Him who made you, stand not on that brink!", Manfred is significantly "not hearing him," and he goes on with his own reflection on suicide. As a matter of fact, when he takes leave of life to leap off the cliff, he bids farewell to the "opening Heavens" in a speech that at the same time renounces and challenges "Him who made you:"

> . . . Farewell, ye opening Heavens!
> Look not upon me thus reproachfully—
> You were not meant for me—   (II. 2. 107-109)

His sadness is mixed with defiance, and he challenges the heavenly regions for having made him a prey to insurmountable conflict:

100

Half dust, half deity, alike unfit
To sink or soar, with our mixed essence make
A conflict of its elements,   (I. 2. 40-42)

Seeing Manfred's torment, the Chamois Hunter offers a prayer for his peace of mind:

...Heaven give thee rest!
And Penitence restore thee to thyself;
My prayers shall be for thee.   (II. 1. 87-89)

The hunter calls on Heaven to grant Manfred Penitence and thereby restore harmony in his divided self. In a typically Byronic mixture of gentleness and pride, Manfred refuses the hunter's prayers, as he refuses any mediator between Heaven and himself. He accepts, however, the hunter's sympathy: "I need them [the prayers] not, But can endure thy pity" (II. 1. 91-92).

Like the hunter, the Abbot of St. Maurice is another pious and benevolent representative of the Father. He admonishes Manfred to "reconcile thee with the true church, and through the church to heaven" (III. 1. 50-51), but Manfred declares:

...whate'er
I may have been or am, doth rest between
Heaven and myself—I shall not choose a mortal
To be my mediator—   (III. 1. 52-55)

Although he endures the hunter's and the abbot's offer of human sympathy, Manfred's energies are directed at a personal confrontation of Heaven, or the "Ruler of the Infinite." In trying to re-unite with Astarte, Manfred engages in unending contention with the supernatural forces. Since he challenges these forces at successively higher and higher level in each scene, it seems as if he wanted to provoke the highest authority of the Maker or the Father to come forth and manifest himself.

There is, however, an unresolved contradiction beyond Manfred's drive for this confrontation and when the Abbot warns him to "reconcile thy self with thy own soul," this would require the resolution of a tragic duality. In the archetypal role of the hero as Adam, Manfred desperately strives for conciliation with the Father; in the role of villain or Satan, he defiantly rebels against the same authority.

The way Manfred conceives of the powers beyond the universe describes a hierarchical, pyramidal structure. Thus in the first encounter with the Spirits, the Seventh Spirit is the last, strongest, and most aggressive. Among the forces of Nature, he occupies the most prestigious position, being the power beyond the stars, particularly of Manfred's ruling star, and thus a force which forms a link to Fate or Destiny.

Manfred's next encounter with the supernatural forces leads to the Witch of the Alps who is a more powerful personage than those before her, since it would be in her power to assist Manfred if he accepted her conditions. Thus the hero's successive encounters with the supernatural delineate an ascending movement of a pyramidal structure, and in the last scene of the second Act, Manfred has to climb to the summit in order to find Arimanes.

Arimanes's realm is also ruled by a hierarchical order of smaller divinities. Manfred encounters here the three Destinies, then Nemesis, and only after these is he introduced to Arimanes, the highest in rank.

Like the gods of the pagan Pantheon, the spirits and divinities surrounding Arimanes assemble on the top of the Jungfrau from where they oversee and control the visible world around them. Unlike the pagan gods, however, Arimanes and his crew are "fiends." They enjoy causing pain and suffering to Man who has been subjected to them at the "Hour" of his fall. Although Mr. Marshall sees an analogy between Byron's Arimanes and Shelley's Demogorgon, closer analysis makes it clear that Arimenes is actually more akin to Shelley's tyrannical skygod, Jupiter. Both Jupiter and Arimanes rule through the power of tyranny and hate. Arimanes is responsible for the forces of Fate, Necessity or Destiny, forces that Byron regards as humiliating or antagonistic to man. A tyrant, Arimanes rules in the "terror of his glory" (II. 4. 45), and is responsible for the agonies that curtail man in his desire for freedom: "Life is his, / With all its Infinite of agonies—And his the Spirit of whatever is!" (II. 4. 14-16).

Quite obviously, neither Manfred's nor Byron's sympathies are with Arimanes. The immediate historical background to the activities of Nemesis and the Destinies is the reign of Napoleon, the circumstances of his coming to power and his defeat. Nemesis complains of the Revolution which had made people dream of freedom, "And mortals dared to ponder for themselves, / To weigh kings in the balance—and to speak / Of Freedom, the forbidden fruit" (II. 3. 69-71). To punish these daring mortals, the Destinies and Nemesis are "repairing shattered thrones" and are busy restoring the world to tyranny. The fact that Nemesis declares Freedom as the "forbidden fruit" has significant implications for Manfred's quest, too. Both the fruit of Knowledge and the fruit of Freedom can be declared "forbidden" only by a tyrannical authority, and the higher

Manfred ascends the pyramid, the more cruel and aggressive the forbidding powers appear.

Yet the fact that Arimanes is a tyrannical ruler over "all that lives," a keeper of slaves, and therefore himself a slave (a notion that Byron seems to share here with Shelley) does not diminish Manfred's real dilemma: Who and where is the "overruling Infinite," the ultimate authority that is also the "Maker" of Arimanes?

Manfred's sense of sin and his defiance are simultaneous expressions of this dilemma of finding his reconciliation with the Father, because the Father, the only authority to answer this question, is emphatically absent from Manfred's cosmos, unable, or unwilling to answer.

Manfred's final confrontation with the supernatural forces culminates in his argument with the infernal spirit who came to take his life. In this scene Manfred presents the ultimate challenge to the absent father, but even now he does not receive the answer to his dilemma. He is neither condemned nor forgiven till the very end.

The spirit is a "dusk and awful figure...like an infernal god, from out of earth." "Robed as with angry clouds," the mist of the blood guilt that symbolizes Manfred's offence against his father, the infernal spirit "stands between" the hero and the Abbot, the potential mediator with the Father.

> I see a dusk and awful figure rise,
> Like an infernal god, from out the earth;
> His face wrapt in a mantle, and his form
> Robed as with angry clouds: he stands between
> Thyself and me—but I do fear him not.   (III. 4. 62-66)

The spirit bears the traditional appearance of Satan, and seems to represent Manfred's eternal damnation, the "immortality of Hell" (III. 4. 78). Yet he is also the essence of Manfred's own being, "the genius of this mortal." He proves to be yet another mirror image of Manfred himself, and the Abbot's question, "Why dost he gaze on thee and thou on him?" succinctly describes this fact.

Manfred acknowledges the presence of this spirit, but denies his debt to the infernal regions:

> ...my past power
> Was purchased by no compact with thy crew,
> But by superior science—penance, daring,
> And length of watching, strength of mind, and skill
> In knowledge of our Fathers—when the earth
> Saw men and spirits walking side by side,
> And gave yee no supremacy: I stand

103

> Upon my strength—I do defy—deny—
> Spurn back, and scorn ye!—   (III. 4. 113-121)

He declares himself not only Satan's rival, but his superior. He claims descent from the "giant sons" born from the shortlived union between earthly and celestial beings, and feels that the "Promethean spark" of the human intellect is a gift from the union between an "undiseased mankind" and the generous spirit of Heaven, Prometheus.

Manfred's argument with the Devil challenges not only Satan but also the authority who uses the evil spirit as its own instrument of punishment. Like Manfred's contention with Arimanes, his contention with the devil is yet another aspect of his challenging the ultimate authority of the Father or the Maker, and of the Judeo-Christian cosmic system.

Unlike Faustus's final emotional plea for mercy, Manfred's argument is presented with cold contempt and in a tone of intellectual superiority. Also unlike Faustus, Manfred denies the right of the infernal spirit to punish him for having claimed the prerogative of deity. In Marlowe's play Faustus accepts both bargain and punishment because he accepts the entire cosmic system based on the distinct reality of Heaven, Nature and Hell. Manfred, however, refuses the criteria of this cosmic system based on an uncontested vision of man's middle position, and hence on his limitations and finitude. Going far beyond Faustus, Manfred asserts his right to the Tree of Knowledge, the "knowledge of our Fathers," claiming it to be man's birthright.

In the next phase of the argument, the infernal spirit interjects that even if Manfred's superior knowledge may have nothing to do with any Faustian pact, and hence is not punishable, Manfred still deserves punishment for his other self-avowed sins:

> Spirit:... But thy many crimes
> Have made thee—   (III. 4. 121-122)

Manfred, once more, interrupts his quasi-supernatural opponent, and delivers a speech which is his last, and therefore rhetorically the most significant.

> ... What are they [my crimes] to such as thee?
> Must crimes be punished by other crimes,
> And greater criminals?—Back to thy hell!
> Thou hast no power upon me, *that* I feel;
> Thou never shalt possess me, *that* I know:
> What I have done is done; I bear within,
> A torture which could nothing gain from thine:

The Mind which is immortal makes itself
Requital for its good or evil thoughts,—
Is its own origin of ill and end.
And its own place and time: its innate sense,
When stripped of this mortality, derives
No colour from the fleeting things without,
But is absorbed in sufferance or in joy,
Born from the knowledge of its own desert.
Thou didst not tempt me; and thou couldst not tempt me;
I have not been thy dupe, nor am thy prey—
But was my own destroyer, and will be
My own hereafter.   (III. 4. 122-140)

Manfred rebukes not only the Devil, but the entire cosmic system based on the eternal punishment of the offender, a system in which "crimes" are punished "by other crimes and greater criminals." Byron's position here is strikingly similar to Shelley's in *The Cenci* and in his essay "Of the Devil and Devils."[5] The plural in the "greater criminals" implies criticism not only against the Devil, but also against the authority behind the Devil's punitive power, the ultimate authority of the forbidding and punitive Father.

Manfred's assertive rhetoric causes the crestfallen Spirit to disappear. The Abbot, to whom Manfred's speech sounded only as the "rattle" of a "gasping throat," implores him once more to "give thy prayers to Heaven—Pray—albeit in thought, but die not thus." The Abbot is not aware that by rebuking the devil's punitive power, Manfred also rejects the concept of Heaven and, therefore cannot pray.

In this last speech Manfred has settled all accounts by claiming his independence even at the risk of dying without an answer to the mystery of redemption. Having rejected both Heaven and Hell, he announces death to be the ultimate solution: "Old man! 'Tis not so difficult to die."

Manfred dares to give up "clinging" to a system he cannot fully believe in. This also implies that his strong sense of sin comes from feeling the guilt of existence, a feeling only death can annihilate by terminating consciousness. In the end, he accepts and affirms this vision with dignity.

By implying that his fall is merely the fall into existence, a fall inflicted upon Man by his Maker, Manfred actually turns the tables, and declares the suffering offender to be greater than the punitive Father responsible for forbidding Man to enjoy the fruits of the Tree.

Byron asserts the "unbounded freedom" of the human spirit, of the "Promethean spark." Coleridge could indeed reprimand Byron, as well as Aeschylus, for the "jumbling together" of the "figures of the Redeemer and Satan" into the figure of Prometheus. Byron, like Shelley, reveals sympathy with the fallen Titan as a cosmic rebel. "Prometheus," Byron's romantic rendering of the myth, makes the fallen Titan superior to the tyrannical Father, the skygod who causes his fall. Ultimately, Byron also exonerates Manfred, his Promethean villain-hero as a cosmic rebel. Sin or villainy is finally attributed to the creating power, held up against "inexorable Heaven / And the deaf tyranny of Fate,"[6] which is responsible for the "curse" of the fall upon the helpless Creature.

IMAGES OF NATURE AND THE COSMIC STRUCTURE

Byron's "Journal" dealing with his Alpine trip reveals his fundamentally allegorical way of observing elements in the natural surroundings. Even in his direct and impressionistic notes, when he writes "Passed whole woods of withered pines, all withered . . . ," he immediately adds that "their appearance reminded me of me and my family."[7] The natural object is of interest mainly as a vehicle for an abstract meaning or significance behind the object.

Once the link between the withered tree and the withering of the family tree has been established in his mind, Byron develops the image in a way to fit in with the rest of the natural-spiritual landscape,

> . . . To be thus—
> Grey-haired with anguish, like these blasted pines,
> Wrecks of a single winter, barkless, branchless,
> A blighted trunk upon a cursed root,   (I. 2. 65-68)

The withered tree with its "cursed roots" now comes to reinforce Cain's and Satan's curse, and thus the image becomes an integral part of the developing hellscape.

The images of Nature serve a primarily intellectual and illustrative function. Thus, Manfred deliberately reaches out for an image from the Alpine scenery to illustrate his fall, comparing himself to "the mountain-cataract . . . having leapt from its more dazzling height." To explain his lonely course, he chooses yet another image from Nature, "for I would not make / But find a desolation. Like the Wind, / The red-hot breath of most lone Simoom" (III. 1. 127-128).

From *Manfred* the energies of Nature emerge as inscrutable or destructive. Through them Nature seems to reveal a will of its own, or indirectly, the will of the Maker responsible for its operations. There is a strong sense of cosmic catastrophes, of "Mountains [that] have fallen, leaving a gap in the clouds," and of energy changing into the "monster" of destruction by changing the "fair and fresh world" into a "comet," a shooting star "without a path, without a course." Natural energies reveal their indifference to man, as if to reveal the indifference or even malice of the Maker. Avalanches

> ...only fall on things that still would live;
> On the young flourishing forest, or the hut
> And hamlet of the harmless villager.   (I. 2. 79-81)

There is a contrast between the "innocent, green valleys" of "harmless villagers" and the destructive forces of Nature. This dramatic contrast between soft and harsh aspects of Nature is also reinforced by the fact that Byron's eye for Nature is greatly influenced (whether directly or indirectly) by Burke's distinction between the beautiful and the sublime. When, in his "Journal" Byron describes the Alpine scenery, he is delighted by the sublime inherent in superhuman proportions and inscrutable energies: "Storm came on, thunder, lightning, hail; all in perfection, and beautiful."[8] He finds sublime beauty in the irregular, the foreboding, the unfathomable.

Although *Manfred* is very much an exploration of man's relationship to Nature, Byron's vision is never minuscule, microscopic, or expressive of the close observation of natural objects. The view is panoramic. Sweeping vistas appear, and unfathomable distances between the mountaintop and the depth of the valley, or the forces of the mountain cataract. The vision reveals the poet in awe of Nature's energy and the infinite magnitude of its forces. Unlike Coleridge and Keats whose images associate the Infinite with infinite delight, Manfred experiences the Infinite through the terror of the sublime. He is like Wordsworth's Oswald who recognized the sublime beauty of Terror in the images of the infinite, the "moonlight desert and the moonlight sea". By contrast, the Infinite revealed in Nature reminds Manfred of man's finitude, and the limitations of his fallen consciousness.

> ...sands on the shore
> Innumerable atoms; and one desert,
> Barren and cold, on which the wild waves break,
> But nothing rests, save carcasses and wrecks,
> Rocks, and the salf-surf weeds of bitterness.   (II. 1. 54-58)

Even in the beauty of the rainbow, an image traditionally associated with the eternal hope to bridge the gap between Earth and Heaven, or Nature and Spirit, Manfred perceives only a reminder of his own finitude and spiritual barrenness. He sees the rainbow itself as the mane on the steed of Death, that is, an image of the Apocalypse.

Yet, there is no doubt that Byron is also aware of the softer and gentler beauties of Nature as opposed to its sublime or more terrifying aspects. In contrast to Manfred's wild energies, Astarte has a gentler beauty associated with Nature's "sweet melancholy sounds / As Music on the waters." In spite of his harsh and militant striving for power, once in a while Manfred stops to express admiration for the gentler and more harmonious beauties of Nature. This shift, however, often appears as a rather abrupt interruption, and the effect between harsh and soft tones can be jarring. Comments on the gentler aspects of Nature are more expressive of Manfred's desire to find beauty, than of his actual ability to do so:

> ... Beautiful!
> I linger yet with Nature, for the Night
> Hath been to me a more familiar face
> Than that of man;   (III. 4. 2-5)

Awareness of the gentler aspects of Nature appears in the form of Manfred's desire for harmony. The sound he hears in the valley is a "breathing harmony, a bodiless enjoyment," and he expresses his wish to melt into this sound, forgetting the self. He turns to Astarte, trying to recapture the "sweet melancholy sounds" of harmony, "And I would hear yet once before I perish / The voice which was my music—speak to me!" (II. 4. 133-134).

Yet, neither Astarte nor Nature can give him this "music," the gift of harmony that would also prove the immanence of the Spirit within Nature, the presence of the Maker in his Creation. Whenever he looks to Nature for softness, beauty and harmony, he finds himself thrown back to the harsh and grating sounds of sheer force and destruction. In vain is he aware of the serenity inherent in the Nature cycle for those who contain themselves within that cycle. His self-hood and individuality make him aspire to the extremes, and he is driven to leave behind the "innocent" or "ripe green valleys." Thus, he is aware that would he be satisfied with the hunter's lot, a non-ambitious and therefore innocent life contained within the natural cycle, he too could enjoy the serenity and softer beauties of Nature. He is aware of the blessings

> Of cheerful old age and a quiet grave,
> With cross and garland over its green turf,

And thy grandchildren's love for epitaph.   (II. 1. 69-71)

Yet such a humble acceptance of the "garland" and the "cross," that is of the Nature cycle and its accompanying religious piety, is made impossible for Manfred. He cannot, or will not, forget that due to a violent catastrophe he is an outsider, "the burning wreck of a demolished world," and cannot partake of these gifts: "My soul was scorched already!"

Juxtaposition between the serene and violent aspects of Nature is a recurring motif in *Manfred*, and although Byron seems to appreciate and desire serenity, there is no doubt that he is more in awe of the violent and "unbounded" energy of Nature. This preference is expressed in the numerous kinetic images of leaping, falling, crushing, destroying and rising—a cyclical or simply chaotic turbulence of the natural energies Manfred bemoans but also celebrates within his own spiritual inscape. There is little doubt that Byron himself regards this energy of chaos as the mainspring of a fundamentally creative suffering, and he identifies with the sublime aspects of Nature, and not with the serenity of the "ripe" and "innocent" green valleys.

Manfred's restless journey between extremities, violence and gentleness, darkness and light, that is, between the extreme heights and depths of the rugged landscape makes the play an interesting work to examine in terms of Northrop Frye's description of the romantic cosmic structure.[9]

According to this description, as discussed earlier, the new mythological construction introduced by the Romantic poet describes a revolutionary reversal of the cosmic structure of the Christian cosmos, which was based on the clearly defined cosmic spaces of Heaven, Nature and Hell. The heights, formerly associated with Heaven and the Father become in this new cosmology associated with a hostile skygod, and symbolic of "alienation." Conversely, the lowest point, formerly associated with Hell, becomes now associated with the highest moral good, self-awareness or "identity."

Frye's concept of the revolutionary reversal does not describe the whole symbolic movement in *Manfred*. This movement here seems to consist of three phases. (1) It begins with the hero's experience of a blurring of all former demarcation lines, (2) followed by the hero's revolutionary defiance against a hostile skygod, and (3) it ends with the collapse of all moral structures in the cosmos.

1.   Manfred experiences the search for the moral good, or "iden-

tity," as an extreme polarity pulling him in both directions, through the extremes of excessive light and darkness, height and depth, "good and ill, extreme in both" (II. 2. 35). When, for example, he evokes the forces of Nature, he significantly turns to both extreme heights and depths, by calling

> ...ye, to whom the tops
> Of mountains inaccessible are haunts,
> And Earth's and Ocean's caves familiar things—
> (I. 1. 32-34)

The direction he maps out for his exploration includes both extreme heights and depths, and the major kinetic images of the play are opposite or contrapuntal ones of "soaring" to the heights and "piercing" into the mysteries below.

Doctor Faustus had to pay for his aspiration for the Infinite because he challenged man's proper station as determined by his "middle" position in the chain of being, between the lowest and the highest cosmic regions. Manfred, the Romantic Doctor Faustus, goes through the same search for the Infinite, but within a different cosmic structure. For him the formerly "middle region" of Nature has gone through an enormous expansion, until it came to contain both the former regions of Heaven and of Hell. As the Romantic Faustus, he asserts that Man should be able to claim experience of both regions with impunity.

Yet the dichotomy between extreme heights and depths is never resolved either in the natural landscape, or in Manfred's spiritual landscape.

In the first outdoor scene, on the Jungfrau, Manfred experiences the tremendous distance between height and depth, and the frustration of being unable to reach up, like the eagle, to the "opening Heavens." Having scaled the mountaintop to whirl himself into the abyss, Manfred is caught by the hunter to whom he complains of vertigo: "The mountains whirl, Spinning around me—I grow blind." His spiritual experience of frustration and incertitude in the face of the Infinite is appropriately accompanied by the sensations of vertigo and blindness.

A similar sensation describes Manfred's reaction to the vanishing apparition of Astarte, after which he "falls senseless," or his falling into convulsion after meeting the Phantom on the summit. He also describes this sensation of vertigo in face of the indeterminate cosmic spaces, in his death scene.

The blurring of the demarcation lines between Heaven, Nature and Hell, and the hero's claim for the infinite expansion of Man's scope is a cause of further complications. It seems that if Man's scope is defined on the scale of the Infinite, the question of moral distinctions becomes indefinite. Although the Romantic hero may indeed refuse Heaven as the region of the punitive and tyrannical Father, after this he may not find a new direction for the good as a moral or spiritual principle in the cosmos.

According to Northrop Frye's interpretation, the direction for the moral principle simply suffered a reversal, pointing now to the depth as to a "deep cosmic center." However, from the tragedies examined in this study, this area of the new, deep, cosmic centre emerges just as alien or even hostile to man. Coleridge's tragic villain dooms himself in a cave, which is a hell-like cosmic centre, while Keats's tragic hero goes insane in the deep dark forest in which he encountered the demonic.

The hero's ambivalent and deeply disturbing experience of the new cosmic centre may take place simultaneously with his expectations of finding there Paradise, as it has been mentioned in Ludolph's search for his bride Auranthe, in *Otho the Great*. "Lamia," "La Belle Dame sans Merci," and the "Fall of Hyperion" also present a double exposure between ecstasy and despair, height and depth, the desire for consummating a sexual union in paradisiac bowers and the awareness that this very moment entails separation, madness and death.

In *Manfred* double exposure between Heaven and Hell has a similar significance. The height of ecstasy is not only the cause, but also the sinister symptom of the collapsing of a moral order. Manfred's and Astarte's love union marks the highest point of the mounting "power and joy" of the hero's Faustian ascent to the Infinite. Yet the highest stage in the flight also becomes identical with the hero's Fall. Height of ecstasy culminates in deepest despair. Finally all structures collapse after the double exposure between Heaven and Hell, as two similarly alien and sinister regions.

2. There is no doubt that the traditional moral associations with Heaven and the Father indeed undergo a "revolutionary reversal" in *Manfred*. In the scene with Arimanes, Manfred comes to scale the highest possible point of the cosmic power pyramid. This summit in its closeness to the sky, is a setting reminiscent of Mount Olympus where Greek mythology placed its deities or of the various strata of the eternal regions where Christianity envisioned its angelic hierarchy.

111

To Manfred, however, the closeness to the sky expresses the highest degree of alienation. The forces of Arimanes are sinister and demonic "fiends" who delight in the suffering they cause to humanity. The "terror" of Arimanes's "glory" consists of his rule over "Infinite agonies." Such negative connotations of height indeed seem to bear out Frye's description of the Romantic poet's revolutionary reversal of the traditional cosmic structure. This is also supported by the fact that Byron describes Arimanes quite deliberately through images which reverse the attitudes traditionally associated with deity. Thus, while God created the world out of the Chaos of elements through Love, Arimanes is the "ruling principle of Hate" at whose "high command" the elements "tear themselves to Chaos" (II. 4. 3-4). As a direct reversal of the cosmic structure of Christianity, the highest point accessible has undeniably turned out to be hostile to Man and to Manfred becomes associated with the realm of the demonic, with alienation, madness, and destruction.

Yet the fact that Manfred rebels against the skygod, Arimanes, does not yet fulfill what Frye calls the Romantics' revolutionary reversal of the cosmic structure. It remains to be determined whether the regions opposite to the heights have indeed assumed the role of a new cosmic centre, whether the depths have indeed become identified as a new direction of the good.

The play contains two scenes which could be associated with the depth as a cosmic centre. These are the valley of the Witch, and the regions of the "infernal god" who emerges "from out the earth" in the last scene.

The valley is the haunt of the beautiful Witch of the Alps, the "Spirit of the Place." In Byron's Alpine cosmos, her haunts could indeed emerge as some kind of a cosmic centre. We find, however that even if the witch has supernatural powers, these are not strong enough to aid the hero, nor is he willing to pay the price she demands for her demonic assistance. In spite of her enticing beauty associated with the sunbow, the witch is the "daughter of the Air," and represents yet another reminder of the demonic "Spirit of the Air," or of the fall of the "erring Spirit." At any rate, when Manfred leaves the valley, he is still dissatisfied in his quest. The valley, then, cannot be associated with a region that signifies the direction of the moral good or the finding of identity.

The other image connected with the lower regions is that of the infernal spirit who arises "from out the earth." There is no doubt that Manfred regards the hell he represents as the region of "criminals," and not the place of the good. This region is, in effect, also teeming with "fiends" or demons, just like the summit inhabited by the fiendish crew of Arimanes.

Manfred defies both the "fiends" of the summit and the "fiends" of the depth. Through his revolutionary defiance of both directions, however, he arrives at a problematic phase that follows cosmic rebellion. He experiences the total collapse of the moral structure in the cosmos. He sees both the extreme heights and the extreme depths as quickened to life by the demonic.

In his tower, symbolic of pride and alienation, Manfred dismisses both representatives of a traditionally conceived Heaven and Hell, that is the Abbot and the Devil, without having established a new moral structure in the place of the old one. In this dismissal he acknowledges the meaninglessness of seeking moral or spiritual guidance, acknowledging the collapse of a morally ordered cosmos. The only thing Manfred can affirm now is his conviction that Man's proper abode is in the limbo of earthly existence, and the mind is the only realm possessing its own values, its own Heaven and Hell.

Yet, when Manfred refused to acknowledge Arimanes as the ultimate power, claiming that he too, must be the creation of a "Maker" who is the "Ruler of the Infinite," implicitly he poses a further question. This question probes into the possible location of the divine power, and the relationship between an ostensibly good Maker and the demonic fiend, Arimanes as his deputy. Is the force of the ultimate authority, the "Ruler of the Infinite" simply at an inaccessible point of the pyramid, or is he outside, beyond or indeed apart and in opposition to the whole world of Nature?

On the evidence of Manfred's final experience of a collapsed cosmic structure, it seems that Byron bears witness to the second alternative. Manfred's tragedy derives from his experience of the insurmountable distance between Creator and Created, the ultimately unalterable alienation of Man, Nature, and Spirit.

VI

"A HIGHER TRUTH":
SHELLEY'S *THE CENCI*

In *The Cenci*[1] Shelley claims to be scrupulously faithful to the data of a sixteenth-century document,[2] which sets the story of Beatrice Cenci in Rome, in the year 1599, under Pope Clement's pontificate. This document is, indeed, the skeleton for the story. In his poetic rendering of this document, however, Shelley is profoundly influenced by his "master passion" to "diffuse [his] opinions and sentiments with regard to human nature and its destiny."[3] It is this "master passion" which turns the individual story into cosmic allegory.

Although the play deals, ostensibly, with the tribulations of Beatrice as an individual character, the poet makes this character represent the Innocence of humanity, and through her fate contemplates a universal philosophical ideal, with profound political, religious and epistemological implications. *The Cenci* explores Man's fall enacted through an innocent heroine's fall from innocence, and through an irreparable offence against the father. As in *Manfred* (and unlike in the plays of Wordsworth, Coleridge or Keats) the heroine's loss of sexual innocence is real and not just a mistaken illusion. It is also significant of this most radically tragic vision, that among the five works, *The Cenci* is the only one in which the offence against the father is not only a symbolic act or a rebellious intention, but a consummated act of parricide.

Unlike Wordsworth, Coleridge and Keats, Shelley does not disguise his cosmic dilemma in the arabesques of Gothic dramatic intrigue, plot and counterplot. If the fundamental elements of a dramatic plot and intrigue are still discernible, they function in conjunction with the main allegorical tendency of the whole work, and not apart from it, or against it, as in the case of the "naive allegory" of the first three works.[4]

As for the plot, it is relatively straightforward once we accept the rather shocking fictional departure into Cenci's inhuman cruelty at the outset (Scene 1). Following this, the sequence of events follows the principles of cause and effect in a chronological order, containing no great surprises, unexpected developments, secrets of hidden identity and melodramatic dénouement of these secrets. The only

114

element reminiscent of Gothic melodrama is the letter intercepted by Orsino, a good point at which to begin examining Shelley's treatment of the intrigue.

Beatrice prepares a letter to the Pope to report her and her family's suffering at the hands of Count Cenci. She entrusts this petition to the priest Orsino, her former suitor. Orsino is still in love with Beatrice, but he does not intend to give up the lucrative priesthood in order to marry her. Neither does he want her to be liberated from Cenci's tyranny and given to someone else in marriage. Therefore he does not deliver her petition.

When he hears of Beatrice's violation by Cenci, Orsino still does not respond to her suffering, but speculates on how to take advantage of it. He decides that by recommending assassins for Cenci's murder he can get rid of Cenci, and make the whole family obliged to him for life. Right after the murder, however, a messenger of the Pope appears with Cenci's arrest warrant. The circumstances of this letter are never explained in the play, since we had heard on several occasions that the Pope, in exchange for considerable sums of Cenci's gold, had shown reluctance to respond to the numerous complaints against him. Judging from his generally benevolent attitude it seems most likely that it is Cardinal Camillo who might be behind this letter of arrest. Yet neither Orsino who intercepted Beatrice's complaint, nor Camillo who might have worked towards contrary ends are ever proven as instrumental in the dénouement. The arrival of the arrest warrant that could have saved Beatrice from committing murder an hour earlier, becomes an instrument of her arrest and execution. It is an ironic stroke of fate or chance, of a malicious or simply indifferent force which is external to human intervention.

Apart from the "action gratuit" of the unexpected arrest warrant, there is only one more event that might test the principles of credibility or probability. It is the fact that the wicked Cenci receives, prior to his giving a banquet, the most welcome news of his two sons' accidental death on the same day. Like the first, this second "action gratuit" also serves to fortify the structure of the allegorical framework. By devising the inopportune arrival of the arrest warrant, Shelley makes us ponder over the forces of Fate, Chance and Necessity as these determine the predicament of Innocence. In the second instance he also raises a fundamental question: What is the relationship between Cenci, the vicious father who prays for his sons' death, and the kind of Deity who so miraculously grants his prayers? In other words, although these two "actions" do not really draw attention to themselves as illogical or incongruous insertions into the plot, they are used to forward the allegorical or mythical structure which proceeds to the examination of the conflicting forces of Good and Evil.

THE INNOCENT HEROINE AS TRAGIC HERO:
EVE WITHOUT ADAM

Like the other innocent heroines of Romantic tragedy, Beatrice is surrounded by aspects of the supernatural. A "perfect mirror of pure innocence," she is the reflection of the divine "light of life" on earth, the very source of earthly light "who made all lovely [she did] look upon." To extinguish her bright sun, Cenci deliberately evokes the raiment of darkness.—In comparison with all the other characters, she is "the one thing innocent and pure / In this black and guilty work," and stands among her fellow-conspirators "like God's angel ministered upon by fiends." Trying to destroy her, Cenci is aware that he wants to destroy all innocence from the Earth, and rejoices that at her fall "There shall be lamentation heard in Heaven / As o'er an angel fallen" (IV. 2. 185-186).

Beatrice's fall from innocence, both in its sexual and spiritual aspects, stands at the very centre of the drama. It raises the question whether we live in a world permeated with the Spirit, in the world of unfallen Nature in which the human being is ultimately perfectible, or whether Man is himself a tragically imperfect flawed being in a fallen world that is irrevocably divorced from the Spirit.

Unlike Wordsworth's Idonea, Coleridge's Teresa, Keats's Erminia, and Byron's Astarte whose union with the hero signals their attainment of earthly Paradise, Beatrice is left alone. The fact that her suitor, the potential Adam of their union, abandoned her is extremely important to the understanding of her tragic incompleteness and helplessness in the face of the world's imperfections. That Orsino abandoned her to become a priest means that given Shelley's ideology, he joined the camp of self-seekers and oppressors, thus betraying Beatrice's innocence to the fallen "world." This "world" in The Cenci is the very locus of the tragic forces that make Beatrice's fall and destruction inevitable.

The two young lovers' meeting place is a garden, and this is the only reference to a garden scene with pleasant connotations throughout the entire play, although we do hear that their past meeting had also taken place out of doors. As two young people in love, their

116

union would have the potential for reaching Paradise, in spite of the obstacles in their way. Yet their very first meeting foreshadows Beatrice's subsequent betrayal. The setting is in the "shadow of cypresses" and the "Mount Palatine," symbols of the corrupt and hence moribund world that overpowers the lovers' Paradise. By becoming a priest, Orsino allows his passion for gain and advancement to prevail over his passion for Beatrice. Once he accepts the ways of the world even his love for Beatrice is degraded into lust, and he decides not to marry but to seduce her, to win her at a lighter price.

Consequently Orsino pursues Beatrice not as the Romantic Adam in search of his Eve, desiring a union of completeness and perfection, but as a seducer who wants to ruin her innocence out of lustful passion.—He now plays the archetypal role of the satanic seducer, which marks his transformation from Adam into Satan. His greed and consequently degraded passion transformed the garden into a place where wild animals pursue their innocent and helpless prey. When describing his passion to the girl, he hypocritically complains of her power over him in the language of the stricken courtly lover "Your image, as the hunter some struck deer, Follows me not whether I wake or sleep?" but when he is alone, he confesses that it is he who is like a "panther" pursuing his prey, the innocent and helpless "antelope" (I. 2. 89-90). In other words, Orsino decides to join the hunt in which the oppressor pursues the oppressed, a hunt in which Cenci describes his own chase of Beatrice as that of a "tiger" for his "prey" (IV. 1. 174). Instead of trying to aid her against her tyrant father, Orsino betrays her confidence. He breaks his promise to mediate with the Pope on her behalf, because were the Pope to marry her off to someone else, she would no longer be accessible to the "plot" her suitor weaves for her seduction. At the end, when he discovers that he is caught in the "net" of his own plot, and has to lose Beatrice entirely, Orsino becomes aware of a sense of shame, like Adam at the loss of Paradise. Although ready to hide himself from his judges, he sees that he will no longer be able to hide from his own shame: "Where shall I / Find the disguise to hide me from myself?" (V. 1. 102-103).

Beatrice, therefore, is left entirely alone, Shelley's innocent Eve is abandoned by a treacherous Adam. Her last song before her death (V. 3. 130-145) is addressed to a "false friend" who is himself like the biblical snake, being responsible for the loss of the lovers garden "There is a snake in thy smile, my dear." Since the last lines of this same farewell song are addressed, without indicating a change in tone, to the "World" she is to part with, the "false friend" and the fallen "World" are used interchangeably, both containing reference to the same betrayal.

To ascertain the significance of Beatrice's loneliness, we should compare her situation with that of the divine couple in *Prometheus Unbound*. The union between Asia, the female principle of love and Nature, and Prometheus the heroic "champion" of humanity, is a sacramental wedding which is symbolic of the restoration of the world to its unfallen condition, a state of Paradise re-gained, or the millennium. Although Beatrice's situation bears close resemblance to that of the oppressed and tortured Prometheus, she is abandoned to loneliness and is deprived of the "eternal love" which is the sole regenerative principle in Shelley's universe. When Beatrice warns the young priest "Speak to me of no love," she also acknowledges the limitations of her own redemptive power. Her renunciation of human love for her male counterpart is inevitable but self-defeating.

Although like Prometheus, she is tyrannized, tortured, and violated by a father who greatly resembles Jupiter the tyrannical sky-god, she is unlike Prometheus in being alone. Being only a mortal, she is thus unable to command the services of the "immortal hours" of the Future which will ultimately hurl Jupiter down from his throne and restore the world to the innocence and perfection of Paradise. A work of celebration, *Prometheus Unbound* projects this moment of regeneration and redemption from human error into a distant, mythical future, a future that is unforeseeable by human beings.

In the meantime, in the fallen world, (as we hear from Demogorgon), things are subject to "Fate, Time, Occasion, Chance, and Change" (*P.U.* IV. 4. 119), the principles of corruption and mutability. Since she is alone and weakened in her "eternal love," Beatrice falls prey to these principles ruling the fallen world which permit the "sad reality" of tragedy. Because it is "real," that is, subject to Time and not in the mythical future, the world is indeed tragic. The forces of "Fate, Time, Occasion, Chance, and Change" are all in opposition to man's claim for perfection, immortality, or Paradise.

Beatrice is indeed asked to contend with these whimsical forces. Had she known that the warrant for Cenci's arrest was on its way, she would not have felt obliged to violently stop him from committing new crimes, and the act of parricide could have been avoided. She had, however, no way of expecting Cenci's arrest. Orsino intercepted her petition, and the Pope had refused Giacomo's plea several times before. Hence it is by moral necessity that she is to choose between two alternatives: to allow Count Cenci to repeatedly violate her and give birth to the "lump of deformity" conceived in hatred, or to stop this violation by another act of violence. Her moral dilemma is whether to acquiesce in the monstrous union of rape and incest, or to choose the monstrous act of parricide.

Shelley emphasizes the parallel between the enormity of these two offences, both of them "incorrect things"[5] that offend against a taboo. Both Cenci and the conspirators against him express anxiety about their enormous and unspeakable crime in the same way: Cenci swears: "It must be done; it shall be done, I swear!" (I. 3. 178) and then sighs, "Would that it were done!" (II. 1. 193), while Lucretia prays in anxiety "Would it were done!" (IV. 3. 38) several times.

It also points to Shelley's awareness of the moral deadlock between the two offences, that neither the act of incestuous rape, nor the ensuing parricide are conceived on the spur of the moment: Cenci's calm resolution to reduce Beatrice to a "lump of destruction" is matched later by her equally calm resolution to have him killed. Having decided on Beatrice's destruction, Cenci boasts that he will be able to sleep most calmly, while after her agreement with Cenci's murderers Beatrice claims the same.

Shelley is quite consistent in emphasizing parallel elements between the two offences, both of them involving the collapse of the moral and natural order. Thus Cenci, when he resolves on the act of violation totters, feels dizzy and suspects the stability of the pavement leading to Beatrice's room (II. 1. 113; I. 2. 141-144). When Beatrice emerges from her room after the violation, in her awakening hatred of her violator she too stumbles to the light and complains of vertigo as if the whole world were reeling and the very pavement feeling unreal under her feet (III. 1. 1-12).

Shelley's emphasis on these parallels draws attention to the parallel enormity of both crimes, while also pointing out the inevitable necessity of establishing a cause-effect relationship between the two. The perception of a moral deadlock between these two offences is at the very centre of the tragedy. As a moral and aesthetic problem it has exercised the wit and ingenuity of countless readers and critics, and Shelley claims that it is this "endless casuistry"[6] inherent in the situation that attracted him to the story in the first place.

In weighing the significance of incestuous rape against Beatrice's act of parricide, Earl Wasserman feels that Shelley condemns the heroine for the latter, because he sees it as an act stemming from her lack of self-knowledge:

119

Count Cenci's rape of his daughter is, of course, an evil deed, but it achieves its evil effect only because Beatrice mistakenly allows herself to believe it dishonors her and demands revenge, instead of recognizing that "no person can be truly dishonoured by the act of another."[7]

Wasserman reads Shelley's treatment of Beatrice's error in the light of the rest of the poet's moral philosophy:

Shelley's tragedy is not rooted in the flaw in character—all human constitutions are flawed—but in the "moral error," as he called it, of believing the "mask" of circumstances to be essential, a "pernicious error" (which, incidentally, is an accurate translation of Aristotle's hamartia). Such circumstances are Giacomo's poverty, insofar as it is unendurable to him because he has been raised in luxury (II. ii. 6-17), and Beatrice's regard for her reputation because she has been taught to prize the world's opinion."[8]

Wasserman's interpretation implies that had Beatrice recognized that her loss of reputation has really no bearing on her as an unfallen being, she should have seen no necessity for committing parricide. At this point, however, one should return to a closer look at the story line, and recognize that Cenci's violation of Beatrice is not a single and isolated incident, but a continuous process meant to break her down gradually and continuously, both in body and spirit. To perpetuate her degradation, Cenci begs nature to be "fruitful in her," so that she should give birth to a child conceived in hatred. It is for the realization of this process that Cenci decided to take Beatrice to the isolated castle on the "savage rock" of Petrella. In terms of the story line, then, it is not Beatrice's feeling of having lost her innocence (whether Shelley would agree or disagree with her assessment of her state), far less a concern about her reputation in the eyes of the world that makes her decide on parricide. She is faced with the repetition and consequences of the act of sexual violation unless she stopped Cenci. This is why she turns to Orsino for help: "Advise me how it shall not be *again*" (III. 1. 147).

Her "pernicious error" or hamartia, if Shelley meant her to have such a flaw, is not translatable to the terms of a moral decision. If she wanted to stop the continuation of evil, she had to have Cenci killed, since begging, praying or asking help from the world were to no avail. From the evidence of the play, there is no indication that Shelley regarded Beatrice's decision as her pernicious error. As a matter of fact, it is her invincibly firm conviction that the killing of Cenci is equivalent to the highest justice (a conviction she never changes throughout the play) that separates her from her fellow-conspirators, and raises her above them as the only tragic figure of heroic stature.

Neither does she accept at any point in the play, as Wasserman indicated, that the "mask" of circumstances is the reality of her essential being. On the contrary, her argument with the Pope's emissary, with Marzio and with her judges indicates just the opposite: she is oblivious to the facts which to others hide the image of Truth like a mask. To her very last moment she insists on the reality of her innocence, of the "sweet folded flower" of her inner self in which she claims to be possessing the reality of a "higher truth." This reality is in contrast to the mere "mask and mantle" of guilty circumstances.

Shelley's approbation of her behaviour is borne out by the emphasis on her superiority in comparison to her fellow conspirators. This is based on the superiority of her motives. By using several well-detailed characters to participate (through a number of sub-plots), in the same act of murder, Shelley draws attention to the difference between the participants: Orsino, the self-seeking councillor; Marzio the hired assassin; Lucretia the loving but pious and weak stepmother, and Giacomo the vengeful and guilt-ridden older son. Each follows vastly different motives and reasoning. Each acts as a foil to Beatrice, the one who suffered most deeply, endured most, and had the most justified of motives. She is Shelley's only contender for the role of tragic hero. On a one-by-one comparison between Beatrice and the others it becomes clear that it was Shelley's design to prove her attitude superior and heroic.

Both Olimpio's and Marzio's motives are based on greed and revenge: "Olimpio [is] the castellan of Petrella...Whom your father degraded from his post," and "Marzio, / That desperate wretch whom he deprived last year / Of a reward of blood, well earned and due!" (III. 2. 64-66). Since "Marzio's hatred matches Olimpio's," they are both delighted to be offered the hundred pieces of gold by Beatrice in addition to having the opportunity to revenge themselves on the object of their hatred. Still, even these hardened criminals have second thoughts when it comes to the murdering of the old man who reminds them of their own father, and by extension, of the wrath of God the Father.

Orsino's part in the murder is not dictated by hate or revenge, yet he is almost as much of a villain as Cenci himself. He bargains with his God, that is, with his own sense of good and evil by promising to be no more wicked than absolutely necessary. Yet it is he who betrays the heroine through greed and calculation and incites Giacomo to do his dirty work for him, betraying his confidence in the end as well. Orsino's crime consists of being aware of the good, yet willingly serving and bargaining with evil.

Giacomo, the oldest son of Count Cenci has many reasons for hating his father. Not only did Cenci deprive him of an innocent and carefree childhood, and denied him his fair share in the family fortune after his marriage, he also managed to borrow from him his wife's dowry (a rather incongruous instance of Giacomo's gullibility at this point) and deprive him of a desperately sought office, also turning his wife against him in the process. Blaming his father for having turned existence into a hell, Giacomo is filled with violent hatred, but he still needs the last push from Orsino before deciding on parricide. Only upon learning about the violation of Beatrice does he start investigating the plan of murder. His motives are hate and revenge, but he is guilt-ridden and uncertain about the justness of their act. Although he turns against Cenci, the tyrannical father, he is profoundly afraid of God whom he sees as a punitive Father, and he allows this fear of punishment to cloud his sense of justice. Since he had acted out of revenge, he is mortally afraid of others who might revenge themselves on him, dreading both his own son, and God the Father:

> ...So wastes and sinks
> Even now, perhaps, the life that kindled mine:
> ...
>
> ...Ha! 'tis the blood
> Which fed these veins that ebbs till all is cold:
> ...
>
> The hours crawl on; and when my hairs are white,
> My son will then perhaps be waiting thus,
> Tortured between just hate and vain remorse;
> (III. 2. 15-27)

Giacomo's regret is connected with his fear of being punished. When the act of parricide is discovered, he bursts out: "It was a wicked thought, a piteous deed, / To kill an old and hoary-headed father." To this the cynical Orsino merely replies: "It has turned out unlucky, in truth." Giacomo's remorse, then, is due not to the justice or injustice of the act, but to his fear of the consequences.

In contrast to Giacomo, Beatrice shows no hesitation or self-reproach, those signs of spiritual cowardice that Orsino mocks Giacomo with. Once she decided on the necessity of parricide, Beatrice remains firm as a rock: "The deed is done, / And what may follow now regards not me / I am as universal as the light; / Free

122

as the earth-surrounding air; as firm / As the world's centre. Consequence to me, / Is as the wind which strikes the solid rock / But shakes it not." (IV. 4. 46-52).

Although bitterly enraged, Giacomo cannot forget that Cenci's fatherly image is similar to his conception of God the Father. He regrets that "this very hand / Must quench life that animated it." He accepts Cenci as his Creator, the source of his existence:

> It is the form that molded mine that sinks
> Into the white and yellow spasms of death:
> It is the soul by which mine was arrayed
> In God's immortal likeness which now stands
> Naked before Heaven's judgement seat! (III. 2. 20-24)

Beatrice, on the other hand, comes to deny that Cenci could be the source of what she defines as the essence of her inner being. Since her innocence has an existence "solid" as a "rock" and as "firm as the world's centre," she argues that Cenci has no title to be called her father—a denial that forms the central sophistry of her argument at the trial: "I am more innocent of parricide / Than is a child born fatherless."

Her kindly, but unthinkingly pious fostermother, Lucretia, offers another contrast here to Beatrice. Like Giacomo, she does not question the substance, and is ready to follow the "form" of her religion. Therefore, in an act that looks like hypocrisy, she kindly approaches her husband to get him to make a confession before she has him murdered. Her belief in the "form" of religion is emphasized further when, considering that Cenci was murdered without having made his confession, she frets about the chances of his salvation. Once more it is Beatrice who voices Shelley's opinion on the absurdity of this "form," by saying that if Heaven is just, Cenci should not be punished for an omission for which he cannot be responsible.

In spite of their individual imperfections and the various degrees of awareness of the distinction between good and evil, each conspirator comes to acknowledge Beatrice's unblemished innocence. The admission is the most puzzling coming from Marzio, the murderer she personally hired, encouraged, and rewarded for the parricide. The understanding of this puzzle is crucial to the understanding of Shelley's concept of innocence, and it warrants a closer look at the scene in which the pure and spotless heroine lies to her judges about the crime we have seen her commit. Contemptuous of her judges, she also denies the instrument of murder she herself had hired: "We never saw him," she claims, and "I know thee! How? Where? When?"

Even if one could accept her superiority as justified contempt for her inhuman inquisitors, it is difficult to justify her attitude to her own hireling Marzio. Yet the paradox can be understood if we come to grips with the peculiar logic behind her denial of the guilt of parricide: "What! Wilt though say That I did murder my own father?" and asks, as the conclusion to her speech of innocence: "Am I or am I not a parricide?"

To this question, in spite of the tortures this will bring him, Marzio answers "Thou art not!" and turns to his judges claiming that he had seen a "higher truth" than those of the apparent rights or wrongs of the case. To resolve this paradox we have to agree that in spite of having Cenci killed, Beatrice is not a parricide, and in spite of having participated in a criminal act, she is not guilty.

> Guilty! Who dares talk of guilt? My Lord,
> I am more innocent of parricide
> Than a child born fatherless . . . Dear Mother
> Your gentleness and patience are no shield
> For this keen-judging world, this two-edged lie,
> Which seems, but is not.   (IV. 4. 111-116)

Since the "sweet folded flower" of her essential inner being does not originate with Cenci, she is indeed "born fatherless." This statement, her first explanation of her participation in evil, contains the essential paradox of Shelley's concept of the Fall of Man. Her basic innocence is not derived from her father, yet she still owes her physical existence to him. Consequently, her essential nature is not of the "world" of existence. This paradox, however, is based on claiming the status of a superior reality for what is the ideal, or even going so far as to deny the reality of the Creation, of the whole "world" which due to the imperfections of existence, only "seems, but is not."

Although this sophisticated argument is essential to the allegorical framework and is fully supportable within that context, Beatrice's behaviour in her confrontation with Marzio still remains an embarrassing dilemma in terms of dramatic action. In this context, winning her argument against Marzio means to seek her life at the cost of his, and when she denies their acquaintance (Innocence is unaware of the power of evil) in dramatic terms she, in effect, tosses him to the judges for further tortures. Although Beatrice's argument may be functional in Shelley's allegorical framework, it is unacceptable outside that framework. In terms of the action, Beatrice's protested innocence and purity breaks down in this confrontation.

In order to accept the justice of her argument with Marzio, we must accept the "higher truth" of the allegorical framework, according to which she is the personification of Innocence. By denying her purity, Marzio would be guilty of allowing the very memory of Innocence to fade away from the world (which would mean letting the image of the Ideal vanish from the world of existence):

> ... there was one
> Who was most pure and innocent on earth;
> ...
>
> What 'tis to blot with infamy and blood
> All that which shows like innocence, and is,
> Hear me, great God! I swear, most innocent,
> So that the world lose all discrimination
> Between the sly, fierce, wild regard of guilt,
> And that which now compels thee to reply
> To what I ask: Am I, or am I not
> A parricide? (V. 2. 137-157)

The paradox of her behaviour is based on her not denying Cenci's murder, but rejecting guilt as a consequence of this act. This is in accord with the point of view that the radically evil Cenci, although the source of her physical existence, should not be rightfully regarded the father of her inner being.

When her brother and stepmother confess themselves guilty on account of this act, Beatrice claims that their admission is a "falsehood" wrung from them through fear of the rack, and calls their admission of guilt a "weak and wicked lie" uttered to "flatter their tormentors."

Beatrice feels that in admitting their guilt the others offended against the higher Truth of their innermost being, against that "eternal honour Which should live / Sunlike, above the reek of mortal fame." By admitting guilt, they really uttered a "falsehood," and by giving up their claim to an unstained name, they betrayed their testament of the human soul's innocence. This testament of her "eternal honour" is by this time the only way Beatrice can conceive of immortality. She mourns that by admitting the "falsehood" of guilt, her relatives betrayed the truth, and have become "false to their deserted selves." While Giacomo and Lucretia beg of her to admit her guilt as the truth ("They will tear the truth ... say thou art guilty now ... Oh speak the truth" (V. 3. 52-55). Beatrice defines her "higher truth" as being true to the testament of human innocence.

When finally she is faced with the Judge's question: "Art thou not guilty of thy father's death?", she answers with the riddle which is based on the insurmountable contradiction between the judge's truth, and her "higher truth" as regards the terms of "guilt" and Cenci's "fatherhood."

> Or wilt thou rather tax high-judging God
> That He permitted such an act as that
> Which I have suffered, and which He beheld;
> Made it unutterable, and took from it
> All refuge, all revenge, all consequence,
> But that which thou hast called my father's death?
> Which is or is not what man call a crime,
> Which either I have done or have not done;
>
> (V. 3. 78-85)

Beatrice does not deny that she was instrumental in the murder, but denies that it should be called a crime ("what men call a crime") and denies that Cenci should be called her father ("which thou hast called my father's death").

After hearing her death sentence, she has strength enough to reiterate her message about the "higher truth" of invincible innocence of her younger brother Bernardo who, symbolically her child, will be her sole survivor and whose memory will serve to maintain the image of the world's innocence.

Wasserman defined Beatrice's "pernicious error" as "her regard for her reputation because she has been taught to prize the world's opinion." Beatrice's behaviour throughout the trial, and her final message to Bernardo reveal a very different attitude. In her defence she applied the "sublime casuistry" of one who does not consider the world's judgement essential. It is not the "reek of mortal fame" that she wants to fight for when begging her relatives to stay "faithful to their deepest selves." Neither does she consider herself subject to the world when she claims that she can bequeath to Bernardo the memory of an innocent life, in spite of the strange mask of guilt.

Yet the question of her reputation, as Wasserman indicates, is worth closer examination. During her trial Beatrice came to a conclusion that her everlasting soul cannot expect any form of after life other than the memory of innocence in the minds of the elect. Admitting the "falsehood" of guilt would be equivalent to allowing the very image of innocence to vanish from the world.

Her last words foreshadow, like those in *Prometheus Unbound*, the final victory of endurance, patience and gentleness, the forces of innocence that are durable enough to bridge the abyss of despair and the rocks of agony:

> ...Err not in harsh despair,
> But tears and patience. One thing more, my child:
> For thine own sake be constant to the love
> Thou bearest us; and to the faith that I,
> Though wrapped in a strange cloud of crime and shame,
> Lived ever holy and unstained   (V. 4. 144-149)

Beatrice's parting words foreshadow the final message about the ultimate triumph of Gentleness, Virtue and Endurance in *Prometheus Unbound*:

> To suffer woes which Hope thinks infinite;
> To forgive wrongs darker than death or night;
> To defy Power, which seems omnipotent;
> To love, and bear; to hope till Hope creates
> From its own wreck the things it contemplates;
> Neither to change, nor falter, nor repent;
> This, like thy glory, Titan, is to be
> Good, great and joyous, beautiful and free;
> This is alone Life, Joy, Empire, and Victory.
> *(P.U.* IV. 570-578)

Yet, the final prophecy of universal renewal in *Prometheus Unbound*, is not borne out by the action in *The Cenci*. This incongruity has two causes, connected respectively with the form of drama and the content of tragedy.

As to the problem pertaining to the genre of drama, Beatrice's characterization reveals a tension between the dramatic credibility and the tendentiousness of allegory. Although Beatrice and each of her fellow sufferers protest her invincible innocence, neither her actions, nor her behaviour at the trial bear out this description. Her hate may have been necessary in activating her moral duty to stop Cenci in the continuation of evil, yet she participated in an act of murder out of hatred when "Hate was the only prayer I could lift up to God." She lies to her judges, and twists her words in a way that looks like lying even to Giacomo and Lucretia. (They both beg of her to tell the truth.) Furthermore, and this appears the most serious moral problem in her action, she denies her own instrument of murder, and attempts to escape the death sentence by abandoning him to torture and execution. Although the reader would be fully in favour of her escape, the sacrifice of her own agent and the denial of her loyalty to him are hard to accept as angelic.

Thus, it seems that in spite of all the protestations, Beatrice's innocence is really a fixed and decorative quality, while her actions create a serious moral dilemma in the eyes of the readers, witness the "restless casuistry" of her numerous critics. The fact that this dilemma finds a consistent solution through Shelley's ideology (and this consistency is proven in Wasserman's essay on *The Cenci*) should not make us blind to the fact that Shelley resolves the dilemma by recourse to an elaborate allegorical framework, and in order to find this resolution, we need all the help we can get out of this framework.

To understand Shelley's attitude to his tragic heroine (to most critics she is the central dilemma in the tragedy), we must rely on the allegorical framework in which Innocence fulfills the kind of role Beatrice fulfills in the play. In effect, Beatrice's character cannot stand alone in terms of a well observed and documented creation of the "dramatic or human Imagination." Acceptance of her behaviour requires our recognition of her allegorical function as a personification of Innocence, or of Man's potential for purity, perfection and immortality. She is, then, primarily an allegorical personification of an abstract quality, and not a human character.

Secondly, the thematic problem concerns the poet's concept of a tragic reality. If, as Beatrice implies, the image of innocence maintains its existence on a level which has a "higher truth" than the apparent evil of factual reality, this is equivalent to denying the existence of radical evil, and dismissing it simply as the "error" of illusion. This philosophical position, however, does not really square with the rest of the story which is based on (as few critics seem to recognize it) the source of all evil, the Father who is responsible for her physical existence, but is in opposition to her essential being. The real enigma of the play is the actively and undeniably evil Count Cenci. No promise of future gentleness and patience can deny the radical existence of Cenci, and no "winged hours" of a mythical future can be expected to hurl him down from his throne (the way Shelley dismissed the tyrannical power of Jupiter in *Prometheus Unbound*). If, therefore, the image of Innocence, in spite of the world's opinion, is more "real" than the "appearance" of evil, then this world itself must be unreal, and to prove this argument is both Beatrice's and Shelley's strategem at the end of the play.

To imply, however, that the world which contains the evil of Cenci is unreal, poses serious philosophical and thematic problems. In the "double action" of tragedy the downward trend is borne out by dramatic action: rape, parricide, physical and spiritual suffering followed by death. The upward trend, however, that is the spiritual knowledge that Innocence is invincible and superior, can become meaningful only in terms of an allegorical framework which is based on an optimistic ideology. This ideology, in turn, might apply to the world of myth, but it does not apply to the "world" as presented by the play itself.

The "faith" in her innocence Beatrice expects from Bernardo is factually contradicted by the final message of the events of the play. This contradiction adds a tragic pathos to Beatrice's parting words. Unlike that in *Prometheus Unbound*, Beatrice's final testimony of innocence follows a series of events that bring in doubt the validity of her message. Can Beatrice indeed leave behind the image of immaculate innocence, the model to be contemplated and ultimately imitated by the survivors? Is Man ultimately perfectible, and does he carry the light of innocence in spite of the "mask and mantle" that enwraps this light in the "cloud" of appearances?

To maintain the reality of Beatrice's innocence in spite of the facts in the third and fourth acts, means to deny all that the fallen world would consider as essential. It means to affirm a hidden "reality" which possesses a higher truth than the "mask and mantle" of circumstances. The "pernicious error" or hamartia that is essential for the making of tragedy, is not a moral error committed by the heroine. It is not she who is wide of the mark through a wrong moral decision. The "pernicious error" in *The Cenci* is the "flaw" or "error" inherent in human existence, as long as this is ruled by "Time, Occasion, Chance, and Change." The source of hamartia, therefore, lies not in Beatrice's weakness or imperfect judgement, but in the tyranny of these principles of Mutability and corruption, external principles imposed upon her innermost being.

Both *Prometheus Unbound* and *The Cenci* ask closely related questions about man's nature and destiny. If *The Cenci* is tragic in mood, it is so because it explores human resistance to evil. Yet Shelley's ideology seems to have no provision for this exploration. Evil in the abstract will be overcome by Good in the abstract and without violent resistance. That this theory is better suited to the ritual re-enactment of a lyrical drama, peopled by mythical figures of fantasy and pure allegory is attested by the immortal figures of Prometheus and Asia. The figure of Beatrice, however, shows that the optimistic myth that informs *Prometheus Unbound* cannot become the moral criteria for human beings whose existence is defined by Time, the ultimate obstacle to Man's claim to Paradise and Immutability.

Beatrice's characterization reveals some pitfalls inherent in Shelley's attempt to reconcile this optimistic, Platonic, Utopian strain in his ideology with an equally strong awareness of our "sad reality." If the mind's notion of the ideal, (like Bernardo's notion of

129

Beatrice's innocence) is sufficient proof of the existence of Innocence, then by the same token, the mind's perception of Cenci's heightened wickedness could also claim connection with a higher truth. Thus, if Beatrice's link with the superhuman realm leads into the direction of the divine reality of Goodness, Cenci's superhuman evil points just as inevitably in the direction of the demonic realm which he proves to be real.

Beatrice's final words of triumphant innocence fail to vindicate the cause of "white romanticism," a cause based on an optimistic, monistic concept of the world. On the contrary, these words force us to confront the dilemma of a divided Manichean world, in which the powers of evil form a demonic realm of their own.

FATHER AS VILLAIN: THE DIABOLIC CREATOR
AGAINST HIS OWN CREATION

In Shelley's *The Cenci* the two major themes of romantic drama achieve their tragic culmination. In this play the innocent heroine falls in actual fact, and instead of a merely symbolic offence against the father, the offspring consummates a well-justified act of parricide.

Both Byron's "Prometheus" and Shelley's *The Cenci* re-phrase the accusation against the Father as a tyrannical and malicious Maker or Creator. Byron's plea against "the inexorable Heaven, / And the deaf tyranny of Fate, / Which for its pleasure doth create / The things it may annihilate" (II. 4-8) sounds very similar to Beatrice's anguished cry: "What if 'tis he who clothed us in these limbs / Who tortures them, and triumphs? (I. 3. 102-103).

In *The Cenci* Shelley offers the most revolutionary interpretation to the myth of Fall and Creation, the fundamental myth behind all five plays in question. In this tragedy the archetypal foursome, Adam and Eve as hero and heroine, their father as the Father, and the villain as Satan, emerge in an entirely new light. The Father is represented by the tyrannical and oppressive Count Cenci, and Shelley makes him fulfill the role of the traditional Satan as well. He is both father and villain, the Maker as well as the diabolical enemy of mankind, the Destroyer of Man's hope for innocence and his claim for Paradise.

In the previously discussed tragedies the hero's offence against the heroine is parallel to his symbolic offence against the father, both of which offences are the result of his spiritual ignorance. In

The Cenci, however, the crime of the incestuous rape (the offence against the heroine) and the crime of parricide (the offence against the father) are not parallel manifestations of humanity's fallen consciousness. Here the two offences are in a cause-effect relationship, illustrative of Shelley's Romantic interpretation of the myth of the Fall: it is not the fallen creature, but the diabolical Father who is responsible.

The major dilemma in the play, therefore, is not whether Beatrice did or did not respond to evil in a psychologically credible and morally justifiable way, the question most critics address themselves to, but the dilemma of Shelley's definition of the original source of the evil Beatrice responds to. The ultimate dilemma is the characterization and motivation of Count Cenci.

Cenci's characterization bespeaks once more Shelley's inner conflict between the optimism of "white romanticism" which would deny the reality of original sin (the world is a sacramental universe permeated with the indwelling Spirit of Nature) and "black romanticism" which bears witness to a demonic universe, because it has to contend with the reality of evil in the human soul. Through the character of Count Cenci the poet will have to resolve the fundamental question: is evil merely an "error" that can be expelled (and is Cenci's sin fundamentally his belief in original sin), or is evil something innate and inexplicable, a flaw which can be approached only by turning to the ultimate source, to the creator of the World who happens to be identical with the creator of evil.

In his analysis of the play, Earl Wasserman offers a comprehensive explanation of Cenci's fundamental "error" as this emerges through the moral and psychological implications of Shelley's optimistic ideology. According to this ideology, all human wickedness stems from a mistaken or erroneous concept of the self which is based upon contempt of the world, and ultimately contempt of the self. Closer examination of the play with its undeniably demonic connotations reveal, however, that it would be useless to seek a psychological or moral explication for a Cenci whose more than human hatred of his own children can hardly be accounted for merely through the "error" of self-contempt.

Whatever else it is, Cenci's desire to violate his daughter is not the result of uncontrollable love or passionate attraction, or of the weakness of self-indulgent lust. Essentially not an act of sexual or sensual nature, Cenci's violation of Beatrice is elevated into the realm of a spiritual act. The decision to rape her is Cenci's challenge to a cosmic opponent to reveal itself or protect the world's light of innocence.

131

Neither is Cenci's desire the result of pathological aberration, at least Shelley shows no sign of the play[9] of regarding Cenci's actions as such. Several speeches in the play prove that the tyrannical father who tortures and destroys his children is regarded not as the pathological exception to the rule of normalcy, but as the most typical representation of the relation between father and children, and Beatrice complains that Cenci tortured her in childhood "as fathers only dare." Cenci's rape of his daughter is also parallel to his equally unnatural desire for the corruption and destruction of his own sons, of all his children.

To analyze the dilemma of Cenci's motivation, one should probably begin with Shelley's discussion on incest, the more so since this discussion sheds light on his opinion not only on the act of incest, but also on the other taboo, parricide. In Shelley's eyes, incest

is like many *incorrect* things a very poetical circumstance. It may be the excess of love or hate. It may be the defiance of everything for the sake of another which clothes itself in the glory of the highest heroism, or it may be that cynical rage which, confounding the good and the bad in existing opinions breaks through them for the purpose of rioting in selfishness and antipathy.[10]

The first version of such "incorrect" passion could appear in a positive light for Shelley, since "incestuous desire of brother and sister motivated by love though incorrect, expresses the desire of the self for union with its own perfection."[11] As such, it is also one of the central metaphors of spiritual marriage in "Epipschydion." It is typical of Shelley's reasoning that if incest were motivated by an excess of love, he would be in sympathy with the offender, whose "defiance" of public norms he is willing to admire as heroic. It is only when the motive for this "incorrect" thing is hatred, that Shelley comes to consider it as morally wrong. He blames the offender for "confounding the good and bad in existing opinions" and breaking through them not to restore the good and eliminate evil, but merely to shock others, that is "for the purpose of rioting in selfishness and antipathy."[12] The breaking of the social taboo is not necessarily evil. What makes it good or evil is the individual's own value system, namely his ability to express love or hatred for others through the act.

Cenci uses incest as a tool of punishment, a tool to express his contempt for a corrupt and cowardly society, and for man in general. He deliberately defies the natural distinction between good and evil. In his discussion of another incestuous character, Shelley also sheds

132

light on Cenci's basic attitude in the play: He is "a prejudiced savage acting what he abhors and abhorring that which is the unwilling party to his crime."[13]

There is little doubt that Cenci's contempt for Beatrice is the consequence of his general contempt for the world, and of his delight in shocking that world through the "rioting" expressions of passionate antipathy. Cenci's relationship to the rest of the world is based on the same contempt or antipathy as his relationship to his children. Both Cenci's first speech with Cardinal Camillo (Act I, Scene 1), and his speech at the banquet (Act I, Scene 3) testify to this contemptuous attitude. But is this contempt and ultimately his self-contempt a sufficient explanation for his motivation to evil? It seems that if contempt of the world were Cenci's fundamental moral "error," Shelley should have presented the world as less worthy of contempt. Yet, although the poet tells us little of the historical or social circumstances of the world in which a Cenci could flourish, he makes sure that it emerges as thoroughly contemptible on account of its cruelty and hypocrisy. Although Cenci openly defies social restraints and breaks taboos by committing "incorrect things," he can do so for a long time with impunity because the society he is so contemptuous of is a similarly evil, if somewhat weaker, mirror image of his own criminality. Thus, when warning Cenci about his latest outrage, Camillo also acknowledges the Pope's receipt of Cenci's "fief that lies beyond the Pincian gate," in exchange for having a murder hushed up. Camillo's speech is a minor masterpiece of Shelley in irony. It expresses the speaker's dignified greed, and his hypocritical observance of the letter of the law which is used to corrupt its original spirit (I. 1. 1-14). Implicitly, Camillo's speech points to the role of the Church as an Institution dedicated to the preservation and perpetuation of corruption.

The way Cenci responds to Camillo's warning is also highly typical of his superior and cynical knowledge of the Pope, Camillo, and their world:

> The third of my possessions—let it go!
> Ay, I once heard the nephew of the Pope
> Had sent his architect to view the ground,
> Meaning to build a villa on my vines
> The next time I compounded with his uncle:
> I little thought he should outwit me so!   (I. 1. 15-20)

He dismisses the moral exhortation, and responds to it only as to a cold and brutal business transaction. He knows that the Pope and his favourites actually encourage his criminality, they expect him to

133

"act the deeds which are the stewards of their revenue." Therefore
Cenci dismisses Camillo's appeal to his conscience, and shows great
contempt for the man who preaches reform, while accepting the
system of corruption:

> For you give out that you half reformed me,
> Therefore strong vanity will keep you silent
> If fear should not; both will, I do not doubt.
>   (I. 1. 74-76)

Because he can be assured of Camillo's silence and co-operation,
Cenci delights in shocking him. He boasts of reckless courage in
defying the natural distinction between good and evil. He talks
about his own evil nature as a man who takes it for granted that if
they dared, all men would take delight in evil deeds. He feels safe
in the assumption that humanity is basically evil and cowardly,
"Sinful indeed, for Adam made all so" (I. 3. 12).

He regards the violation of Beatrice as his supreme achievement,
because it answers his diabolic need to re-assure himself of the
whole world's corruptibility. He also regards himself a "fiend" who
"chastises" mankind for the "sins of an unremembered world" and
boasts on several occasions of being a diabolical "scourge" in the
hand of an angry God.

That Cenci is a malicious old man full of mocking contempt for
his audience, all of them potential victims, cannot be denied. Yet his
contempt and self-contempt achieve a mythical significance in the
light of his superior power over the world which he seems to rule, as
the embodiment of worldly and cosmic forces of Authority or
Power. He can afford to shock his audience because the power of
God, the tyrannical Father is vested in him. When boasting that
God the Father answered his prayer by killing his two rebellious
sons, he claims, in effect, to be his privileged representative ("when
a parent from a parent's heart / Lifts from this earth to the great
Father of all / A prayer."). He boasts, with justification in the play,
of the "most favouring providence" that manifested his link with
the Father "even in the manner of their [his sons'] deaths." By
fulfilling Cenci's prayer in this most miraculous fashion, the "great
Father of all" shows himself in favour of the Father's tyranny
against his innocent young sons. The death of both sons on the same
night is a sinister miracle, since there is no indication in the plot that
their wicked father was responsible for their deaths in any other way
than through his prayers to the "great Father."

Although Cenci's prayers sound like a mockery and blasphemy in

the eyes of the pious, until the last moment of his life Cenci claims to
be representative of the real divinity whose existence and omnipo-
tence is borne out through all the evil actions in the play. Even when
he tastes the bright wine as the "mingled blood" of his dead sons
(in a gesture that is the blasphemous mockery of the mass, since he
pledges it to the "mighty Devil in Hell,") Cenci acts as a person
allied, or even identical with his image of deity. This divinity
assumes, however, the double image of Father and Satan, and Cenci
indeed feels secure in being backed not only by the Father who so
readily answered his prayers, but also by Satan "Who, if a father's
curses . . . / Climb with swift wings after their children's souls, / And
drag them from the very throne of Heaven, / Now triumphs in my
triumph!" (I. 3. 84-87).

Hearing Cenci's triumphant announcement of the death of his
two children, Beatrice turns to the assembled guests for protection.
In her plea she describes her fear of Cenci as of a satanic divinity,
the universal accusation against the Father who is responsible not
only for the creation, but also for the torturing of his children:

> What, although tyranny and impious hate
> Stand sheltered by a father's hoary hair?
> What, if 'tis he who clothed us in these limbs,
> Who tortures them, and triumphs!   (I. 3. 100-103)

In spite of her outcry, the triumph of this divinity is assured in the
world. The guests dare not oppose him, and Cenci dismisses
Beatrice with a threat:

> . . . My brain is swimming round;
> Give me a bowl of wine! Thou painted viper!
> Beast that thou art! Fair and yet terrible!
> I know a charm shall make thee meek and tame,
> Now get thee from my sight!   (I. 3. 164-168)

Having dismissed Beatrice, he turns to the wine he takes symbolically
as the mingled blood of his own children, the source of the "charm"
of his prowess. He is the mythical father as ogre, who, since their
infancy, had to be restrained from devouring his children (the Cenci
children express their gratitude to Lucretia for "keeping our father
not to murder us"). Now he offers a sacrifice of his two sons' blood
to extend his own life span by drinking it as the elixir of his own
sense of power (like Uranus devouring his son Chronos):

> Be thou the resolution of quick youth
> Within my veins, and manhood's purpose stern,
> And age's firm, cold, subtle villainy;

As if thou wert indeed my children's blood
Which I did thirst to drink! (I. 3. 173-177)

After this invocation he feels that he has regained the strength of a magician to work "the charm" on Beatrice, the deed that even he cannot mention: "The charm works well; / It must be done; it shall be done, I swear!" (I. 3. 177-178).

Cenci is a diabolical divinity who un-creates the world through hate. Like Byron's Arimanes at whose will the elements "tear themselves to chaos," Cenci also evokes the "ruling principle of Hate." He deliberately creates darkness out of light, in order to eliminate the distinction between good and evil or to "confound both night and day." An enemy of the light, he evokes the darkness for his deed against Beatrice who is the reflection, and even the source of spiritual light:

> The all-beholding sun yet shines; I hear
> A busy stir of men about the streets;
> I see the bright sky through the window panes:
> It is a garish, broad, and peering day;
> Loud, light, suspicious, full of eyes and ears,
> And every little corner, nook, and hole
> Is penetrated with the insolent light.
> Come darkness! Yet, what is the day to me?
> And wherefore should I wish for night, who do
> A deed which shall confound both night and day?
> 'Tis she shall grope through a bewildering mist
> Of horror: if there be a sun in heaven
> She shall not dare to look upon its beams;
> Nor feel its warmth. Let her then wish for night;
> The act I think shall soon extinguish all
> For me: I bear a darker deadlier gloom
> Than the earth's shade, or interlunar air,
> Or constellations quenched in murkiest cloud,
> In which I walk secure and unbeheld
> Towards my purpose.—Would that it were done!
> (II. 1. 174-193)

A sinister Creator not of light but of darkness, Cenci spreads the mist of horror that will create further darkness and error in Beatrice's mind. He extinguishes the sun of the bright and unfallen world when un-creating this world through hatred.

Having celebrated the death of his sons "whom in one night merciful God cut off," he now proceeds to cut off his daughter from Nature and from the Spirit, and contaminate and destroy her physically and spiritually. Therefore, when he talks about a God "merciful" to his prayers, he means just the opposite of the traditional meaning of "mercy." The tragic irony is that Beatrice would ask for real mercy of a God who stands behind, condones, and as we are ultimately to discover, is identical to Count Cenci. "O that the earth would gape! Hide me, O God!", she cries after her violation.

Wasserman argues that the poet identifies Cenci with a Satanic Creator in order to illustrate the absurdity of our concept of an anthropomorhic Creator. He states that Shelley always refused belief in a "creative Deity," and that

However he was to define the "world," Shelley never wavered in rejecting a Creator after he first arrived at that decision in "The Necessity of Atheism": "It is easier to suppose that the Universe has existed from all eternity, than to conceive a being capable of creating it."[14]

Indeed, there is no doubt that to some extent the character of Count Cenci illustrates Shelley's opinion on the image men worship as Jupiter or Jehovah. For Shelley the image of an angry and tyrannical Father supersedes the monstrosity of the Devil. Worship of this oppressive image of the punitive Father, (as Shelley describes it, for example in "On the Devil and Devils,")[15] is conducive to the political structure of tyranny, as well as the rigid habits it imposes on man's mind.

It is also evident from several of his prose works, that Shelley refuted what he called the "received hypothesis" of Judeo Christianity about an anthropomorphic God whose moral nature represents the tyranny of the "Power who tempted, betrayed, and punished the innocent beings who were called into existence by his sole will." Shelley declares that:

The received hypothesis of a Being resembling men in moral attributes of His nature, having called us out of non-existence, and after inflicting on us the misery of the commission of error, should superadd that of the punishment and the privations consequent upon it, still would remain inexplicable and incredible.[16]

Yet, the dramatic presence of a Count Cenci can never be satisfactorily explained without recognizing that he embodies not only man's mistaken notion of the Creator, but the Creator himself (as if the poet himself were unable to explain away the existence of such a presence, or substitute anything else for the monstrosity of the "received hypothesis"). From the play it is evident that Cenci personifies the very attributes of that tyrannical and unjust "Power" or "Being" whom Shelley identifies interchangeably as the tyrannical Jupiter or Jehovah the angry Father.

137

Yet the pathos of the tragedy, and the moral dilemma facing Beatrice follows from the undeniable fact that Count Cenci, the ogre and satanic deity, is indeed omnipotent on earth. What is more, he is also responsible for "having called into existence" both the daughter he violates, and the sons whom he tortures. Although he is their torturer, he is also responsible for "clothing them into limbs," and the plight of the Cenci children sounds like the outcry of the tortured creature against the source of his existence. At the same time, being "clothed" into matter is also like being arrayed in the "cloak and mantle" of circumstance, a departure from naked Truth, or one's essential being. Thus Shelley also implies that the moment of Man's Creation is simultaneous with fall from spiritual innocence.

One cannot accept fully Wasserman's statement that Shelley uses the horror of Count Cenci merely to express his detestation of the concept of an anthropomorphic divinity. In his poetry Shelley himself is often unable to withhold some kind of an anthropomorphic or personal quality from the Spirit of the Universe. He may present this spirit beyond Nature as a kind of Mother goddess (as he does in the "Sensitive Plant" and in the "Witch of Atlas"), but his attitude to the puzzling paradox remains the same. If Creation is a boon, why is the suffering and the decay of Mutability inflicted upon the innocent Creature? Thus, in the "Sensitive Plant" the Lady of the Garden fulfills the role of a protective and creative mother, calling forth her children, the flowers of the garden, and cradling them in a protective embrace throughout the Spring and Summer. In the Winter, however, the Lady abandons her creatures in an attitude that the poet regards as both sinister and inexplicable. In the "Sensitive Plant" he directs a protest against this deity in very much the same way as towards a Creator. There is a pathos of the personal approach directed against the goddess of Nature who creates only to annihilate the innocent creatures, a reproach against the creative deity of a basically cruel or sinister design. What is significant to establish here is that the Creature's pathetic and reproachful tone to a Nature goddess assumes the same personal relationship between the two, as Beatrice's relationship to an anthropomorphic male tyrant of a Creator.

Beatrice's following words, spoken in the moment of her deepest despair of man, depict the world of Nature as cruelly indifferent and even malicious, being deaf and blind to the suffering Creature's plight:

> ... Plead with the swift frost
> That it should spare the eldest flower of spring:
> Plead with the awakening earthquake, o'er whose couch
> Even now a city stands, strong fair, and free;
> Now stench and blackness yawn, like death. Oh, plead
> With famine, or wind-walking Pestilence,
> Blind lightning, or the deaf sea, not with man!
> Cruel, cold, formal man: righteous in words,
> In deeds a Cain.   (V. 4. 101-109)

Mother Nature who creates and destroys without apparent design, and without any regard for human and ethical values, is just as frightening an image as the anthropomorphic image of the Creator, presented through the cruel Father of Beatrice.

In the final analysis of Shelley's tragic vision, it seems that it is the very fact of being created, "clothed into limbs" or "called into existence" that is ultimately being questioned. Whether the Creator appears as a male tyrant (Shelley's view of the anthropomorphic concept of Judeo Christianity) or as a deceptively cruel Mother Goddess (the image of Nature as the Mother who calls the Creature into being but also deserts it in the season of Winter), the poet accuses the Deity of having created, and, through the act of Creation, also having doomed, the innocent creature to be fallible and subject "to the misery of the commission of error."

Beatrice's major difference from the other "fantastic creatures" of the poet's "fancy" consists of her tragic misfortune of existing under Time, and hence being faced with the unresolvable dilemma. Instead of receiving the divine and regenerative embrace of the immortal Asia and Prometheus (in which embrace they re-assert the claim for "the divinity in man," and hence man's claim for Paradise in the moment of his liberation from the tyrannical father, Jupiter) Beatrice is raped and violated by the same father himself. Yet the fact that Cenci is a tyrannical and cruel representative of authority does not eliminate the fact that he is also the one to whom she owes the dubious gift of being "called into existence." It is therefore highly significant that in Shelley's play the villainous Father is responsible both for the heroine's physical existence and for her loss of innocence. Ultimately, therefore, it seems that the very act of its creation also entails the destruction of Paradisiac Innocence. (The paradox works in a somewhat similar way in *Manfred* where, through the telescoping of Fall and Creation into the very same "Hour," Creation also brought about the loss of Paradise.)

When compared to the mythical and optimistic vision of *Prometheus Unbound*, the tragic world of *The Cenci* founders on the very question of the incarnation of Innocence, as if here Shelley had to face the major contradiction or limitation of his myth of "white romanticism." Being under Time and accepting the process of being "clothed into matter," means the inevitable fall from innocence and perfection. What in Christian mystical literature is described as the divine wedding between the feminine Soul and its male Creator (the image that also functions as the attainment of Paradise), becomes in *The Cenci* an act of rape, a parody of the sacramental wedding. Although his philosophical leanings would make Shelley want to celebrate the soul's potential for perfection in an unfallen world of Nature (the celebration of Man's wedding to the Spirit through Nature, the vindication of a sacramental universe), his tragedy leads him to admit to a demonic universe. He comes to accuse the Father of the rape of his own daughter, grieving over the soul's inevitable fall from innocence and perfection by power of the very force that bestowed upon it the curse of physical existence.

IMAGES OF NATURE: THE COSMIC STRUCTURE

Expressive of the optimistic myth of "white romanticism," *Prometheus Unbound* takes place entirely in a natural setting, where even the palatial abodes are light-flooded caves, that is, constructs created by Nature. In contrast, the world of *The Cenci* is realized almost exclusively through indoor scenes, in the halls, fortresses and dungeons of tyranny. There are only two scenes in the play in which the natural landscape receives any attention, the garden scene with the two young lovers, Orsino and Beatrice, and the rocky landscape of the chasm that the Cenci family has to pass on its way to the "savage rock" of the castle of Petrella.

The images of the garden and of the rough rocky landscape serve as a point counterpoint between the softly inviting and the savage aspects of Nature, which also implies duality between these two aspects in human nature. Beatrice's desire for realizing the promise of innocence, the paradisiac perfection of the inner self is picked up by recurring references to the grassy turf, the "flowers of this departed spring," and the "sweet folded flower" of her inner being. Her actual predicament on the other hand, that is her journey through the "sad reality" of tragedy takes its course through the emblematic elements of the other landscape which centres in the rock of agony hanging over the chasm of despair, under a solid roof of shade created by the tangled hair of the impenetrable foliage, error.

Shelley claims that he used the image of the rocky landscape exclusively for its beauty, and calls it the only instance of such an indulgence.

I have avoided with great care in writing this play the introduction of what is commonly called mere poetry, and I imagine there will scarcely be found a detached simile or a single isolated description, unless Beatrice's description of the chasm appointed for her father's murder should be judged to be of that nature.[16]

In spite of this admission, however, the image plays a vital part in the action and characterization and becomes an expressive example of the tendency for allegory beyond Shelley's powerful visual imagination.

Although in its composite effect the landscape works as an emblem, its vividness prevents it from fading into a static or lifeless illustration of an abstraction. On the contrary, the most salient feature of the landscape is that is suggests Nature being alive, and throbbing with the vitality of its creator.

> ... But I remember
> Two miles on this side of the fort, the road
> Crosses a deep ravine; 'tis rough and narrow,
> And winds with short turns down the precipice;
> And in its depth there is a mighty rock,
> Which has from unimaginable years,
> Sustained itself with terror and with toil
> Over a gulf, and with the agony
> With which it clings seems slowly coming down;
> Even as a wretched soul hour after hour,
> Clings to the mass of life; yet clinging, leans;
> And leaning, makes more dark the dread abyss
> In which it fears to fall: beneath this crag
> Huge as despair, as if in weariness,
> The melancholy mountain yawns ... below,
> You hear but see not an impetuous torrent
> Raging among the caverns, and a bridge
> Crosses the chasm; and high above there grow,
> With intersecting trunks, from crag to crag,
> Cedars and yews, and pines; whose tangled hair
> Is matted in one solid roof of shade
> By the dark ivy's twine. At noonday here
> 'Tis twilight, and at sunset blackest night.
> ...
>
> ... [Cenci] must never pass
> The bridge of which we spoke.   (III. 1. 243-273)

In the context of the tragic dilemma—incestuous rape versus parricide—the image of rock, torrent and abyss work as a sexual landscape. A central symbol for Beatrice's and Cenci's relationship, the image combines the masculinity of the mighty rock with the feminity of the abyss shaded by entangled mats of hair, the abyss which is raging with the torrent of blood that should separate instead of uniting the two of them. When Cenci sends for Beatrice after he violated her, Beatrice's answer reiterates these connotations of the landscape:

> 'Go tell my father that I see the gulf
> Of Hell between us two, which he may pass,
> I will not.' (IV. 1. 97-99)

and

> ...She said, 'I cannot come;
> Go tell my father that I see a torrent
> Of his own blood raging between us.'
> (IV. 1. 112-114)

Although the emblematic landscape functions primarily as a sexual landscape evocative of the horror of Cenci's relationship to Beatrice, elements of the same landscape also recur in the speech and characterization of most of the other characters, which draws attention to the more universal tenor beyond the sexual-physical "vehicle" of the metaphor. This also suggests that the rape itself has profound spiritual implications. In the relationship between Father and Child, Cenci's sexual assault of Beatrice is also used to point to a more universal spiritual offence committed by the diabolic Creator against his innocent Creations.

The rock evokes the feeling of being exposed to suffering without recourse to the higher justice or clemency of Heaven—a fairly consistent connotation throughout Shelley's poetry, and an equally well known archetypal usage of this image. (This image of the naked rock of agony is also used by Wordsworth in *The Borderers* where the innocent captain meets his death through being exposed to the elements on a barren rock, while the innocent old father, Herbert also finds his death through exposure, on the rocky heath.) In *Prometheus Unbound* the rock of the suffering Titan becomes the locus of the fallen world's agony, and of man's existential loneliness. In *The Cenci* Giacomo complains about experiencing a moment of such agony before coming to the decision about his father's murderer: "Upon the brink on which you see me stand," he feels compelled by his own despair, and consequently he is thrust deeper and

142

deeper into criminality, which to Shelley is equivalent to deeper and deeper suffering.—Lucretia also echoes the tragic elements of this landscape when describing the daughter-father relationship as an unbridgeable "gulf of obscure hatred." By the end of her plight, as if recognizing this landscape of existential despair as the only reality, Beatrice dismisses hope because hope would only make the rock, which is destined to fall, "cling" to life, and hence make the fall into the "yawning abyss" more of an agony:

> Worse than the bitterness of death, is hope:
> It is the only ill which can find place
> Upon the giddy, sharp and narrow hour
> Tottering beneath us.   (V. 4. 98-101)

As Shelley gratefully acknowledges, the image takes its origin in Calderon's *El Purgatorio de San Patricio*.[17] For Shelley, however, the emblematic landscape becomes a hellscape of man's existence under Time, with the rock as the agony of man's loneliness and finitude, over the abyss of despair. The rock is in the process of falling (although it has "for unimaginable years sustained itself over the gulf"), because it is weighed down, by necessity, through its pathetic "clinging" to existence, and it is this very "clinging" that makes the inevitable fall from the precipice into the yawning gulf more horrible an agony.

The recurring use of the emblematic elements in this landscape also relates it to the language of moral parable, with the bridge over the abyss standing for the only desirable or possible escape. Through the play all the characters are brought to face their existence pecariously verging over this abyss, and when they are brought to the gulf, they are unable to pass the bridge. By deciding to hurl Cenci down, and not allow him to pass the bridge, they themselves fall into the irredeemable but also inevitable trap of "error," criminality.

Beatrice's moment of greatest agony is set against the fortress located on top of the "lonely" and "savage" rock of Petrella. This is the place where Cenci, having contaminated her innocent body, now proceeds to her spiritual destruction. Therefore, it is in contending for the purity of her spirit, for the "immortal soul," that she is forced into the act of parricide. Yet, ironically, it is through this decision that she has to turn from victim into active participant in evil, and thus loses her spiritual innocence as if to fulfill Cenci's design. Her crime, however, is initially the crime of the Father or Creator, since the human being is tempted and betrayed into error through the very Being who called it into existence. External punishment only compounds that suffering which follows the human being's recognition of his own error. Being created, to fall into error is the very substance of Beatrice's suffering on the "crags of agony."

Even Olimpo and Marzio, these lowliest beings whose motivation for murder was greed and revenge, are associated with the "savage rock" of ultimately undeserved suffering. After the murder they are discovered "lurking among the rocks" (IV. 4. 81).

The last element of this landscape, the "tangled hair of the trees" that is "matted in one solid roof of shade" is also worth closer attention, in the context of Shelley's allegorical use of some related images. In *Prometheus Unbound* the intricately woven branches of foliage creating a shelter for light is a recurring motif, and it reaches its culmination in Prometheus's final abode which is a cave of light. In contrast, in *The Cenci* the "tangled hair" of branches created not a shelter for welcoming or transfusing, light. "Matted in one solid roof of shade," the branches lock out the light. Consequently, the entire landscape is steeped quite consistently in darkness, symbolic of Man's lack of insight, or lack of hope at the chasm of despair, or over the crags of agony: "At noonday here / 'Tis twilight, and at sunset blackest night."

Beatrice's "entangled hair" is another of the recurring images of the play. She is "dragged by the hair" by Cenci, and after her violation she feels as if blinded by the "wandering strings" of her "entangled hair" ("How comes this hair undone? / Its wandering strings must be what blind me so"). She also complains of the "mist" which is "clinging" and contaminating her awareness of her own and Nature's purity.[18] The fact that she feels herself "blinded" by this "mist" is also connected with her "entangled hair" which blocks her vision into the true light of the "pure and inmost spirit of life," together with the "mist" of suffering and error:

> ... There creeps
> A clinging, black contaminating mist
> About me ... 't is substantial, heavy, thick,
> I cannot pluck it from me, for it glues
> My fingers and my limbs to one another,
> And eats into my sinews, and dissolves
> My flesh to a pollution, poisoning
> The subtle, pure and inmost spirit of life!
> (III. 1. 16-23)

Once she decides on Cenci's murder, she claims that she has disentangled her "entangled will," and also can see more clearly. In this "higher truth" she stands firm to the end. By then the image of her entangled and then disentangled hair is also connected with her ability to transcend the painful darkness and confusion of her passions by the clear insight into a higher order. She finally accepts her fate as inevitable and turns to her weak foster mother with gentle reassurance, trying to transplant into her also the quiet dignity of her own "higher truth":

> ... Here, Mother, tie
> My girdle for me, and bind up this hair
> In any simple knot; ay, that does well.
> And yours I see is coming down. How often
> Have we done this for one another; now
> We shall not do it any more.   (V. 4. 159-164)

In these last words she claims to have transcended the blinding "mist" created by her entangled hair. Being able to give up hope for life, she is no longer in agony, "clinging" to life. Hence she is able to adjust her sight to the eternal light of man's innocence, and recognize the "pure and inmost spirit of life" beyond the "cloud" of crime: to see the real form in spite of its being enwrapped by and hidden under the "mask and mantle of circumstances."

Yet, in spite of these words which affirm the vision of transcendent Innocence, the Infernal landscape as the emblem of existence did not gain different significance. Through the mist of her entangled hair, the mist of error, Beatrice is as much part of the general moral landscape as is Count Cenci: both the oppressed and the oppressor are inextricably linked in the net of "error" Shelley describes here as the fallen and violent world of Nature and of human nature.

The last element of the moral landscape deals with the growth of trees whose "tangled hair is matted in one solid roof of shade," thereby creating the shade of impenetrable darkness over the whole area. For a fuller interpretation of this image, we should look at Shelley's poem on the Medusa, one of the most striking among his shorter works.[19] In this poem he meditates upon the portrait of the Medusa, a young woman who is in many ways a mirror image (if possibly also a negative image) of Beatrice Cenci. The similarity between Shelley's rendering of the two portraits is striking. The Medusa suffers, and thereby inflicts suffering, yet in her face Shelley celebrates beauty being born out of the horror: "Yet it is less the horror than the grace / Which turns the gazer's spirit into stone."— Beatrice, for reasons not explained in the story, is called "viper" by her angry father, who also drags her by the hair, causing the disarray of her entangled hair, making her feel blinded with blood and filled with hatred.

Even more than Beatrice, the Medusa evokes a sense of horror. Yet Shelley insists that there is a "hue of beauty thrown athwart the darkness and the glare of pain / Which humanize and harmonize the strain," while Beatrice wears the "mask and mantle" of external evil thrown over the radically opposite and pure substance of her inner being.

There is no doubt that in Shelley's poetry the snake is symbol of the poisonous "error" of hatred, and both Beatrice's "wandering strings" and the Medusa's serpent locks reiterate this error of their fallen condition. When Giacomo describes the Cenci children as "scorpions ringed with fire," he describes their predicament as being inextricably and irredeemably entangled in their hate, and hence destructive of their own selves. Yet, when meditating upon the "inextricable error" which is inherent in the Medusa's serpent locks," the poet is bewildered by a "tempestuous loveliness" which shines through the error. Like a female Satan, the Medusa looks at her triumphant tormentor (who cursed her by making her wear these serpent locks of hatred) with heroic defiance: hence her "brazen glare" shines through the darkness of horror. The onlooker is both repelled and in awe of the Medusa, because, although she demonstrates the inextricable error of hatred, she also manifests invincible defiance of her triumphant tormentor. Shelley, therefore, is in sympathy with the fallen creature whom he sees as a victim first tempted into error, and then punished by Heaven, the seat of tyranny she gazes at with reproachful defiance:

> 'Tis the tempestuous loveliness of terror;
> For from the serpents gleams a brazen glare
> Kindled by that inextricable error,
> Which makes a thrilling vapour of the air
> . . .
>
> A woman's countenance, with serpent-locks,
> Gazing in death on Heaven from those wet rocks.
> ("On the Medusa of Leonardo da Vinci in the
> Florentine Gallery," 33-40)

It is typical of Shelley's vision that Satan in his serpentine beauty is presented here as woman, just as in *The Cenci* he appoints Beatrice to the dual role of Prometheus as the potential redeemer of mankind, and the rebellious fallen spirit.

Although the head of the Medusa bears the inextricable error which makes her face freeze into the mask of defiant hatred, the real source of her error is in the foreboding and unresponsive regions of Heaven that threw her onto the "crags of agony," upon the "wet rocks" of existence. Through the horror of the Medusa's frozen glance, existence reveals itself as Hell. Therefore the poem ends with a note of defiance and disdain against Heaven, ultimately the source of all evil.

The serpentine female's reproachful gaze at Heaven demonstrates that in Shelley's universe Heaven became the real seat of evil, and this seems to verify Northrop Frye's suggestion about the romantic poets' "new mythological construction."[20] According to Frye, the romantic poet-hero experiences a reversal of the traditional cosmic structure, together with the reversal of the "moral principle incorporated into" this structure. Consequently, he establishes a new direction for the "good," the finding of "identity," not in the height, but in an inward or downward movement, in a "deep cosmic center."

The revolutionary reversal is indeed one of the fundamental movements of the symbolic action in all five tragedies under discussion, but it is not the final or ultimate stage of that action. As a matter of fact, on the basis of *The Borderers*, *Remorse* and *Otho the Great*, it seems that the tragic experience does not culminate in revolutionary reversal. Rather, it culminates in a sense of loss which signifies that the recently established revolutionary order either failed in making manifest a cosmic centre, or this new centre failed to establish the direction of the moral good. Consequently, these three plays demonstrate that these poets are unable to deal with the "double nature" of tragic action, to deal with an insurmountable loss, but also affirm a new moral-spiritual insight, or a new light being born out of this loss.

In Shelley's and Byron's works, however, there is an attempt to deal with the "double nature" of tragic action, to affirm a third stage that may follow in the wake of the total collapse of moral directions, after the revolutionary reversal.

Shelley's *The Cenci* shows the three-stage process of (1) reversal, (2) collapse, and (3) need for new affirmation in most complete detail.

1. The first phase, that of the revolutionary reversal, begins with Beatrice's violation and her ensuing decision that retaliation is necessary or inevitable. This movement begins in the Cenci palace which, with its proud arches, dark corridors and dungeons stands for the tyranny of the Judeo-Christian cosmic structure, an edifice of the tyrannical Father's power over the world. That Shelley associates the high arches of this palace, with the "arches of hell," foreshadows the association of height with depth, and the revolu-

tionary reversal of the entire traditional cosmic structure, with its built-in moral principle.

Yet in this play the initially violent reversal of the moral structure has been accomplished not by the revolutionary offspring, but by the Father himself. By becoming the rigid personification of "Power," it is the skygod or the Father himself who upsets the moral order. Shelley's description of how Christ's "sublime" teachings were distorted and reversed through institutional religion sheds light on his idea of this reversal.

The sublime human character of Jesus Christ was deformed by an imputed identification with a Power, who tempted, betrayed, and punished the innocent beings who were called into existence by His sole will;[24]

Although Cenci, the father is the symbol of Power or Authority who rules from the very centre of tradition, from the Cenci palace in Rome, Shelley also makes him responsible for the creation of chaos, for the violent overthrow of the natural moral structure. An unchecked tyrant, Cenci turns into a savage "rioting" against the natural distinction between good and evil.

Through her violation, Beatrice falls victim to Cenci's reversal of the moral order. She experiences this as a reversal of the cosmic structure: her world is turned upside down, light is changed into darkness, the light of the Spirit into the dark blood and pollution of crime. This moment of agony is her "darkness at noon." Even the "sunshine on the floor is black," and she is thrust from a state of innocence into a world she now sees as radically fallen and evil.

> ...O horrible!
> The pavement sinks under my feet! The walls
> Spin round! I see a woman weeping there,
> And standing calm and motionless, whilst I
> Slide giddily as the world reels....My God!
> The beautiful blue heaven is flecked with blood!
> The sunshine on the floor is black!   (III. 1. 8-14)

She experiences the shock of reversal in a sense of vertigo, and a feeling of having gone mad: the physical and psychological symptoms of experiencing the reversal of the cosmic order. If the "beautiful blue heaven" beheld her violation without intervention, God either does not exist, or is on the side of the violator.

The world of Nature, previously of paradisiac purity, appears now not only a fallen world, but the nightmare image of Hell.

> ...The air
> Is changed to vapours such as the dead breathe

148

In charnel pits! Pah! I am choked! There creeps
A clinging, black contaminating mist
About me... 'tis substantial, heavy, thick,
I cannot pluck it from me, for it glues
My fingers and my limbs to one another,
And eats into my sinews, and dissolves
My flesh to a pollution, poisoning
The subtle, pure and inmost spirit of life!

(III. 1. 14-23)

The "clinging, black, contaminating mist" is the mist of error that clouds her vision to the true light hidden within Nature, or beyond Nature. That this fallen condition follows her violation by her biological father also implies, however, that suffering is really the inevitable result of the fall into physical existence, as willed by a diabolical heavenly Father. By the end of her stay in the Cenci palace (Act III, Scene 1), her world is turned upside down, and the realm of Heaven abandoned by the benevolent and just Father.

Upon the "lonely and savage rock" in the Castle of Petrella (Act IV, Scene 2), she turns this experience of a morally reversed universe into revolutionary action: Turning away from Heaven which beheld her violation, she takes the cause of justice into her own hands, and announces herself the earthly angel of avenging heaven. In doing so, she claims that the direction of the highest moral good or justice lies within her, within the centre of the human heart, the deep cosmic centre which is also the centre of the indwelling Spirit within Nature. She declares herself "Solid" as a "rock," and "firm as the world's centre."

The reversal between highest and lowest has been accomplished. Beatrice declares that to thrust down the tyrannical father is a "high and holy deed," and that the "higher truth" resides in seeing its justice. When Cenci is murdered, she celebrates her triumph as the liberation of light that is now to emerge out of the very depth of the new cosmic centre: "The world / Is conscious of a change. Darkness and Hell / Have swallowed up the vapour they sent forth / To blacken the sweet light of life" (IV. 3. 40-42).

Had the play ended here, it would not be a tragedy, but a cosmic drama of celebration, like *Prometheus Unbound* which indeed ends on this point of revolutionary reversal in the cosmic structure. Prometheus is liberated, and the light of Spirit rises up from the deep cosmic centre of Demogorgon's cave. The reversing of the traditional cosmic structure results there in the emergence of another sacramental universe.

149

2. Beatrice's tragedy, however, has another phase in Act V, following this reversal. This phase is concerned with the question whether the new, that is the deep inner cosmic centre is indeed a valid direction for the moral good. Failing to see a new moral direction emerge from the depth of this new centre, is tantamount to the loss of both old and new moral principles, and hence to the collapse of any moral order. The experience of such a collapse is essential to Beatrice's tragedy.

Having abandoned faith in divine justice, Beatrice turns her gaze down. While awaiting justice in the depth of her prison cell, she hopes for earthly justice, born from the inherent justice in the human heart.

She has to find out, however, that she cannot hope for justice from either direction. Now she bewails a universe left without moral dimensions: "No difference has been made by God or man / Or any power moulding my wretched lot. 'Twixt good and evil, as regarded me."

Man's cruelty and inhumanity reflects the cruel indifference of Nature. The heart of "cruel, cold, formal man" reflects the centre of the fallen world of Nature, a world abandoned by the Spirit. Nature is deaf and blind to man's plight, and to the questions of right and wrong. The "quick frost" ruthlessly kills the "innocent flowers of spring," while "famine, pestilence, blind lightning" and the "deaf sea" also reiterate the notion of inscrutable cruelty, or even malice against Man. Man's heart, consequently, reflects the very forces of a fallen Creation.

In her despair Beatrice has a nightmare vision in which the space of the deep emerges as also the seat of evil. In this vision Cenci, the diabolical father, grins at her both from above and below, reaching out for her from the very centre of the earth, to embrace her in his "hellish arms."

> ...If there should be
> No God, no Heaven, no Earth in the void world;
> ...
>
> If all things then should be...my father's spirit,
> His eye, his voice, his touch surrounding me;
> The atmosphere and breath of my dead life!
> If sometimes, as a shape more like himself,
> Even the form which tortured me on earth,
> Masked in gray hairs and wrinkles, he should come
> And wind me in his hellish arms, and fix
> His eyes on mine, and drag me down, down, down!
> For was he not alone omnipotent

On Earth and ever present? Even though dead,
Does not his spirit live in all that breathe,
And work for me and mine still the same ruin,
Scorn, pain, despair? Who ever yet returned
To teach the laws of Death's untrodden realm?
Unjust perhaps as those which drive us now,
Oh, whither, whither? (V. 4. 57-75)

It seems that Cenci has finally succeeded in his promise to bring forth a demonic world, as forecast in his invocation:

...and upon Earth
All good shall drop and sicken, and ill things
Shall with a spirit of unnatural life
Stir and be quickened... (IV. 2. 186-189)

Through his "unnatural" but omnipotent power to evil, Cenci succeeded in making Beatrice lose the vision of innocence. She sees both the heights and the depths "quickened" to life by the demonic, and can find no perceptible direction for the good or for the divine.

After her nightmare vision of a demonic cosmic centre to which Cenci's hellish arms are dragging her "down, down, down," she awakens with a "chill of death." This death refers to her hopes of finding the Spirit in the Judeo-Christian cosmic structure, or in the earth-oriented structure of white romanticism which expected to find the moral good within the human heart, or through the indwelling Spirit, within the world of Nature.

Beatrice experiences not only the reversal of the traditional order, but a total collapse, a loss of any moral or spiritual directions in the universe, the lack of any moral or ethical dimension in the world. This final and total loss, the experience of nothingness that follows the collapse, is the essence of her tragedy, and it forms the most weighty downward movement in the tragedy's "double action."

But how about the counter movement, or the ascending motif in great tragedy which wrings spiritual victory out of the tragic loss?

3. This question leads us to Beatrice's final reaction to her experience and to the problem of catharsis.

Having accepted the collapse of a morally ordered cosmos, Beatrice indeed emerges with a sense of new dignity. Accepting the futility of awaiting divine or earthly justice, in the last scene Beatrice reaches the calm after all passion spent. No longer "clinging" to life, she turns to embrace death as the annihilation of consciousness, and welcomes the finality of natural death as the embrace of a "gentle mother" who rocks her child to sleep. She faces death with no hope for after life. What she can salvage for her immortal soul is exclu-

151

sively the fame of her unstained name, the image of invincible Innocence that may become realized in the distant future.

Her resignation and renunciation of the transcendental reality of an afterlife seems to foreshadow the emergence of the existential hero of modern tragedy: after experiencing the collapse of a morally ordered cosmos, Beatrice is thrust into the loneliness and finitude of her individual existence, with no external moral guideline to follow. The human being has to make his own values, undertake his own commitment. There are some weighty considerations in Beatrice's position that would approximate the basic stance of existentialism.

Yet, when Beatrice insists that she is entitled to the afterlife of her eternal name through the "higher truth" of her innocence, she insists upon a world beyond or opposite to the world of existence. She claims "higher reality" for the One, for the Spirit, in opposition to the "sad reality" of experience, of physical existence.

There is no doubt that it is by her own father that she has been driven to accomplish the ultimate revolutionary reversal, parricide. Yet, in contending for the immortality of her spirit, she was also forced to turn against the source of her physical existence, and to declare this as separate and in opposition to the "sweet folded flower" of her inner, and hence more "real," spiritual being. She can insist on the "higher reality" of her Innocence only by denying the "sad reality" of appearances. She claims that when devoid of the ideal, the world is only a mirage, "where nothing is but all things seem," and this is certainly a very different position from that of existentialism.

She is driven to annihilate her Father through the forces of Fate, Chance and Necessity, all of these accidental or alien to her inner core of being. Yet after this revolution she can expect to find no sense of at-onement between her own Soul and Body, between the Creator and the Created, or between Spirit and Nature. In her tragic battle for the immortality of Innocence she is made to further enhance a central dichotomy. In spite of her agonized desire for becoming one with the "pure and inmost spirit of life" (Shelley's yearning for the optimistic monism of "white romanticism,") she is condemned to remain irredeemably a product of her father's "divided being" (IV. 1. 117). Witnessing the collapse of a morally ordered cosmos, she suffers then the alienation between Existence and Innocence, Nature and Spirit, Body and Soul, attesting to the irrevocable verdict that their "sweet bond [is] broken" (V. 4. 137). In other words, she can liberate herself from the burden of her fall only by finally denying the unity between body and soul, or between Man, Nature and the Spirit.

152

VII

CONCLUSION

Although Wordsworth may refer only to himself when speculating on his greater affinity with the "allegorical spirit" of Milton's and Spenser's "enthusiastic meditative Imagination" as opposed to Chaucer's and Shakespeare's "human and dramatic Imagination,"[1] he is, in effect, speaking on behalf of all the major English poets of his period. None of the five poets under study excel in that "dramatic" or "human" imagination which creates memorable, psychologically modulated and credible human character.[2]

While the Romantic Movement on the Continent produced strong and successful drama, it is, as though, having watched the revolutionary upheaval from across the channel, the English romantics have translated Revolution and Counter-Revolution into an almost exclusively cosmic, metaphysical dilemma. This is not to say that Goethe, for example, participated any more actively in political events than the English romantics. Still, the revolution had immediate social and political implications for the Continental poets, and they have often managed to translate the crucial Romantic dilemma, millennium via revolutionary upheaval, into psychologically and socially credible human situations. With the English Romantic playwrights, the same dilemma emerges on an almost exclusively cosmic, metaphysical level and is best sustained as such.

Schiller's *Robbers*, *Mary Stuart*, and *Louisa Miller*, or Victor Hugo's *Hernani*, *Ruy Blas*, and *Le roi s'amuse* are plays not only of poetic, but also of dramatic power. Goethe's *Faust*, while having cosmic significance, still translates the mythical aspects of the romantic quest into socially and psychologically valid human interaction. The claim for Paradise and the rebellion against the father, the characteristic themes of the Romantic Movement, are symbolically maintained within the Continental dramas, but they are part and parcel of the structure and the imagery. Moreover, these themes do not detract from the quality of the drama as credible conflict between closely observed human characters. The interaction of these characters is portrayed against a socially and politically recognizable background, whereas the tragic characters of Wordsworth, Coleridge, Keats, Byron and Shelley emerge against a stark, purely cosmic background. As a matter of fact, whether or not these authors are aware of it, each of the five plays reads more as a vehicle for cosmic allegory, than that of historical drama.

The characters of Marmaduke, Alvar, and even Manfred, Beatrice or Count Cenci are larger-than-life projections of the good and evil forces familiar from allegory, rather than being multi-dimensional characters whose actions are motivated by the psychology of human behaviour. All these characters, even the evocative figures of Beatrice and Cenci are more reflective of the poet's inner spiritual conflict, and embody ideas or various impulses of the poet's own psyche. As such, they differ significantly from Chaucer's or Shakespeare's characters of "dramatic" or "human" imagination.

In the worst of these five plays, the poet lacks control over an overwhelming allegorical tendency, and is unaware how this tendency plays havoc with his alleged intent to write historical drama or costume play. The result is incongruity and failure, as demonstrated by *The Borderers*, *Remorse*, and *Otho the Great*. At its best, in *Manfred* and in *The Cenci*, the same tendency achieves a magnificent system of cosmic allegory,[3] probably worthy of the best poetry produced by the "allegorical spirit," or the "enthusiastic, meditative Imagination."

Regardless of the varying merits of their achievement, each of the five tragedies use characters to externalize their poets' inner, spiritual conflict, the conflict between absolute affirmation and absolute despair. Through the often erratic interaction of fundamentally four stock characters from Gothic melodrama, these five romantic tragedies enact Man's fall from innocence, and question his potential for re-gaining Paradise by forming the proper relationship with Spirit and Nature.

a.   In terms of the stock characters of Gothic melodrama, the hero sins by offending against an innocent heroine and their common father. (Symbolically or through close family ties both hero and heroine regard the same man as their father.) Both offences are instigated by the fourth stock character, the villain.

b.   In terms of the underlying myth of a Romantic Paradise Lost, these figures act out the same drama as Adam's loss of Eve, and his offence against their Father or Maker. The aftermath of his offence —his fall—is succumbing to the villain who represents Satan.

c.   In terms of the Romantic poet's cosmos, the union between Adam and Eve signifies the potential wedding between Man and

154

unfallen Nature, a wedding which also signifies Man's union with the Spirit through Nature. Failing to achieve this union, the hero loses his chances for entering into a sacramental universe, or Paradise, and he enters the realm of the Demonic alienation between Man, Nature and Spirit.

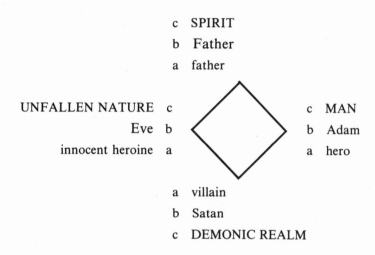

c SPIRIT
b Father
a father

UNFALLEN NATURE c   c MAN
Eve b   b Adam
innocent heroine a   a hero

a villain
b Satan
c DEMONIC REALM

The hero's success in establishing the relationship with heroine and father stands for the harmonious union between Adam, Eve and their Father, or for the harmony between Man, Nature and Spirit. This relationship implies Man's attainment of paradise.

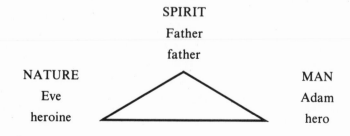

SPIRIT
Father
father

NATURE   MAN
Eve   Adam
heroine   hero

The hero's failure to "wed" the heroine and attain their father's

155

blessing implies Man's fall, his succumbing to the villain's intrigue, and hence his fall to alienation or the Demonic realm.

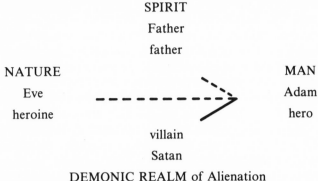

SPIRIT

Father

father

NATURE   MAN

Eve   Adam

heroine   hero

villain

Satan

DEMONIC REALM of Alienation

Each of the five tragedies ask fundamentally the same questions about the central conflict between limitless hope and limitless despair concerning Man and his predicament. Yet, the tragedian's spiritual dilemma assumes a different shape and resolution in each of the five plays.

Wordsworth's *The Borderers* fits the above diagrams in its entirety. The hero, Marmaduke, is tricked by the ruthless villain to murder the father, and as a consequence he loses the heroine. Having done so, he succumbs to alienation, the realm of the satanic villain, but only temporarily. Impelled by remorse and compassion for his innocent victim, he starts on a new journey, with the "spectre of this innocent man my guide." In Wordsworth's tragedy, then, the romantic rebellion against the father leads to the loss of Paradise, to madness, guilt and alienation, but also to a remorseful search for atonement.

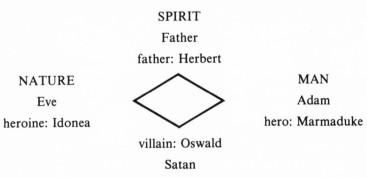

SPIRIT

Father

father: Herbert

NATURE   MAN

Eve   Adam

heroine: Idonea   hero: Marmaduke

villain: Oswald

Satan

DEMONIC REALM of Alienation

In Coleridge's *Remorse* the two major romantic themes, rebellion and the claim to Paradise, receive a significantly different solution. The solution is characteristic of Coleridge's own dilemma between romanticism, and his quite orthodox religious, convictions. At a first glance, the successful wedding between Alvar and Teresa, blessed by their father, seems to affirm a belief in man's chance to attain Paradise. The wedding achieves harmony between Adam, Eve and their Father, or between Man, Nature and Spirit. Yet, upon closer scrutiny, we find that the character of the father, Lord Valdez, is only a figurehead, and his blessing of the young couple at the end does not carry its appropriate weight. It is, interestingly, the older brother, Alvar, who represents the spiritual attributes normally associated with the father. Coleridge is reluctant to act out the romantic son's rebellion against the father. Instead, he transposes the conflict between a sinful younger, and a saintly and fatherly older brother.

Perhaps we can better understand the nature of Coleridge's ambivalence if we take into consideration the two versions of his play. In the first, the father is not only the weak and gullible old man of the second version, but he is also quite clearly in alliance with the treacherous and tyrannical authority of clerical oppression, represented by 'Father' Monviedro, the Inquisitor. In this case, both 'fathers' are also allied with the villain to the extent of forcing the heroine's acceptance of the villain as husband. In the second version the alliance between the Inquisitor and the father is less clear; this allows Coleridge to act out the father-son conflict in two different phases.

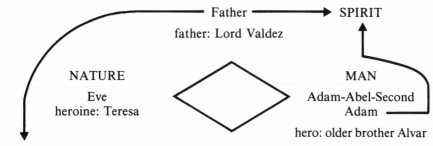

Father ⟶ SPIRIT
father: Lord Valdez

NATURE
Eve
heroine: Teresa

MAN
Adam-Abel-Second Adam
hero: older brother Alvar

'Father' Monviedro, Inquisitor

villain: younger brother Ordonio

Satan-Cain-Judas

DEMONIC REALM of Alienation

157

The hero rebels against the tyranny of authority and oppression by turning against the Inquisitor, himself a father substitute. At the same time, the villain, Ordonio acts out the spiritual-religious aspect of the same rebellion. In a typically Coleridgian rendering of the father-son conflict, the guilty son becomes a murderous Cain, a rebellious 'younger' brother raising his hand against the saintly and fatherly Abel. He pays with his life for the offence.

Coleridge's ambivalence about these romantic themes is also illustrated in his presentation of the search for Paradise. Although hero and heroine achieve their union and exude cosmic joy at the elimination of all evil, the reader suspects that this joy is really quite unjustified in their world. The reasons for this suspicion are numerous. The entire intrigue of the play was directed at redeeming the villain, but he, in effect, dies in despair, with no hope of forgiveness.

Both the lovers and their father proceed to the celebration of the wedding, as it were, averting their eyes from the dead body and so avoiding the unresolved tragic dilemma. Neither is the world free from evil after the villain's death. The Inquisitor, responsible for the hero's imprisonment, is still alive and unchecked, and the violence of the villain was stopped only by another act of violence (that of Alhadra killing Ordonio as an act of revenge). There are, then, several false notes in this symphony of universal celebration, and the pious homily delivered by the hero at the close of the play does not improve upon this effect.

In *Otho the Great* the allegorical relationship between father and

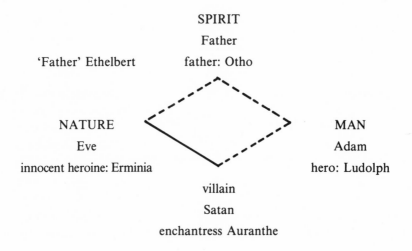

son shows closer similarity to Wordsworth's play. The son's rebellion is followed by guilt, and then by a desire for reconciliation. Somewhat similarly to Coleridge, Keats also relies on a 'secondary father figure,' so to speak, in this case on 'Father' Ethelbert, against whom the hero plays out the romantic son's deep-seated hostility and defiance of age and authority.

As for the relationship between hero and heroine, or the question of Man's claim to Paradise, it appears here with a slight variation. There are two heroines. Both the innocent Erminia and the enchantress, Auranthe, represent different aspects of Nature, and the hero is torn between these two. His dilemma seems to point at the tragic irresolution in the poet's mind about the paradisiac and the demonic aspects of Nature.

At a first glance it would seem futile to look for the four stock characters of hero, heroine, villain and father in Byron's tragedy. Upon closer scrutiny, however, one realizes that Manfred indeed 'doubles' in the roles of villain and hero. As for the angry father and the innocent heroine, they may be absent from stage, but not from the "mental theatre" of Manfred's mind. It also becomes apparent that Manfred's drama does, indeed, take place in the 'mental theatre' of an inner conflict, still acted out between these four dramatic-allegorical entities of hero, heroine, father and villain.

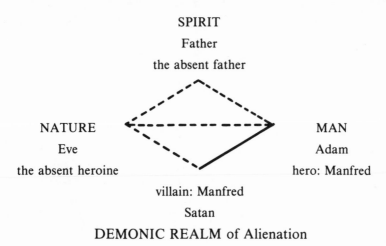

SPIRIT

Father

the absent father

NATURE   MAN

Eve   Adam

the absent heroine   hero: Manfred

villain: Manfred

Satan

DEMONIC REALM of Alienation

In effect, Manfred's whole ordeal consists of his struggle to overcome the absence of the heroine, Astarte, and to find conciliation, through punishment or forgiveness from the father. That is to say, he, too, acts out the romantic quest for the harmonious union between Adam, Eve and their Father, or Man, Nature and Spirit. Yet, because Manfred does fulfill the double role of villain and hero, Satan and Adam, he cannot realize either of his goals; he cannot attain harmony. Because of his duality, he remains alone and alienated. The conclusion of his quest is that Man is unable to achieve the paradisiac union with Spirit and Nature, and has to accept alienation, the traditional realm of the satanic villain, as his only refuge.

In Shelley's *The Cenci* the central diagram of the cosmic allegory shows yet another variation. Here it is the father who 'doubles' in the usually contradictory roles of father and villain. The highest spiritual authority, the Creator, and Satan the destroyer, are one and the same.

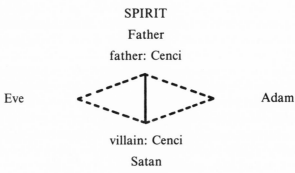

SPIRIT

Father

father: Cenci

Eve   Adam

villain: Cenci

Satan

DEMONIC REALM of Alienation

It is due to this duality that Cenci most effectively cuts off his daughter from her own mate, and leaves her alienated both from Spirit and from Nature. This is the most clear-cut and drastic separation of Man from the promise of Paradise in the five plays, and through it Shelley suggests the most radically pessimistic conclusion about the relationship between the Creator and the world of the Created: he denies the possibility of a harmonious union between Man, Nature and Spirit.

Throughout the five plays, the greater pessimism of the second generation of romantic tragedians keeps coming into relief. This is also demonstrated by the fate of the heroes and the nature of their tragic error.

160

In *The Borderers* the hero commits an "atrocious crime" due to the villain's machinations, but he survives his error, even if only as a lonely wanderer. In Coleridge's play the hero celebrates his triumph over the villain in a joyful wedding with the heroine, and his joy is not significantly shadowed by his brother's death in despair. Keats', Byron's and Shelley's tragic heroes, however, die at the end of their ordeal.

This increased sense of pessimism if also demonstrated by the poet's presentation of the hero's tragic error. In Wordsworth's, Coleridge's and Keats's play the hero offends against the innocent heroine through ignorance, or through an error in judgement. In *Manfred*, however, the hero commits his double offence against heroine and father not out of ignorance, but out of passion. Manfred knowingly and proudly follows his passion as his tragic fate, and does so in defiance of the power responsible for predetermining that fate.

In *The Cenci* the romantic hero's defiance finds an even more revolutionary expression, if at all possible. Both themes of romantic tragedy find their ultimate enactment here. To begin with, the reponsibility for the conflict between father and child is entirely attributed to the father. This is the only play where it is not the offspring, whether he is blindly or knowingly rebellious, but the tyrannical father himself, who commits the initial offence. Beatrice, the violated daughter, is forced to murder her father in order to stop him from further acts of violence. As a consequence, she is, indeed, irretriveably drawn to the realm of madness, alienation and death; the satanic villain, the destroyer, is also her father and creator.

Another significant measure of the poet's characteristically individual response to central romantic themes is his use of cosmic imagery. As Northrop Frye pointed out, the romantic cosmology introduces the revolutionary reversal of the Judeo-Christian cosmic system, each having a unifying moral purpose "built into it" as a spatial principle. Northrop Frye points out that while in the traditional cosmology the 'good' of Heaven or Paradise is associated with heights, in the romantic version height becomes symbolic of the evil of alienation. Simultaneously, the depths often become symbolic of the good forces, of the search for identity in a deep and new "cosmic center."

When we examine this statement in the context of the five romantic tragedies, we find that Frye's outline of the revolutionary reversal is of great importance. Just as important, however, is the fact that none of these romantic tragedies end merely with a revolutionary reversal, which simply substitutes an old with a new moral principle. What Frye describes as the romantic discovery of a new cosmic centre remains either unrealized, as in *The Borderers*, or this centre emerges as double-faced, ambivalent. In Coleridge's *Remorse*, for example, the depth of the subterranean caverns is the location both of liberation and of the demonic powers of evil.

The after-effects of the revolutionary reversal are even more far-reaching in *Manfred* and in *The Cenci*. As a matter of fact, here the after-effects are more significant to the resolution of the tragedy, than the reversal itself. Although both Byron's and Shelley's heroes discover that the heights are associated with the demonic forces of evil, when they turn their glance to the depth for a possibly new "cosmic center," they find this region also quickened by the demonic. What emerges from their experience, then, is not only the reversal of the old, but the total collapse of both traditional and revolutionary cosmic systems, the collapse of any cosmos which contains a sustaining moral spiritual principle.

After this collapse there can be no new revelation of a spiritual nature. There will be no "higher truth" emerging out of the depth of darkness. To echo Wordsworth's hero, romantic tragedy is "darkness deepening darkness."[4]

FOOTNOTES

CHAPTER I

[1] M. H. Abrams, "Structure and Style in the Greater Romantic Lyric," in *From Sensibility to Romanticism*, ed. F. W. Hilles and Harold Bloom (New York: Oxford Univ. Press, 1965), p. 755.

[2] Allardyce Nicoll, *British Drama: an Historical Survey from the Beginnings to the Present Time*, 5th ed. (New York: Barnes and Noble, 1962), pp. 211-215; R. M. Fletcher, *English Romantic Drama, 1795-1843: A Critical History* (New York: Exposition Press, 1947).

[3] All of these various points have been treated exhaustively, and therefore we are not entering into them here. The problem of a poetic idiom is part of most critical works, but E. Gosse's "The Revival of Poetic Drama" and R. Peacock's *Poet in the Theatre* are paying particularly close attention to it. Useful for the discussion of the whole problem are J. O. Bailey's *British Plays of the Nineteenth Century*, and of course, A. Nicoll's *British Drama*. (Fully cited in bibliography)

[4] In Wordsworth's *The Borderers* the villain's intrigue begins with his making the hero believe that Idonea, the innocent heroine, was sold to a lecher by her own father. Also in Coleridge's *Remorse*, the plot begins with the hero testing the heroine's innocence whom he suspects of being "stained in soul and body." In Keats's *Otho the Great* the innocent Erminia loses her reputation due to the villain's slander. To prove her innocence she has to reveal the corruption of the villainess, and this is the mainspring of the intrigue.

In Byron's *Manfred* the heroine's loss of innocence is more than just a rumour; Manfred and Astarte did consummate an incestuous union and Astarte is destroyed as a consequence. In Shelley's *The Cenci* it is also the heroine's loss of innocence, her violation by her wicked father, which sets the dramatic machinery in motion.

[5] In Wordsworth's *The Borderers* the hero loves the heroine's blind old father as his own. In Coleridge's *Remorse* the hero's father fulfills the role of guardian to the orphaned heroine. Consequently both hero and heroine call the same man "Father" and they also consider their love for each other as that of "twins." In Keats's *Otho the Great* the innocent Erminia is the orphaned niece of the hero's father, the Emperor Otho, who also fulfills the role of her guardian and protector. In *Manfred* both hero and heroine have a common father.

[6] In *The Borderers* the hero causes the father's murder because he believes that the old man sold his innocent daughter to a lecher. In *Remorse*, the villain attempts to murder his older brother, a father figure in this case, to obtain the innocent heroine, Teresa. In *Otho the Great* the son takes arms against the father because the father insisted on his marrying the innocent Erminia.

In the last two plays the crime against the father is related to the heroine's loss of innocence even more directly. In *Manfred* the incestuous union between Manfred and Astarte signifies their loss of innocence and their offence against their father's blood at the same time. In *The Cenci* the connection between the two themes is even tighter. The heroine becomes a parricide on account of the violation of her innocence. The loss of innocence, here, is the direct cause of the offence against the father.

[7] At first glance the happy ending in Coleridge's *Remorse* seems to be an exception. Here the play ends with the lovers' marriage, the victory of the hero and the defeat of the villain. Yet in this play the villain is the only potentially tragic character (as it will be apparent from the discussion in Chapter 3). His inability to "wed" the heroine and atone for sinning against his older brother remains an illustration of Man's inability to achieve harmony with Nature and with the Spirit.

8 In Wordsworth's *The Borderers* the hero murders God's image in his own heart when he murders the venerable old father. In *Remorse*, too, the villain attempts to murder his older brother who is his "Maker's image undefac'd." The act of murder amounts to an offence against the Spirit, that is, an act of spiritual suicide.

9 Sidney Lamb, *Tragedy* (Toronto: CBC Publications, 1965), p. 3.

10 Karl Jaspers, "The Tragic: Awareness; Basic Characteristics: Fundamental Interpretations," in *Tragedy: Modern Essays in Criticism*, ed. Laurence Michel and Richard B. Sewall (Englewood Cliffs, N.J.: Prentice Hall, 1963), pp. 14-15.

11 M. H. Abrams, "English Romanticism: The Spirit of the Age," in *Romanticism Reconsidered: Selected Papers from the English Institute*, ed. Northrop Frye (New York: Columbia Univ. Press, 1963), p. 54.

12 M. H. Abrams, "Coleridge and the Romantic Vision," Wed., Dec. 5, 1973, Sir George Williams Univ., Montreal, *verbatim*.

13 I borrowed the term "white romanticism" from Leslie Fiedler who contrasts Emerson's and Thoreau's optimistic vision of a light-flooded universe with the dark and demonic emphasis of Melville and Hawthorne, pointing out a contrast between "white" and "black" romanticism. (In his *Love and Death in The American Novel* (New York: Stein and Day, 1966).) In this study the term, "white romanticism" is associated with the romantic poets' heritage of the optimistic belief in man's perfectibility, in a monistic universe. White romanticism also stands for an epistemological idealism, and the Platonic and utopian strain of the Romantic Movement which denies the existence of radical evil and emphasizes the possibility of reaching the perfection of Truth through higher and higher degrees of light, or knowledge. The term "black romanticism," in contrast, stands for the vision that often follows the heightened expectations, of "white romanticism." It signifies metaphysical pessimism and obsession with darkness in the universe and in the human psyche.

14 Ernst Cassirer, *The Philosophy of the Enlightenment*, trans. F. C. A. Koellin and J. Pettegrove (Princeton: Princeton Univ. Press, 1951), pp. 135-136.

15 *Ibid.*, p. 141.

CHAPTER II

NOTE: All quotations from *The Borderers* are taken from Wordsworth's *Poetical Works*, ed. T. Hutchinson, rev. E. de Selincourt (London: Oxford Univ. Press, 1936).

1 O. J. Campbell and Paul Mueschke, "*The Borderers* as a Document in the History of Wordsworth's Aesthetic Development, "*Modern Philology*, 28, 1925-1926, 482.

2 *Ibid.*

3 Ernest de Selincourt, *Oxford Lectures on Poetry* (Oxford: Clarendon Press, 1934), p. 160.

4 E. Légouis, *The Early Life of William Wordsworth, 1770-1798*, trans. J. W. Matthews (London: Dent, 1897).

5 H. W. Garrod, *Wordsworth: Lectures and Essays* (London: Oxford Univ. Press, 1927), pp. 105-106.

6 P. Thorslev, "Wordsworth's *Borderers* and the Romantic Villain-Hero," *Studies in Romanticism*, 5, 1966, p. 88.

7 C. J. Smith, "The Effect of Shakespeare's Influence on *The Borderers*," *Studies in Philology*, 50, 1953, 625-639.

8 G. Hartman, "Wordsworth, *The Borderers* and Intellectual Murder," *Journal of English and Germanic Philology*, 62 (Oct. 1963), 761-768.

9 P. Thorslev, "Wordsworth's *Borderers* and the Romantic Villain-Hero," *Studies in Romanticism*, 5, 1966, 84-103.

10 Allardyce Nicoll, *British Drama: An Historical Survey from the Beginnings to the Present Time*, 5th ed. (New York: Barnes and Noble, 1962), p. 212.

11 Macbeth's hesitation before committing murder, Lear's love for Cordelia, his despair in the heath scene, and Iago's betrayal of Othello come readily to mind as parallels with Marmaduke's, Herbert's and Oswald's situation respectively.

12 W. Wordsworth, "Essay Supplementary to the Preface," in *Poetical Works* (London: Oxford Univ. Press, 1936), p. 745.

13 W. Wordsworth, "Preface to the edition of 1815," in *Poetical Works* (London: Oxford Univ. Press, 1936), p. 745.

14 *Ibid.*

15 Cleanth Brooks, "Wordsworth and Human Suffering, Notes on Two Early Poems," in *From Sensibility to Romanticism*, ed. R. W. Hilles and Harold Bloom (New York: Oxford Univ. Press, 1965), p. 365.

16 Melvin M. Rader, *Wordsworth: A Philosophical Approach* (Oxford: Clarendon, 1967), p. 47.

17 Geoffrey Hartman, "A Poet's Progress: Wordsworth and the Via Naturaliter Negativa," *Modern Philology*, 59, 1962, p. 224.

18 W. Wordsworth, [Preface to *The Borderers*] in *Poetical Works of William Wordsworth*, vol. I. *Poems Written in Youth: Poems Referring to the Period of Childhood*, ed. E. de Selincourt (Oxford: Clarendon Press, 1940), p. 317.

19 *Ibid.*, p. 348.

20 Eric Donald Hirsch, *Wordsworth and Schelling: A Typological Study of Romanticism* (New Haven: Yale Univ. Press, 1960), p. 45.

21 W. Wordsworth, [Preface to *The Borderers*] in *Poetical Works of William Wordsworth* (Oxford: Clarendon Press, 1940), v. 1, p. 345.

22 Geoffrey Hartman, "Wordsworth, *The Borderers* and Intellectual Murder," *Journal of English and Germanic Philology*, 62 (Oct. 1963), 761-768.

23 W. Wordsworth, [Preface to *The Borderers*] in *Poetical Works of William Wordsworth*, (Oxford: Clarendon Press, 1940), v. 1, p. 346.

24 A. C. Shaftesbury, *Characteristics of Men, Manners, Opinions, Times*, 5th ed. 3 vols. (London, 1732), v. 2, p. 71.

25 W. Wordsworth, "Preface to the edition of 1815," in *Poetical Works* (London: Oxford Univ. Press, 1936), p. 755.

26 David Perkins, *Wordsworth and the Poetry of Sincerity* (Cambridge: Harvard Univ. Press, 1964), p. 116.

27 Northrop Frye, *A Study of English Romanticism* (New York: Random House, 1968), p. 46.

28 *Ibid.*, pp. 24-25.

29 *Ibid.*, p. 46.

CHAPTER III

NOTE: All quotations from *Remorse* and *Osorio* are taken from Coleridge's *Complete Poetical Works*, ed. E. H. Coleridge, V. 2. (Oxford: Clarendon, 1912).

1 M. H. Abrams, *Natural Supernaturalism: Tradition and Revolution in Romantic Literature* (New York: Norton, 1971), pp. 183-187.

[2] S. T. Coleridge, "Milton," in *Selected Poetry and Prose*, ed. Donald A. Stauffer, Modern Library College ed. (New York: Random House, 1951), p. 481.

[3] S. T. Coleridge, footnote to line 215 of his "Religious Musings," in *Poems of Coleridge* (London: Oxford Univ. Press, 1912), p. 117.

> By a priest I mean a man who holding the scourge of power in his right hand and a bible... in his left... produces that temper of mind which leads to Infidelity—Infidelity which judging of Revelation by the doctrines and practices of established Churches *honours God by rejecting Christ.*

[4] When referring to the code of the religion of love, I am indebted to Leslie A. Fiedler's *Love and Death in the American Novel* (New York: Stein and Day, 1966), especially to Chapters 2-4, "The Novel's Audience and the Sentimental Love Religion," "Richardson and The Tragedy of Seduction," and "The Bourgeois Sentimental Novel and the Female Audience," to C. S. Lewis's *The Allegory of Love* (London: Oxford Univ. Press, 1936), and to Mario Praz's *The Romantic Agony*, 2d. ed. (London: Oxford Univ. Press, 1970).

[5] S. T. Coleridge, "Preface to the MS. of *Osorio*," in *The Complete Poetical Works of Coleridge*, ed. E. H. Coleridge, 2 vols. (Oxford: Clarendon Press, 1912), v. 2, p. 114.

[6] Coleridge announces his desire to "compose a sacred drama, for the purpose of elucidating the character of Judas," and describes the process of Judas's degradation as original hostility against Christ, compounded by confusion. *Inquiring Spirit*, ed. Kathleen Coburn (New York: Pantheon, 1951), p. 165.

[7] S. T. Coleridge, "The Wanderings of Cain," in *Poems of Coleridge* (London: Oxford Univ. Press, 1912), pp. 285-292.

[8] Beverly Fields, *Reality's Dark Dream: Dejection in Coleridge* (Kent, Ohio: Kent State Univ. Press, 1967), p. 36.

[9] Arnold Fox, "Political and Biographical Background to Coleridge's Osorio," *Journal of English and Germanic Philology*, 61, 1962, p. 263.

[10] S. T. Coleridge, *Specimens of the Table Talk*, May 8, 1824, 4th ed. (London: Murray, 1851), p. 29.

> "Prometheus in the old mythus, and for the most part of Aeschylus, is the Redeemer and the Devil jumbled together."

[11] S. T. Coleridge, *Specimens of the Table Talk*, May 1, 1830, 4th ed. (London: Murray, 1851), p. 61.

> "A Fall of some sort or other—the creation, as it were, of the non-absolute—is the fundamental postulate of the moral history of Man. Without this hypothesis, man is unintelligible."

[12] S. T. Coleridge, *Complete Works*, ed. W. G. T. Shedd, 7 vols. (New York: Harper, 1856), v. 1, pp. 195-196.

> "I profess a deep conviction that man was and is a fallen creature, not by accident or bodily constitution or any other cause, which human wisdom in the course of ages might be supposed capable of removing: but as diseased in his will, in that will which is the true and only strict synonyme of the word, I, or the Intelligent Self."

[13] A. C. Shaftesbury, *Characteristics of Men, Manners, Opinions, Times*, 3 vols. (London: 1771), v. 1, p. 17.

[14] *Ibid.*, p. 16.

[15] The names of the major characters in

	Osorio	and in	*Remorse*
the father:	Marquis Velez		Marquis Valdez
the hero:	Albert		Alvar
the heroine:	Maria		Teresa

the villain:	Osorio	Ordonio
the villain's agent:	Ferdinand	Isidore
his wife:	Alhadra	Alhadra
the Inquisitor:	Francesco	Monviedro

[16] S. T. Coleridge, footnote to line 320 of his "Religious musings," dated 1797, in *Poems of Coleridge*, ed. E. H. Coleridge, Oxford Standard Authors (London: Oxford Univ. Press, 1912), p. 121.

[17] When he served on the Committee of Drury Lane, Byron encouraged Coleridge to submit a play there. Byron's belief in Coleridge's great promise as a tragedian reflects the opinion of many of their contemporaries:

"Oh—your tragedy—I do not wish to hurry you, but I am indeed very anxious to have it under consideration. It is a field in which there are none living to contend against you and in which I should take a pride and pleasure in seeing you compared with the dead." (Letter to S. T. Coleridge, Oct, 18, 1815, in *Byron: A Self-Portrait*, ed. Peter Quennell, v. 1, p. 317.)

Coleridge's contemporaries, Wordsworth, Keats and Byron included, had a high regard for *Remorse*, which was, according to Byron "the best play for years." (Byron, *Works, Letters, Journals*, ed. Prothero, London, Murray, 1922), v. 3, p. 191.

Unlike the other four plays in question, *Remorse* also had a good measure of stage success. When "performed in January, 1813, it ran for twenty nights." (W. J. Bate, *Coleridge*, London, Macmillan, 1968), p. 127.

[18] S. T. Coleridge, *Letters, Conversations and Recollections of Coleridge*, ed. Thomas Allsop (London: Farrah, 1864), Aug. 8, 1820, pp. 57-58.

[19] S. T. Coleridge, "Allegoric Vision," in *Poems of Coleridge* (London: Oxford Univ. Press, 1912), p. 594.

"Among the rest he [Superstition] talked much and vehemently concerning the infinite series of causes and effects, which he explained to be—a string of blind men, the last of whom caught hold of the skirt of the one before him, he of the next, and so on till they were all out of sight, and that they all walked infallibly straight, without making one false step though all were alike blind. Methought I borrowed courage from surprise, and asked him—Who then is at the head to guide them? He looked at me with ineffable contempt, not unmixed with angry suspicion, and then replied, 'No one! The string of blind men went on for ever without any beginning; for although one blind man could not move without stumbling, yet infinite blindness supplied their want of sight. I burst into laughter, which instantly turned to terror..'"

[20] "Opposite the passage in M.S. II the following is written in the transcriber's hand: "Ce malheur dites-vous, est le bien d'un autre être—
...
(Désastre de Lisbonne. P.W. 1893, p. 491, Editor's Note."

Cited in *Osorio*, in Coleridge's *Complete Poetical Works*, ed. E. H. Coleridge, 2 vols. (Oxford: Clarendon, 1912), v. 2, p. 559, footnote no. 4.

[21] Northrop Frye, "The Unity of Literature," Montreal, Loyola of Montreal, Feb. 22, 1974, Lahey Lecture. *Verbatim*.

[22] Northrop Frye, "The Drunken Boat: The Revolutionary Element in Romanticism," in *Romanticism Reconsidered*, ed. Northrop Frye (New York: Columbia Univ. Press, 1963), p. 19.

CHAPTER IV

NOTE: All quotations from *Otho the Great* are taken from *Keats's Poetical Works*, ed. W. H. Garrod (London: Oxford Univ. Press, 1970).

1 John Keats, Letter to Fanny Brawne, Aug. 5-6, 1819, no. 180, *Letters of John Keats*, ed. Hyder Edward Rollins, 2 vols. (Cambridge, Mass.: Harvard Univ. Press, 1958), v. 2, p. 137.

2 John Keats, Letter to Fanny Brawne, July 15, 1819, no. 176, *Letters*, v. 2, pp. 130.

3 John Keats, "Ode to Fanny," VI. 8; VII. 5; I. 8.

4 Amy Lowell, *John Keats*, 2 vols. (Boston: Houghton Mifflin, 1925), v. 2, p. 293.

5 *Ibid.*, pp. 289-291; 294.

6 Werner W. Beyer, *Keats and the Daemon King* (New York: Oxford Univ. Press, 1947), p. 16.

7 *Ibid.*, p. 391

8 *Ibid.*, p. 392.

9 *Ibid.*

10 *Ibid.*

11 *Ibid.*

12 John Keats, Letter to the George Keatses, April 21, 1819, no. 159, *Letters*, v. 2, p. 102.

13 *Ibid.*, p. 103.

14 *Ibid.*, p. 102.

15 *Ibid.*

16 John Keats, Letter to John Taylor, Nov. 17, 1819, no. 211, *Letters*, v. 2, p. 234.

17 John Keats, Letter to Benjamin Bailey, Aug. 14, 1819, no. 181, *Letters*, v. 2, p. 139.

18 John Keats, Letter to Richard Woodhouse, Sept. 22, 1819, no. 118, *Letters*, v. 1, pp. 386-387.

19 *Ibid.*, p. 387.

20 John Keats, Letter to Richard Woodhouse, Sept, 22, 1819, no. 194, *Letters*, v. 2, p. 174.

21 Richard Woodhouse, Letter to John Taylor, Oct. 27, 1818, no. 119, *Letters*, v. 1, pp. 389-390.

22 John Keats, Letter to John Taylor, Nov. 17, 1819, no. 211, *Letters*, v. 2, p. 234.

23 John Keats, Letter to Richard Woodhouse, Oct. 27, 1818, no. 118, *Letters*, v. 1, p. 387.

24 John Keats, Letter to John Taylor, Jan. 30, 1818, no. 57, *Letters*, v. 1, p. 218.

CHAPTER V

NOTE: All quotations from *Manfred* are taken from Byron's *Selected Poetry*, ed. L. A. Marchand (New York: Random House, 1951).

1 Although he knows that "Goethe made a comparison between Faust and Manfred," Byron denies having read that work at all. As a matter of fact he writes to Murray for "a translation of Faust together with Goethe's biography" several months after the publication of *Manfred*. (Letter to John Murray, in *Byron: A Self-Portrait*, v. 2, p. 696, p. 684.) This would deny the direct, and minimize the indirect influence of Goethe's *Faust*, yet Byron cannot deny the influence of Marlowe's *Doctor Faustus*, even though he insists that it was

"The Staubach [*sic*] and the Jungfrau, and something else, much more than Faustus, that made me write *Manfred*. The first Scene, however, and that of *Faustus*, are very similar.

(Letter to John Murray, in *Byron: Works, Letters and Journals*, v. 5. p. 37.)

[2] Johann Wolfgang Goethe (Extract from a review on Manfred), in *Byron: The Critical Heritage*, ed. A. Rutherford (New York: Barnes and Noble, 1970), pp. 119-120.

"Johann Wolfgang von Goethe (1749-1832) wrote a review of *Manfred* in 1817, which was not published until 1820. It was translated for Byron, at his eager request, by R. B. Hoppner, the British Consul at Venice. The following extract from his version is reprinted from LJ. V. 506. Byron was delighted by the favourable opinion of the 'Greatest man of Germany—perhaps of Europe' (LJ. V. 36), although he was amused by the 'Florentine husband-killing story' (op. cit., p. 113) which illustrates the wildly inaccurate accounts of Byron current in Europe before the publication of Moore's *Life*. For a detailed account of Goethe's views on Byron, and Byron's on Goethe, see E. M. Butler, *Byron and Goethe*, 1956." A. Rutherford, ed., *Byron: The Critical Heritage*, p. 119.

[3] Wilson Knight, *Lord Byron's Marriage: The Evidence of Asterisks* (London: Routledge and Kegan Paul, 1957).

[4] Oscar Wilde, "The Ballad of Reading Gaol," VI. 13.

[5] Shelley, "On the Devil and the Devils," in *Complete Works*, ed. R. Ingpen and W. E. Peck, 10 vols. (London: Benn, 1965), v. 7, p. 94.

[6] Byron, "Prometheus."

[7] Byron [A Journal] Sept. 23, 1816, in *Byron: A Self-Portrait*, v. 1, p. 353.

[8] *Ibid.*, Sept. 22, p. 352.

[9] Northrop Frye; *A Study of English Romanticism* (New York: Random House, 1957), pp. 24-47; "The Drunken Boat: The Revolutionary Element in Romanticism," in *Romanticism Reconsidered*, ed. Northrop Frye (New York: Columbia Univ. Press, 1963), p. 19; "The Unity of Literature," Montreal, Loyola of Montreal, Feb. 22, 1974, Lahey Lecture, *Verbatim*.

CHAPTER VI

NOTE: All quotations from *The Cenci* are taken from Shelley's *Poetical Works*, ed. T. Hutchinson, rev. ed. G. M. Matthews (London: Oxford Univ. Press, 1970).

[1] Stuart Curran's *Shelley's The Cenci: Scorpions Ringed with Fire* (Princeton: Princeton Univ. Press, 1970) has an extensive and conclusive summary on the play's critical fortunes.

[2] Shelley, "Preface (to *The Cenci*)," in *Poetical Works* (London: Oxford Univ. Press, 1970), p. 278.

[3] Mary Shelley, "Note on *The Cenci*," Shelley's *Poetical Works*, ed. Thomas Hutchison, rev. ed. G. M. Matthews (London: Oxford Univ. Press, 1970), p. 337.

[4] Byron considered *The Cenci* "undramatic" but "a work of power and poetry" (*Byron: A Self-Portrait*, Murray, 1967), v. 2, p. 601.

[5] Shelley, Letter to Maria Gisborne, Nov. 16, 1819, *Complete Works*, R. Ingpen and W. E. Peck, 10 vols. (London: E. Benn, 1965), v. 10, pp. 124-125.

[6] Shelley, "Preface (to *The Cenci*)," in *Poetical Works* (London: Oxford Univ. Press, 1970), p. 276.

[7] Earl Wasserman, *Shelley: A Critical Reading*, pp. 108-109.

[8] *Ibid.*, p. 117.

169

[9] Although Shelley also says, "Crime is madness. Madness is disease," in his "A Vindication of Natural Diet," in *Complete Works*, v. 6, p. 10.

[10] Shelley, Letter to Maria Gisborne, Nov. 16, 1819, in *Complete Works*, v. 10, pp. 124-125.

[11] Earl Wasserman, *Shelley: A Critical Reading*, p. 85.

[12] Shelley, Letter to Maria Gisborne, Nov. 16, 1819, in *Complete Works*, v. 10, pp. 124-125.

[13] *Ibid.*

[14] Earl Wasserman, *Shelley: A Critical Reading*, p. 135.

[15] Shelley, "On the Devil and Devils," in *Complete Works*, v. 7, p. 94.
"If the Devil takes but half the pleasure in tormenting a sinner which God does, who took the trouble to create him, and then to invent a system of casuistry by which he might excuse himself for devoting him to external torment, this reward must be considerable.... [It is] God's government [which is responsible for] the exertions of the Devil, to tempt, betray, and accuse unfortunate man."

[16] Shelley, "Notes on Hellas," footnote no. 2, in *Poetical Works*, p. 478.

[17] Shelley, "Preface [to *The Cenci*]," in *Poetical Works*, p. 277.

[18] *Ibid.*, p. 277.

[19] Shelley, "On the Medusa of Leonardo da Vinci in the Florentine Gallery," 33-40. Text reference to the poem will be indicated as "M."

[20] Northrop Frye, *A Study of English Romanticism* (New York: Random House, 1968), Chapter I.

CHAPTER VII

[1] W. Wordsworth, "Preface to the edition of 1815," in *Poetical Works* (London: Oxford Univ. Press, 1936), p. 755.

[2] The one exception is, possibly, Byron, whose various self-portraits do create a memorable character.

[3] It becomes evident that while the main intent is allegorical in all five plays, the more direct the poet's cosmic concern and resulting allegorical method become, the more successful the work appears to be.
In these plays attempts at historical authenticity or realistic psychology are unsuccessful, mainly because these only call attention to their function as camouflage. The plays either work as allegorical poems, or hardly at all. Hence the historical costume plays are contrived and incongruous in most respects, while the overtly allegorical plays are not, a case supported by their respective critical standing. *The Borderers*, *Remorse* and *Otho the Great*, that is, the "costume plays," are usually dismissed as unsuccessful drama and not greatly significant among their authors' works, while *Manfred* and *The Cenci* achieve the stature of magnificent cosmic allegory, and have received a great deal of critical attention and acclaim.
The same contrast between historical-psychological and cosmic-allegorical perspectives is also applicable to the individual playwright's works. Byron, for example, produced a great number of "historical" plays, and these represent his deliberate breaking with the worst characteristics of the Gothic tradition. Still, these works remain lifeless, or, at their best, rather uninteresting self-confessions, such as *Sardanapalus*, *The Two Foscari*, *Marino Faliero* and *The Transformed Deformed*. *Cain* and *Manfred*, however, his two cosmic or metaphysical dramas, are undisguisedly of an allegorical nature, and they are, if not masterpieces of drama, nevertheless recognizable high peaks of romantic tragedy.

⁴ This inability to resolve the contradiction between absolute affirmation and absolute despair is also significant to the understanding of the romantic poet's aesthetic theory on tragedy. On the basis of Wordsworth's, Coleridge's, Keats's and Shelley's aesthetics, the romantic *Ars Poetica* seems to be based on an Enlightenment optimism and epistemological idealism which postulates that poetry is the highest form of knowledge, and the poet, at the height of his intuitive knowledge, possesses insight to a world of potential perfection, a world of Paradise. The loss of this moment of paradisiac insight has been dreaded and bewailed in innumerable romantic poems which assume that the loss of Paradise is equivalent to the loss of creativity.

It seems, then, that the romantic poet cannot regard the disappearance of Paradise as a loss which could lead to a higher level of understanding. To him the moment of alienation is the moment in which creativity is lost. This leads to absolute despair, even if only temporarily. For the romantic poet there exists no philosophical basis for a poetic theory which could include the basic tenets of tragedy.

BIBLIOGRAPHY

The Romantic Movement

Abrams, M. H. "Coleridge and the Romantic Vision." Montreal: Sir George Williams Univ., Dec. 5, 1973. *verbatim*.

Abrams, M. H., ed. *English Romantic Poets*. Modern Essays in Criticism. New York: Oxford Univ. Press, 1960.

Abrams, M. H. *The Mirror and the Lamp: Romantic Theory and the Critical Tradition*. New York: Norton, 1958.

Abrams, M. H. *Natural Supernaturalism: Tradition and Revolution in Romantic Literature*. New York: Norton, 1958.

Auerbach, Erich. *Mimesis: The Representation of Reality in Western Literature*. Princeton: Princeton Univ. Press, 1953.

Babbitt, Irving. *Rousseau and Romanticism*. Boston: Houghton Mifflin, 1919.

Bernbaum, Ernest. *Guide through the Romantic Movement*. New York: Ronald Press, 1949.

Bloom, Harold. *The Visionary Company: A Reading of English Romantic Poetry*. New York: Doubleday, 1963.

Bowra, C. M. *The Romantic Imagination*. Cambridge: Harvard Univ. Press, 1957.

Bush, Douglas. *Mythology and the Romantic Tradition*. Cambridge: Harvard Univ. Press, 1937.

Fiedler, Leslie. *Love and Death in the American Novel*. New York: Stein and Day, 1966.

Frye, Northrop, ed. *Romanticism Reconsidered*. Selected Papers from the English Institute. New York: Columbia Univ. Press, 1963.

Frye, Northrop. *A Study of English Romanticism*. New York: Random House, 1957.

Hilles, F. W., and Bloom, Harold, eds. *From Sensibility to Romanticism*. Essays to F. A. Pottle. New York: Oxford Univ. Press, 1965.

Hulme, Thomas Ernest. "Romanticism and Classicism." *Speculations: Essays on Humanism and the Philosophy of Art*. Ed. Herbert Read. London: Routledge and Kegan Paul, 1924.

Praz, Mario. *The Romantic Agony*. Tr. Angus Davidson. London: Oxford Univ. Press, 1937.

Quennell, Peter. *Romantic England: Writing and Painting*. New York: Macmillan, 1970.

Wellek, René. "Romanticism Re-examined." *Concepts of Criticism*. New Haven: Yale Univ. Press, 1963.

Philosophical Background

Becker, Carl. *The Heavenly City of the Eighteenth Century Philosopher.* New Haven: Yale Univ. Press, 1937.

Cassirer, Ernest. *The Philosophy of the Enlightenment.* Trans. F. C. A. Koelln and J. Pettegrove. Princeton: Princeton Univ. Press, 1957.

Cassirer, Ernest. *Rousseau, Kant and Goethe.* Trans. J. Gutman et al. Princeton: Princeton Univ. Press, 1945.

Grean, Stanley. *Shaftesbury's Philosophy of Religion and Ethics: A Study in Enthusiasm.* Athens: Ohio Univ. Press, 1967.

Lively, Jack. *The Enlightenment.* London: Longmans, 1966.

Mead, George. *Movements of Thought in the Nineteenth Century.* Ed. M. Moore. Chicago: Univ. of Chicago Press, 1963.

Owen, H. P. *Concept of Deity.* London: Macmillan, 1971.

Rockwood, Raymond, ed. *Carl Becker's Heavenly City Revisited.* Hamden, Conn.: Anchor Books, 1968.

Shaftesbury, Anthony Ashley Cooper, Earl of. *Characteristics of Men, Manners, Opinions, Times.* 5th ed. 3 vols. London: 1732.

Romantic Drama

Bailey, J. O. *British Plays of the Nineteenth Century: An Anthology to Illustrate the Evolution of Drama.* New York: Odyssey Press, 1966.

Bair, George. "The Plays of the Romantic Poets: their Place in Dramatic History." Dissertation, Univ. of Pennsylvania, 1951.

Donohue, Joseph W. *Dramatic Character in the English Romantic Age.* Princeton: Princeton Univ. Press, 1970.

Evans, Bertrand. *Gothic Drama from Walpole to Shelley.* Berkeley: Univ. of California Press, 1947.

Fletcher, Richard M. *English Romantic Drama, 1795-1843: A Critical History.* New York: Exposition Press, 1947.

Gosse, Sir Edmund. "The Revival of Poetic Drama." *Atlantic Monthly*, 90, 1902, 156-166.

Kauvar, Gerald B. *Nineteenth-century English Verse Drama.* With introductions and ed. by G. B. Kauvar and Gerald C. Sorensen. Rutherford, N.J.: Farleigh Dickinson Univ. Press, 1973.

Nicoll, Allardyce. *British Drama: An Historical Survey from the Beginnings to the Present Time.* 5th ed. New York: Barnes and Noble, 1962.

Nicoll, Allardyce. *A History of Early Nineteenth-century Drama 1800-1850.* Cambridge: Cambridge Univ. Press, 1930. 2v.

Otten, Terry. *The Deserted Stage: The Search for Dramatic Form in Nineteenth-century England.* Athens: Ohio Univ. Press, 1972.

Peacock, Ronald. *Poet in the Theatre.* New York: Harcourt, Brace, 1946.

Watson, Ernest B. *Sheridan to Robertson: A Study of the Nineteenth-Century London Stage.* Cambridge: Harvard Univ. Press, 1926.

173

Critical Thought on Drama, Tragedy and Allegory

Aristotle. "Poetics." *Criticism: The Major Texts.* Ed. W. J. Bate. New York: Harcourt Brace, 1952.

Burke, Edmund. *A Philosophical Enquiry into the Origin of Our Ideas of the Sublime and Beautiful.* Ed. J. T. Boulton. London: Routledge and Kegan Paul, 1958.

Collingwood, R. G. *The Principles of Art.* New York: Oxford Univ. Press, 1958.

Criticism: The Major Texts. Ed. W. J. Bate. New York: Harcourt Brace, 1952.

Else, Gerald. "Classical Poetics." *Encyclopedia of Poetry and Poetics.* Ed. Alex Preminger. Princeton: Princeton Univ. Press, 1965.

Frye, Northrop. "Allegory." *Encyclopedia of Poetry and Poetics.* Ed. Alex Preminger. Princeton: Princeton Univ. Press, 1965.

Frye, Northrop. *Anatomy of Criticism: Four Essays.* Princeton: Princeton Univ. Press, 1957.

Heilman, R. B. *Tragedy and Melodrama: Versions of Experience.* Seattle: Univ. of Washington Press, 1968.

Hussey, Christopher. *The Picturesque: Studies in Point of View.* London: Putham, 1927.

Jaspers, Karl. "The Tragic: Awareness; Basic Characteristics; Fundamental Interpretations." *Tragedy: Modern Essays in Criticism.* Englewood, Cliffs, N.J.: Prentice Hall, 1963.

Lamb, Sidney. *Tragedy.* Toronto: CBC Publications, 1965.

Lewis, C. S. *The Allegory of Love: A Study in Medieval Tradition.* London: Oxford Univ. Press, 1936.

Lucas, Frank Lawrence. *Tragedy: Serious Drama in Relation to Aristotle's Poetics.* New York: Collier, 1957.

Michel, Lawrence, and Sewall, Richard B. *Tragedy: Modern Essay in Criticism.* Englewood Cliffs, N.J.: Prentice Hall, 1963.

Olson, Elder. *Aristotle's Poetics and English Literature: A Collection of Critical Essays.* Patterns of Literary Criticism. Chicago: Univ. of Chicago Press, 1965.

Plato. [From Book X of] *The Republic. Criticism: The Major Texts.* Ed. W. J. Bate. New York: Harcourt Brace, 1952.

Telford, Kenneth. *Aristotle's Poetics: Translation and Analysis.* Chicago: Henry Regnery, 1965.

Warren, Austin, and Wellek, René. *Theory of Literature.* New York: Harcourt Brace, 1949.

Wellek, René. *Concepts of Criticism.* New Haven: Yale Univ. Press, 1963.

Wimsatt, William, and Brooks, Cleanth. *Literary Criticism: A Short History.* New York: Random House, 1957.

Wordsworth

Primary Sources

Wordsworth, William. *Poetical Works*. Ed. T. Hutchinson, rev. ed. Ernest de Selincourt. London: Oxford Univ. Press, 1936.

Wordsworth, William. *The Poetical Works of Wordsworth*. Eds. Ernest de Selincourt and Helen Darbishire. 5 vols. Oxford: Clarendon, 1949-1958.

Wordsworth, William. *The Early Letters of William and Dorothy Wordsworth*. Ed. Ernest de Selincourt. Oxford; Clarendon, 1935.

Brooks, Cleanth. "Wordsworth and Human Suffering: Notes on Two Early Poems." *From Sensibility to Romanticism*. Essays Presented to F. A. Pottle. Eds. F. W. Hilles and Harold Bloom. New York: Oxford Univ. Press, 1965.

Campbell, O. J., and Mueschke, Paul. "The Borderers as a Document in the History of Wordsworth's Aesthetic Development." *Modern Philology*, 23 (1925-1926), 465-482.

Clarke, Colin. *Romantic Paradox: An Essay on the Poetry of Wordsworth*. London: Routledge and Kegan Paul, 1962.

Garrod, H. W. *Wordsworth: Lectures and Essays*. London: Oxford Univ. Press, 1927.

Grierson, Sir Herbert. *Milton and Wordsworth*. Cambridge: Cambridge Univ. Press, 1937.

Grob, Alan. "Wordsworth and Godwin: A Reassessment." *Studies in Romanticism*, 6 (Autumn 1966), 98-119.

Hartman, Geoffrey. "A Poet's Progress: Wordsworth and the 'Via Naturaliter Negativa.'" *Modern Philology*, 59 (Feb. 1962), 214-224.

Hartman, Geoffrey. *Wordsworth's Poetry: 1787-1814*. New Haven: Yale Univ. Press, 1964.

Hartman, Geoffrey. "Wordsworth, The Borderers and Intellectual Murder." *Journal of English and Germanic Philology*, 62 (Oct. 1963), 761-768.

Hirsch, Eric Donald. *Wordsworth and Schelling: A Typological Study of Romanticism*. New Haven: Yale Univ. Press, 1960.

Légouis, Emile. *The Early Life of William Wordsworth, 1770-1798*. Tr. J. W. Matthews. London: Dent, 1897.

Légouis, Emile. *William Wordsworth and Annette Vallon*. London: Dent, 1922.

Owen, W. J. B. *Wordsworth as Critic*. Toronto: Toronto Univ. Press, 1969.

Perkins, David. *The Quest for Permanence: The Symbolism of Wordsworth, Shelley and Keats*. Cambridge: Harvard Univ. Press, 1959.

Perkins, David. *Wordsworth and the Poetry of Sincerity*. Cambridge: Harvard Univ. Press, 1964.

Rader, Melvin M. *Wordsworth: A Philosophical Approach*. Oxford: Clarendon, 1967.

Selincourt, Ernest de. *Oxford Lectures on Poetry*. Oxford: Clarendon, 1934.

Thorslev, Peter. "Wordsworth's *Borderers* and Intellectual Murder," *Studies in Romanticism*, 5, 1966, 8-103.

Zall, Paul M. *Literary Criticism of Wordsworth*. Lincoln: Nebraska Press, 1966.

Coleridge

Primary Sources

Coleridge, Samuel Taylor. *Coleridge on the Seventeenth Century*. Ed. Roberta Florence Brinkley. Introd. Louis Bredvold. London: Cambridge Univ. Press, 1955.

Coleridge, Samuel Taylor. *Complete Poetical Works*. Ed. E. H. Coleridge. 2 vols. Oxford: Clarendon, 1912.

Coleridge, Samuel Taylor. *Complete Works*. Ed. W. G. T. Shedd. 7 vols. New York: Harper, 1856.

Coleridge, Samuel Taylor. *Notebooks*. Ed. Kathleen Coburn. London: Routledge and Kegan Paul, 1957.

Coleridge, Samuel Taylor. *Poems of Coleridge*. Ed. E. H. Coleridge. Oxford Standard Authors. London: Oxford Univ. Press, 1912.

Coleridge, Samuel Taylor. *Selected Poetry and Prose*. Ed. Donald A. Stauffer. Modern Library College Ed. New York: Random House, 1951.

Appleyard, J. A. *Coleridge's Philosophy of Literature: The Development of a Concept of Poetry, 1798-1819*. Cambridge: Harvard Univ. Press, 1965.

Barfield, Owen. *What Coleridge Thought*. Middleton, Conn.: Wesleyan Univ. Press, 1971.

Barth, J. Robert. *Coleridge and Christian Doctrine*. Cambridge: Harvard Univ. Press, 1969.

Bate, Walter Jackson. *Coleridge*. Masters in World Literature. Ed. L. Kronenberg. London: Macmillan, 1968.

Bayard, K. Morgan. "What happened to Coleridge's *Wallenstein?*" *Modern Language Journal*, 6, 1959, 195-201.

Bretl, R. L. *S. T. Coleridge*. Writers and their Background. London: Bell, 1971.

Coburn, Kathleen, ed. *Coleridge: A Collection of Critical Essays*. Twentieth Century Views. Englewood Cliffs, N.J.: Prentice Hall, 1967.

Coburn, Kathleen, ed. *Inquiring Spirit*. New York: Pantheon Books, 1951.

Encoe, Gerald. *Eros and the Romantics*. Paris: Mouton, 1957.

Ewen, Frederick. *The Prestige of Schiller in England, 1788-1859*. New York: 1952.

Fields, Beverly. *Reality's Dark Dream: Dejection in Coleridge*. Kent, Ohio: Kent State Univ. Press, 1967.

Fogle, Richard. *The Idea of Coleridge's Criticism.* Berkeley: Univ. of California Press, 1962.

Fox, Arnold B. "Political and Biographical Background to Coleridge's *Osorio. Journal of English and Germanic Philology*, 61 (1962), 258-267.

Fruman, Norman. *Coleridge, the Damaged Archangel.* New York: Braziller, 1971.

Hamilton, Marie Padget. "Wordsworth's Relation to Coleridge's *Osorio.*" *Studies in Philology*, 34, 1937, 429-437.

Jackson, J. R., ed. *Coleridge: The Critical Heritage.* London: Routledge and Kegan Paul, 1935.

Lowes, John Livingston. *The Road to Xanadu: A Study in the Ways of the Imagination.* Boston: Houghton Mifflin, 1927.

McFarland, Thomas. *Coleridge and the Pantheist Tradition.* Oxford: Clarendon, 1969.

Rader, Melvin. *Wordsworth: A Philosophical Approach.* Oxford: Clarendon, 1969.

Richards, I. A. *Coleridge on Imagination.* New York: Harcourt Brace, 1935.

Schneider, Elizabeth. *Coleridge, Opium and Kubla Khan.* Chicago: Univ. of Chicago Press, 1953.

Walsh, William. *Coleridge: The Work and the Relevance.* London: Chatto and Windus, 1967.

White, R. J. *The Political Thought of Samuel Taylor Coleridge.* London: Cape, 1938.

Woodring, Carl R. "Two Prompt Copies of Coleridge's *Remorse.*" *Bulletin of the New York Public Library*, 65 (1961), 229-235.

Yarlott, Geoffrey. *Coleridge and the Abyssinian Maid.* London: Methuen, 1961.

John Keats

Primary Sources

Keats, John. *Poetical Works.* Ed. W. H. Garrod. London: Oxford Univ. Press, 1970.

Keats, John. *The Letters of John Keats: 1814-1821.* Ed. Hyder Edward Rollins. 2 vols. Cambridge: Harvard Univ. Press, 1958.

Bate, Walter Jackson. *John Keats.* Cambridge: Harvard Univ. Press, 1963.

Bate, Walter Johnson, ed. *Keats: A Collection of Critical Essays.* Twentieth Century Views. Englewood Cliffs, N.J.: Prentice Hall, 1964.

Beaudry, Harry R. *The English Theatre and John Keats.* Salzburg: Univ. of Salzburg, 1973. (Salzburg Studies in English Literature)

Beyer, Werner. *Keats and the Daemon King.* New York: Oxford Univ. Press, 1947.

Bloom, Harold. *The Visionary Company: A Reading of English Romantic Poetry*. New York: Doubleday, 1961.

Bowra, C. M. *The Romantic Imagination*. Cambridge: Harvard Univ. Press, 1949.

Bush, Douglas. *John Keats: His Life and Writings*. New York: Macmillan, 1966.

Bush, Douglas. *Mythology and the Romantic Tradition in English Poetry*. Cambridge: Harvard Univ. Press, 1937.

Finney, Claude L. *The Evolution of Keats's Poetry*. 2 vols. Cambridge: Harvard Univ. Press. 1936.

Fogle, Richard H. *The Imagery of Keats and Shelley: A Comparative Study*. Hamden, Conn.: Archon Books, 1949.

Gittings, Robert. *The Mask of Keats: A Study of Problems*. Cambridge: Harvard Univ. Press, 1956.

Jack, Ian. *Keats and the Mirror of Art*. Oxford: Clarendon, 1967.

Lowell, Amy. *John Keats*. 2 vols. Boston: Houghton Mifflin, 1925.

Matthews, G. M., ed. *Keats: The Critical Heritage*. London: Routledge and Kegan Paul, 1971.

Murry, John Middleton. *Keats*. London: J. Cape, 1955.

O'Neill, Judith, ed. *Critics on Keats: Readings in Literary Criticism*. London: Allen and Unwin, 1967.

Patterson, Charles I. *The Daemonic in the Poetry of John Keats*. Urbana: Univ. of Illinois Press, 1970.

Perkins, David. *The Quest for Permanence: The Symbolism of Wordsworth, Shelley and Keats*. Cambridge: Harvard Univ. Press, 1959.

Ridley, M. R. *Keats's Craftsmanship: A Study in Poetic Development*. New York: Russell and Russell, 1967.

Slote, Bernice. *Keats and the Dramatic Principle*. Nebraska: Univ. of Nebraska Press, 1958.

Stillinger, Jack. "The Hoodwinking of Madeline: Skepticism in 'The Eve of St. Agnes'," *Studies in Philology*, 63 (1961), 533-555.

Wasserman, Earl. *The Finer Tone: Keats's Major Poems*. Baltimore: John Hopkins Press, 1953.

Byron

Byron: A Self-Portrait: Letters and Diaries, 1798-1821. Ed. Peter Quennell. 2 vols. London: Murray, 1967.

Byron, George Gordon, Lord. *Selected Poetry*. Ed. Leslie A. Marchand. Modern Library College Ed. New York: Random House, 1951.

Byron, George Gordon, Lord. *Works, Letters and Journals*. Ed. Rowland E. Prother. 6 vols. London: Murray, 1922.

Ashton, Thomas L. *Byron's Hebrew Melodies*. London: Routledge and Kegan Paul, 1972.

Barzun, Jaques. *The Energies of Art*. New York: Random House, 1967.

Butler, E. M. *Byron and Goethe: Analysis of a Passion*. London: Bowes and Bowes, 1956.

Buxton, John. *Byron and Shelley: The History of a Friendship*. London: Macmillan, 1968.

Calvert, William. *Byron: The Romantic Paradox*. New York: Russell and Russell, 1962.

Chew, Samuel. *The Dramas of Lord Byron: A Critical Study*. New York: Russell and Russell, 1915.

Cooke, M. G. *The Blind Man Traces a Circle: On the Patterns and Philosophy of Byron's Poetry*. Princeton: Princeton Univ. Press, 1969.

Gleckner, Robert F. *Byron and the Ruins of Paradise*. Baltimore: John Hopkins Press, 1967.

Gunn, Peter. *My Dearest Augusta: A Biography of the Hon. Augusta Leigh, Lord Byron's Half-Sister*. London: Bodley Head, 1968.

Jeffrey, Francis. [Unsigned Review] *Edinburgh Review*, 28 (Sept. 1817), 418-413.

Knight, Wilson. *Byron and Shakespeare*. London: Routledge and Kegan Paul, 1966.

Knight, Wilson, *Lord Byron: Christian Virtues*. London: Routledge and Kegan Paul, 1952.

Knight, Wilson. *Lord Byron's Marriage: The Evidence of Asterisks*. London: Routledge and Kegan Paul, 1957.

Macaulay, Thomas Babington. "Review of Thomas Moore's *Letters and Journals of Lord Byron*," Edinburgh Review, 53 (June 1831), 544-572.

Marchand, Leslie. *Byron: A Biography*. 2 vols. London: Murray, 1957.

Marchand, Leslie. *Byron's Poetry: A Critical Introduction*. Riverside Studies in Literature. Boston: Houghton Mifflin, 1965.

Marlowe, Christopher. *Doctor Faustus*. Ed. John D. Jump. London: Macmillan, 1962.

Marshall, William M. *The Structure of Byron's Major Poems*. Philadelphia: Univ. of Pennsylvania Press, 1967.

Praz, Mario. *The Romantic Agony*. Trans. Angus Davidson. London: Oxford Univ. Press, 1933.

Quennell, Peter. *Byron in Italy*. London: Collins, 1941.

Quennell, Peter. *Byron: The Years of Fame*. Rev. ed. Hamden, Conn.: Archon Books, 1967.

Russell, Bertrand. *History of Western Philosophy, and Its Connection with Political and Social Circumstances from the Earliest to the Present Day*. London: Allen and Unwin, 1946.

Rutherford, A., ed. *Byron: The Critical Heritage*. New York: Barnes and Noble, 1970.

179

Thorslev, Peter. *The Byronic Hero: Types and Prototypes*. Minneapolis: Univ. of Minnesota Press, 1962.

Whitmore, Allen Perry. *The Major Characters of Lord Byron's Dramas*. Salzburg: Univ. of Salzburg, 1974. (Salzburg Studies in English Literature)

West, Paul, ed. *Byron: A Collection of Critical Essays*. Englewood Cliffs, N.J.: Prentice Hall, 1963.

Whipple, A. B. C. *The Fatal Gift of Beauty*. New York: Harper, 1964.

Wilson, John. [Unsigned Review] *Blackwood Magazine*, 1 (June 1817), p. 289.

Shelley

Primary Sources

Shelley, Percy Bysshe. *Complete Works*. Eds. Roger Ingpen and W. E. Pack. 10 vols. London: E. Benn, 1965.

Shelley, Percy Bysshe. *Notebooks*. Ed. Buxton Forman. Princeton: Princeton Univ. Press, 1968 (1911).

Shelley, Percy Bysshe. *Poetical Works*. Ed. Thomas Hutchinson, new ed. G. M. Matthews. London: Oxford Univ. Press, 1970.

Baker, Carlos. *Shelley's Major Poetry: The Fabric of a Vision*. Princeton: Princeton Univ. Press, 1948.

Baker, Joseph E. *Shelley's Platonic Answer to a Platonic Attack on Poetry*. Iowa: Iowa Univ. Press, 1965.

Bloom, Harold. *Shelley's Mythmaking*. New York: Yale Univ. Press, 1959.

Bloom, Harold. *The Visionary Company*. New York: Doubleday, 1961.

Bush, Douglas. *Mythology and the Romantic Tradition in English Poetry*. Cambridge: Harvard Univ. Press, 1937.

Cameron, Kenneth Neill, ed. *Shelley and His Circle, 1773-1827*. Cambridge: Mass.: Harvard Univ. Press, 1970.

Curran, Stuart. *Shelley's Cenci: Scorpions Ringed with Fire*. Princeton: Princeton Univ. Press, 1970.

Flagg, John. "Shelley and Aristotle: Elements of the *Poetics* in Shelley's Theory of Poetry." *Studies in Romanticism*, 9 (1970), 44-67.

Fogle, Richard. *The Imagery of Keats and Shelley: A Comparative Study*. Hamden, Conn.: Archon Books, 1949.

Frye, Northrop. *A Study of English Romanticism*. New York: Random House, 1968.

Lamb, Sidney. *Tragedy*. (Toronto, CBC Publications, 1964).

May, Rollo, ed. *Symbolism in Religious Literature*. New York: Braziller, 1961.

Perkins, David. *The Quest for Permanence: The Symbolism of Wordsworth, Shelley and Keats*. Cambridge: Harvard Univ. Press, 1959.

Praz, Mario. *The Romantic Agony*. Trans. Angus Davidson. London: Oxford Univ. Press, 1933.

Ridenour, George, ed. *Shelley: A Collection of Critical Essays*. Englewood Hill: Prentice Hall, 1965.

Smith, Paul. "Restless Casuistry: Shelley's Composition of *The Cenci*." *Keats-Shelley Journal*, 13 (Winter 1964), 77-85.

States, Bert. O. "Addendum: The Stage History of Shelley's 'The Cenci'," *PMLA*, 72 (1957), 633-644.

Underhill, Evelyn. *Mysticism: A Study in the Nature and Development of Man's Spiritual Consciousness*. 12th rev. ed. London: Methuen, 1930.

Wasserman, Earl. *Shelley: A Critical Reading*. Baltimore: John Hopkins Press, 1971.

White, Newman Ivey. *Portrait of Shelley*. New York: Knopf, 1945.

White, Newman Ivey. *The Unextinguished Hearth: Shelley and His Contemporary Critics*. New York: Octagon Books, 1966.

Whipple, A. B. C. *The Fatal Gift of Beauty*. New York: Harper, 1964.

Woodman, Ross Greig. *The Apocalyptic Vision in the Poetry of Shelley*. Toronto: Toronto Univ. Press, 1964.

Yeats, William Butler. *The Philosophy of Shelley's Poetry: Ideas of Good and Evil*. New York: Russell, 1963.

INDEX

Abrams, M. H., 10-11
Augustine, Saint, 10

Bacchus, 86
Beyer, W., 78-79
Brown's contribution to Keats's *Otho the Great*, 107
Brawne, Fanny, 73
Burke, Edmund, *On The Sublime*, 28, 29, 41, 107
Byron, George Gordon, Lord
  Cain, 170
  Marino Faliero, 170
  "*Prometheus*," 106, 130
  Sardanapalus, 170
  The Transformed Deformed, 170
  The Two Foscari, 170
  Manfred, 7-9, 72, 92-113, 138, 147, 159-62, 163, 170
    Abbot, 101, 102, 105
    Arimanes, 102-03, 111-13, 136
    Astarte, 93-113, 116
    Hunter, 100-01
    Manuel, 98
    Manfred, 58, 93-113, 154
    Seventh Spirit, 96, 101
    Witch of the Alps, 102, 112

Cain, 55, 56, 106, 170
Calderon de la Barca, Pedro
  El Purgatorio de San Patricio —Influence on Shelley's *The Cenci*, 143
Campbell, O. J., 14
Coleridge, Samuel Taylor
  "Allegoric Vision," 64
  Ancient Mariner, 37
  "Dejection: An Ode," 59-60
  "The Destiny of Nations," 51, 67
  Osorio, 47, 62, 65
  "Religious Musings," 46, 47, 67
  "The Wanderings of Cain," 56
  Remorse, 7, 9, 45-71, 72, 74, 89, 98, 107, 114, 147, 154, 157-58, 161, 163, 170
    Alhadra, 46, 66-71, 158
    Alvar, 45-71, 77, 154, 158, 172, 177
    Isidore, 45, 46, 59, 60, 76, 116
    Monviedro, Inquisitor, 62-65
    Ordonio, 45-71, 158, 164
    Teresa, 45-71, 116
    Valdez, 49, 61-65

Dostoievski, Feodor, 15, 42

Frye, Northrop, 69, 109, 111, 112, 147, 161, 162

Garrod, H., 14
Godwin, W.
  Influence on Wordsworth, 14
Goethe, J. W. von,
  Faust, 153
  influence on Byron, 95, 168-69

Hugo, Victor
  Hernani, 153
  Le roi s'amuse, 153
  Ruy Blas, 153
Hartman, Geoffrey, 20
Hume, David, 12

Ibsen, Henrik, 9

Judas, 55, 166

Keats, John
  "La Belle Dame sans Merci," 72, 111
  "The Fall of Hyperion," 72, 111
  "Lamia," 72, 79, 89, 111
  Otho the Great, 7, 9, 72-91, 114, 147, 154, 161, 162, 163, 170
    Albert, 74-85
    Auranthe, 74-85
    Conrad, 74, 91
    Erminia, 74-85, 116
    Ethelbert 88-90
    Gersa, 74, 86-91
    Ludolph, 72-91
    Otho, 74, 86-91
Knight, Wilson, 98

Légouis, E., 14
Locke, John, *tabula rasa*, 11

Marlowe, Christopher
  Doctor Faustus—Influence on Byron's *Manfred*, 92, 93, 104, 110
Milton, John, 153
  Paradise Lost—Influence on Wordsworth's *The Borderers*, 17, 18, 28, 31, 32
Mueschke, P., 14

Napoleon, 102
Nicoll, A., 16

Oxford Platonists, 12

Prometheus, 57, 65, 70, 106, 118, 129, 139,
  146, 166

Rousseau, J. J., 12

Schiller, Friedrich
  Louisa Miller, 153
  Mary Stuart, 153
  Robbers, 153
Shaftesbury, Anthony Ashley Cooper,
  Earl of, 15, 34, 41, 61
Shakespeare, William, 7, 9, 153, 154
  Influence on Wordsworth's *The Border-
  ers*, 17, 165
Shelley, Percy Bysshe
  "Epipsychidion," 132
  "The Sensitive Plant," 138
  "On the Medusa," 145-47
  "The Witch of Atlas," 138
  "Prometheus Unbound," 118, 126, 127,
    128, 139-44, 149
  On the Devil and the Devils, 105
  The Cenci, 7, 9, 114-52, 160-63, 170
    Beatrice, 114-52
    Bernardo, 129
    Count Cenci, 57, 105, 114-52

Camillo, 115, 133, 134
Giacomo, 122, 123, 125, 126, 142
Lucretia, 123-26, 135, 143, 145
Marzio, 121, 123-25, 144
Olimpio, 121, 144
Orsino, 115-22, 140
Smith, C., 14
Spenser, Edmund, 53
  The Faerie Queene—Influence on Words-
  worth's *The Borderers*, 17-27, 33

Thorslev, P., 15

Vallon, Annette, 14
Voltaire, 12, 168

Wasserman, Earl, 119-20, 126-29, 131
Wieland
  Oberon, 78-79
Wordsworth, William, 65, 66, 114
  "Preface to *The Borderers*," 27
  "The Prelude," 16, 22, 24, 26, 32, 33, 37,
    38, 40, 41, 42
  The Borderers, 14-44, 45, 72, 89, 98, 142,
    147, 154, 156, 161, 163, 170
    Idonea, 16-26, 48, 50, 116
    Herbert, 16-44, 66
    Marmaduke, 16-44, 66, 72, 77, 154,
      156, 162, 164
    Oswald, 23, 27-44, 57, 66

O3